I can't really speak French, but I cook in French…
The fistfuls of garlic and thyme… the ethereal
creaminess of a *soufflé*… The merging of
classic French cuisine and the food I grew up
eating in Brooklyn is the foundation of how
I approach cooking—and the raison d'etre of
this book. To me, the cuisines are not two
distinct things, but seamlessly intertwined
into a glorious whole.
—From the Introduction

France was Melissa Clark's first love. Every summer when she was a child, her family decamped to a different region in the nation. They devoted their days to cooking and eating, visiting vast outdoor markets with just-harvested produce, restaurants that beckoned with classic preparations, and tiny shops with breads and pastries and meats that would become perfect, simple meals.

Dinner in French marries the cuisine that Melissa loves with the weeknight-friendly techniques and ingredients she relies on in her Brooklyn kitchen. Distinctly Gallic in organization—eggs, cheese, salads, soups, quiches and tarts, fish, meats, vegetables, and desserts—these recipes are French at heart and meant for the way we cook today: the Ratatouille Sheet-Pan Chicken is a game-changing weeknight number; the Tahini Omelet marries traditional and modern; golden and puffy Cornmeal and Harissa Soufflé resembles a southern spoon bread; Chicken Liver Mousse has strong notes of bourbon. Classics include simple Roasted Tarragon Chicken with Crispy Mushrooms, Scalloped Potato Gratin, Seared Steaks with Basil Béarnaise, Jam-Filled Sablés, and Apricot Tarte Tatin.

French cooking is foundational for the relaxed and eclectic recipes for which Melissa Clark is beloved, and *Dinner in French* is a thrilling resource for dinner every night or every occasion.

Dinner in French

Dinner in French

Melissa Clark

My Recipes by Way of France

CLARKSON POTTER / PUBLISHERS
New York

Copyright © 2020 by Melissa Clark
Photographs copyright © 2020 by Laura Edwards

Published in the United States by Clarkson Potter/Publishers, an
imprint of Random House, a division of Penguin Random House LLC,
New York. clarksonpotter.com

CLARKSON POTTER is a trademark and POTTER with colophon is a
registered trademark of Penguin Random House LLC.

Library of Congress Cataloging-in-Publication Data
Names: Clark, Melissa, author.
Title: Dinner in French: my recipes by way of France / Melissa Clark.
Description: First edition. | New York : Clarkson Potter/Publishers,
    [2020] | Includes index.
Identifiers: LCCN 2019013485 (print) | LCCN 2019018378 (ebook) |
    ISBN 9780553448269 (ebook) | ISBN 9780553448252 (hardcover)
Subjects: LCSH: Cooking, French.
Classification: LCC TX719 (ebook) | LCC TX719 .C469 2020 (print) |
    DDC 641.5944--dc23
LC record available at https://lccn.loc.gov/2019013485

ISBN 978-0-553-44825-2
Ebook ISBN 978-0-553-44826-9

Printed in China

Book and cover design by Marysarah Quinn
Photographs by Laura Edwards

10 9 8 7 6 5 4 3 2 1

First Edition

To my parents,
for making France
such a vital part
of my life

CONTENTS

Introduction

I can't really speak French, but I cook in French. For years, I studied conjugations and the *passé simple,* practiced pronouncing *yaourt* and *grenouille,* but try as I might I just couldn't seem to master it beyond the essentials like *"deux pains au chocolat, s'il vous plaît."*

In the kitchen, however, I am fluent. The fistfuls of garlic and thyme, the pebbly feel of grey *sel marin de Guérande* between my fingers, and the lushness of an emulsifying sauce are now so ingrained, I can cook in French without thinking. The ethereal creaminess of a *soufflé,* the anchovy funk of a *pissalardière,* the caramelized depth of *bœuf Bourguignon* are as deeply part of me as the bagels and lox we ate in Brooklyn every Sunday.

That merging of classic French cuisine and the food I grew up eating in Brooklyn is the foundation of how I approach cooking—and the raison d'être of this book. To me, the cuisines are not two distinct things, but seamlessly intertwined into a glorious whole, because I learned about them at the same time. Yes, we waited in line for Di Fara's pizza, Lundy's clams, and chicken feet and tripe at our favorite dim sum palace. And we also spent countless weekends fussing over Julia Child's terrines and Jacques Pépin's *coq au vin,* which my mother might slather on leftover challah, and my dad might spike with soy sauce (sorry, Jacques). It wasn't irreverence so much as an intense culinary curiosity, a playful exploration of the delicious. All of these influences are so essential to the way I think about food that they're the touchstones of every recipe I create. I might start by asking myself, would adding chicken schmaltz to *ratatouille* be a good thing? The full answer is on page 176. The short answer is: Yes!

None of this would have happened if my Great-Aunt Martha and Uncle Jack hadn't dragged my parents on their first trip to Europe—seven countries in twenty-five days—after medical school in 1960. My dad, whose ideal vacation up until then was fishing in the Catskills, didn't want to go. But they went and fell hard for France, getting hooked on *escargot*, extra crispy *frites*, and the high culture of Monet-filled museums and Gothic cathedrals, all so astoundingly ancient and different from the Yeshiva-centric Brooklyn they grew up in. My parents went back every year, first by themselves, then with my sister and me in tow.

The planning began in January. At first my parents rented houses. But at some point they started house exchanging to economize. Less money spent on lodging meant more on the Michelin-starred meals my parents mapped into their own stellar universe. The year began with the arrival of a thick catalog in the mail: HomeAway, bursting with options. We swapped our old wood-framed Victorian in Flatbush for stone-walled farmhouses in Burgundy, cabins in the Dordogne, stucco split-levels near Nîmes. It was the 1980s, and it was still the custom for a psychiatrist to take off the entire month of August.

This was back before the internet, back before cell phones, even before fax machines. My parents typed letters on blue onionskin paper, then sent them via airmail. There was no way to look up references and no background checks from the HomeAway company. We packed our valuables into a locked closet, printed out instructions for the care of the cats, and caught a cheap charter flight to Paris, hoping for the best.

It always worked out, though some years better than others. There were the lifelong friends we made with the people whose homes we exchanged for ours, like the Lamontagnes, gourmets to the core, whose pantry filled with jars of homemade quince jam and pork rillettes was rival to our own.

On the other end of the spectrum were the shady characters who used our Brooklyn house and Volkswagen Rabbit while we got their marble-clad apartment in Nice, their white Mercedes convertible, and their National Front pamphlets next to a loaded gun in their bedside table. We came home to find the odometer of the car disconnected, the wineglasses broken, and the cat gone. We never did figure out what happened, but always wondered if the mezuzahs on our doors sparked the sabotage.

Meanwhile, behind all the closed doors of our house exchanges, my mother, an incorrigible snoop, opened high cupboards and poked around closets, hoping for menorahs, seder plates, yarmulkes—looking for a clue, any indication of kindred spirits. Sometimes a bookshelf revealed a volume of translated Philip Roth or Saul Bellow, which led to speculation and a little spark.

Our true connection to the French was through our mutual obsession with the food—learning about it, exploring it, and preparing lavish feasts with it. When we weren't cooking, we were planning the next meal, chasing the daily markets from small town to even smaller town, reveling in the figs, the sausages, the incredible cheeses we couldn't get at home.

We also went to fancy restaurants. It was my dad's quest to eat in every Michelin-starred restaurant in France, and he came pretty close, despite getting lost along the way. Pre-GPS, losing our way on tiny country roads was just a normal part of the journey to a meal. When my kindergarten teacher asked me what I did with my parents every August in France, I said, "First we get lost, then we have lunch."

That cute reply was the original title for this book. But as I cooked and wrote down my recipes, I realized that I wasn't lost anymore. I knew where I was going with every recipe. They're quirky and personal, streamlined and practical, seasoned with a dose of Brooklyn moxie to augment all that buttery *haute cuisine*. Yes, there are times I might meander down a seemingly dead end of harissa *gougères* only to end up with a buoyant *soufflé* (page 34). I always find my way because, really, I'm not going very far. It's all right there, rooted in my New York–Jewish–Francophile DNA. And my cooking ends up playfully and unmistakably French. At our house, the conversation might be in English, but dinner's in French.

Twice-Baked Cheese Soufflés, page 32

Eggs

French Baked Eggs with Smoked Salmon and Tarragon Cream

SERVES 4

Is it at all surprising that when the French bake eggs, they do so in a bath of cream? Here that cream is seasoned with fresh tarragon and lemon zest, and stirred into a nest of buttery sautéed leeks before being spooned into individual ramekins along with the eggs. Then everything is baked until the yolks are still liquid while the whites turn just firm enough to hold their shape on your spoon. Because it's hard for me to think about brunch without smoked salmon, I add a few slices here as a garnish, along with some capers for a salty tang. I would never say this is better than bagels and cream cheese, but it's awfully good in its own French-leaning way.

Thinking Ahead

Leek and cream sauce: You can make the sauce up to 2 days in advance and store it in a sealed container in the refrigerator. Pour off any excess water before distributing it among the ramekins.

2 tablespoons unsalted butter, plus more for the ramekins

1 large leek (white and light green parts only), halved lengthwise, cleaned, and thinly sliced

Fine sea salt

10 tablespoons heavy cream, divided

2 tablespoons crème fraîche

1 tablespoon chopped fresh tarragon leaves

¾ teaspoon finely grated lemon zest

8 large eggs, room temperature

Freshly ground black pepper

4 ounces thinly sliced smoked salmon

1 tablespoon chopped capers

Crusty bread or toast, for serving (optional)

1. Heat the oven to 400°F. Brush four 8-ounce ramekins with butter and place them on a rimmed baking sheet.

2. Melt the butter in a large skillet over medium heat. Stir in the leeks and ¼ teaspoon salt, and cook until they are very soft, 15 to 20 minutes, reducing the heat if necessary. You are aiming for melted leeks with the barest touch of gold at the edges but no browning.

3. Stir in 6 tablespoons of the cream, the crème fraîche, tarragon, and lemon zest, and remove the skillet from the heat. Divide the mixture among the ramekins.

4. Crack 2 eggs into each ramekin and sprinkle with salt and pepper. Float 1 tablespoon of the remaining cream on top of each one, and bake until the egg whites are just set and the yolks are still runny, 13 to 17 minutes (it will look jiggly in the center and that's okay—the eggs will continue to cook out of the oven). Remove from the oven and let cool slightly. Top each ramekin with salmon and capers. Serve with bread or toast.

Oeufs à l'Aioli *(Eggs with Aioli)*

A classic aioli starts with pounding garlic with a mortar and pestle until the cloves nearly dissolve to a soft, pungent paste, then dribbling in good Provençal olive oil, drop by greenish drop, until the whole thing emulsifies into a creamy, mayonnaise-like sauce. It looks silky and smooth, but it packs a wallop on the palate, especially if you use all three garlic cloves. In Provence, aioli is typically served with a mix of raw and boiled vegetables, and sometimes fillets of poached fish, but I love it smeared over pieces of ripped-up baguette, savoring the way its pungent unctuousness contrasts with the mild bread.

You get a similar flavor contrast dolloping aioli over the jammy yolks of not-quite-hard-cooked eggs. It's a play on the classic French appetizer *oeufs à la mayonnaise*. Capers make for a bright and saline garnish here, but any number of salty things could also work—salmon roe, chopped pickled peppers, sliced olives or cornichons, or anchovies or bits of sardine. Serve these with drinks at the aperitif hour, as an appetizer with a ruffle of green salad on the plate, or even with bacon for brunch.

FOR THE AIOLI

  1 to 3 garlic cloves, finely grated

  1 teaspoon fresh lemon juice, plus more to taste

  ⅛ teaspoon fine sea salt, plus more to taste

  1 large egg

  1 large egg yolk

  ¾ cup mild extra-virgin olive oil (or for a mellower flavor, substitute ¼ cup neutral oil, such as grapeseed, for some of the olive oil)

FOR THE EGGS

  12 large eggs

FOR THE GARNISH

  Capers, anchovies, salmon roe, olives, slices of cornichons, or bits of sardines

Thinking Ahead

Aioli: You can make the aioli (without the garnish) up to 1 week in advance. Store it, covered, in the refrigerator.

Eggs: You can cook the eggs up to 3 days in advance. Peel and store them in a covered container in the refrigerator.

1. **Make the aioli:** Combine the garlic, lemon juice, and salt in a blender or food processor and let the mixture sit for a minute or two to mellow the garlic. Then add the egg and egg yolk and blend until combined. With the machine running, drizzle in the oil in a thin, steady stream. Start dribbling the oil in slowly, then more quickly as the emulsion takes hold after 20 to 30 seconds. The whole thing should be completed quickly, in under a minute. Taste for seasoning and add more lemon juice and/or salt if necessary. The consistency should be that of a light mayonnaise; it will thicken in the fridge. (For more tips, see the mayonnaise recipe on page 21).

   You can also use a mortar and pestle if you like, pounding the garlic, lemon juice, salt, egg, and egg yolk and then pounding in the slow stream of oil. The consistency will be slightly thicker than that from the blender because there will be less air whipped in.

2. **Cook the eggs:** Place the eggs in a medium saucepan and cover them with cold water. Over medium-high heat, bring the water to a boil. The second you see big bubbles forming, take the pan off the heat and cover it. Let it sit for 8 to 9 minutes (8 minutes gives you jammy, barely set yolks; 9 minutes gives you creamy yolks).

3. Meanwhile, fill a bowl with water and ice and set it aside.

4. Uncover the saucepan and use a slotted spoon to transfer the eggs to the bowl of ice water. When they are cool enough to handle, crack the eggs all over and peel away the shells. Halve the eggs and arrange them on a platter. Dollop with the aioli and sprinkle with capers or other garnishes.

Homemade Mayonnaise

MAKES ABOUT ¾ CUP

When the French serve a little bowl of mayonnaise for dipping artichoke leaves or tiny pink shrimp, chances are it's homemade. Of course you can buy mayo in any French supermarket, but no self-respecting host would serve that to guests, especially when everyone knows how incredibly easy it is to whip up.

I've adopted that mayo-at-any-moment mind-set, always ready to whirl together a batch. When my daughter asks for a BLT, the first thing I do is pull out the blender.

That said, it took me a while to master making mayonnaise in the blender. Afraid of breaking the emulsion, I'd drip in the oil so slowly that the blender motor caused the whole thing to overheat and separate anyway. I've since learned that the trick to blender mayo is not to overblend.

Sometimes, instead of using just an egg yolk, I use a whole egg because I'm too lazy to separate it. This gives you a slightly runnier mayo, which is good for dips and as the base for salad dressings. If you choose to use the whole egg, eliminate the water in this recipe.

1 large egg yolk, room temperature

2 teaspoons fresh lemon juice, plus more to taste

1 teaspoon Dijon mustard

¼ teaspoon fine sea salt, plus more to taste

1 teaspoon cold water

⅔ cup mild extra-virgin olive oil (or, for a mellower flavor, use half olive oil and half neutral oil such as grapeseed or sunflower)

1. *To make this in a blender,* blend the egg yolk, lemon juice, mustard, salt, and water until well mixed. With the blender on a medium speed (mine says "blend"), drizzle in the oil in a thin, steady stream. Start dribbling the oil in slowly, then more quickly as the emulsion takes hold after 20 to 30 seconds. The whole thing should be completed quickly, in under a minute.

   If you're making this by hand, choose a large or medium bowl; you'll need room to maneuver the whisk. Whisk together the egg yolk, lemon juice, mustard, salt, and water. Whisking constantly, slowly drizzle in the oil, little by little, until the mixture is emulsified and thickened. (This will take longer than using a blender.) You can steady the bowl between your legs or by nestling it on a rolled-up damp dish towel.

2. Taste the mayonnaise and add more salt and/or lemon juice if needed.

Thinking Ahead

Mayonnaise can be made up to 1 week in advance and stored, covered, in the refrigerator.

Deviled Eggs with Crème Fraîche and Roquefort

SERVES 4 TO 6

The French don't, as a rule, devil their eggs. A little mayonnaise spooned on top turns a modest jammy-yolk egg into a killer appetizer (homemade mayo helps the cause). However, if they ever go the deviling route, I wouldn't be surprised to see this very Gallic combination of crème fraîche and Roquefort cheese mashed into the yolks. More piquant than the usual potluck offering, these are sophisticated and highly appealing—elegant enough to nibble with champagne at a cocktail party, casual enough to serve in your backyard at a cookout. They're the best of both worlds.

Thinking Ahead

Eggs: You can cook the eggs up to 3 days in advance. Peel and store them in a covered container in the refrigerator.

6 large eggs

3 tablespoons crème fraîche

1 tablespoon mayonnaise, homemade (see page 21) or store-bought

2 teaspoons chopped fresh chives

½ teaspoon Dijon mustard

Large pinch of fine sea salt

¼ cup (1 ounce) crumbled Roquefort cheese

1. Place the eggs in a medium saucepan and cover them with cold water. Over medium-high heat, bring the water to a boil. The second you see big bubbles forming, take the pot off the heat and cover it. Let it sit for 9 minutes for creamy yolks.

2. Meanwhile, fill a bowl with water and ice and set it aside.

3. When the eggs are done, uncover the saucepan and use a slotted spoon to transfer the eggs to the bowl of ice water. When they are cool enough to handle, crack the eggs all over and peel away the shells. Halve the eggs and scoop the yolks into a medium bowl.

4. Mash the yolks with a fork, then fold in the crème fraîche, mayonnaise, chives, mustard, and salt. Spoon the mixture back into the egg whites. Crumble the Roquefort on top of the eggs, and serve.

A French omelet is iconic, and making a perfect one is often held up as the test of a French chef's skill. Fluffy in the center, with large billowing curds barely contained by a thin, firm exterior, omelets really don't need anything substantial as a filling. A little cheese or some herbs can set off their eggy richness nicely.

That said, I can never resist adding garlic pretty much everywhere there's an opportunity (blame my parents—it's how I was brought up). I got the idea for the garlicky tahini sauce, indirectly, from Yotam Ottolenghi. His brilliant Middle Eastern–inspired recipes drastically increased my tahini consumption, and I've been using the sesame paste in ways far beyond the usual hummus. For this omelet, after folding in the tahini and garlic sauce, I douse the whole thing with an herbed yogurt sauce. It's more assertively flavored than most other omelets, with a distinctive Mediterranean flair.

If making an omelet seems too fussy—all that folding and flipping *can* take some concentration—just scramble your eggs and drizzle them with the tahini sauce and yogurt. It may be sloppier looking, but it will be just as satisfying to eat.

Tahini Omelet

SERVES 2

2 tablespoons fresh lemon juice

1 small garlic clove, finely grated or minced

Fine sea salt

¼ cup tahini

4 to 5 tablespoons cold water, divided

½ cup plain yogurt, for serving

2½ tablespoons chopped fresh dill (or mint, cilantro, or parsley) leaves, divided, plus more for serving

6 large eggs

Freshly ground black pepper

4 tablespoons (½ stick) unsalted butter, divided

Sweet paprika, for serving (optional)

Flaky sea salt, for serving

1. In a small bowl, combine the lemon juice, garlic, and ½ teaspoon fine sea salt. Let the mixture sit for 5 minutes (to let garlic mellow in the acidic lemon juice), then whisk in the tahini. Whisk in cold water, 1 tablespoon at a time, until very smooth (2 to 3 tablespoons water total). The sauce should be as thick as crème anglaise and just as silky.

2. In another small bowl, whisk together the yogurt, 1½ tablespoons of the herbs, and a pinch of salt. Set aside.

3. In a medium bowl, whisk together the eggs, remaining 1 tablespoon herbs, 2 tablespoons cold water, and a large pinch of salt and pepper.

4. In a large nonstick skillet set over medium-high heat, melt 2 tablespoons of the butter until foaming. Then pour in half the egg mixture and reduce the heat to medium. Stir briefly with the flat back side of a fork, to agitate the eggs and keep them from immediately setting. Cook until the eggs are mostly set on the bottom, 45 seconds to 1 minute and 15 seconds, then drizzle them with a quarter of the tahini sauce. Fold the omelet using a heat-proof spatula and carefully transfer it to a plate. Repeat with the remaining 2 tablespoons butter, egg mixture, and another quarter of the tahini sauce.

5. Drizzle the omelets with the remaining tahini sauce, sprinkle with the paprika, if using, and flaky sea salt, and add a dollop of the yogurt sauce. Serve immediately, topped with more herbs.

Thinking Ahead

Tahini sauce: You can make and refrigerate the sauce, covered, up to 2 days in advance. Bring to room temperature before serving.

Yogurt sauce: You can make and refrigerate the sauce, covered, up to 3 days in advance. Drain off any excess water before serving. This sauce is also great on fish or chicken.

Spicy Egg, Tomato, and Leek Toasts

MAKES 6 TOASTS

Think of this dish as a simpler, spicier, and more vegetable-forward eggs Benedict. You've got the runny-yolk egg, which is fried rather than poached. There's the rich sauce: here, a tangy Sriracha and ginger–spiked mayonnaise in place of the subtler hollandaise. Slices of ripe, juicy tomato, nestled cozily under the egg, stand in for the Canadian bacon. And as a crunchy base, I use thick slices of olive oil and garlic–rubbed crostini instead of toasted English muffins. The final garnish of soft, caramelized leeks may seem superfluous, but it really creates a memorable dish, increasing the vegetable quotient and making the whole thing a little sweeter and more complex. Although this is simple enough to make for brunch (no egg poaching or hollandaise blending!), I actually prefer it as a light dinner, with a spinach salad and a really good cru Beaujolais.

2 medium leeks (white and light green parts only), halved lengthwise, cleaned, and thinly sliced

3 tablespoons extra-virgin olive oil, divided, plus more for drizzling

3 sprigs fresh thyme (lemon thyme is nice here but not necessary)

Fine sea salt

6 thick slices country bread

2 garlic cloves, divided

½ cup mayonnaise, homemade (see page 21) or store-bought

2½ teaspoons soy sauce, plus more to taste

2 teaspoons fresh lime juice, plus more to taste

2 teaspoons Sriracha, plus more to taste

1 teaspoon grated fresh ginger

6 thin slices of tomato (from 1 very large ripe tomato)

6 large eggs

1. Heat the oven to 400°F. On a rimmed baking sheet, toss the leeks with 2½ tablespoons of the olive oil, the thyme sprigs, and a large pinch of salt. Roast, tossing occasionally, until the leeks are browned and crispy, about 20 minutes. When they are done, set them aside.

2. While the leeks are cooking, arrange the bread slices in an even layer on a separate rimmed baking sheet, drizzle them with oil, and sprinkle lightly with salt. Bake (along with the leeks in the same oven) until golden on the edges, 6 to 10 minutes. Transfer the toasts to a rack to cool slightly (until you can pick them up without burning your hands). Cut 1 garlic clove in half, and immediately rub it lightly over the tops of the warm toasts. Transfer the toasts to a serving platter or plates.

Thinking Ahead

Leeks: You can roast the leeks up to 4 hours ahead and leave them, loosely covered, at room temperature.

Sauce: You can make the sauce and refrigerate it, covered, up to 2 days in advance.

3. Make the sauce. Grate or press the remaining garlic clove into a medium bowl, then whisk in the mayonnaise, soy sauce, lime juice, Sriracha, and ginger. Taste and adjust the seasonings if necessary.

4. Spread each toast with a little of the mayonnaise, then top it with a tomato slice and sprinkle lightly with salt.

5. Heat the remaining ½ tablespoon oil in a large nonstick skillet over medium-low heat. Crack the eggs into the skillet, working in batches if they don't all fit at once. Cook until the whites are set but the yolks are still runny, 2 to 4 minutes. Transfer each egg to a toast. Top the eggs with the leeks and a dollop of the mayo.

Egg Yolk Shakshuka

SERVES 4

I learned how to make an egg yolk shakshuka from Mourad Lahlou, the famous San Francisco chef originally from Morocco. As Mourad sees it, the egg whites in a shakshuka merely imprison the yolks, preventing them from gushing gleefully into the sauce, mingling freely with the peppers, tomatoes, and spices. Here, the merest tap of a fork releases the yolks' richness without any whites holding them back. Flavored with preserved lemon (if you've got it) and goat cheese, this is more decadent and more complex than the usual shakshuka. Be sure to save the whites to use in meringues and buttercreams; they will keep in the freezer for up to a year.

Thinking Ahead

Tomato sauce: You can make the sauce (through step 2) up to 4 days in advance and store it, covered, in the refrigerator. Warm it in a skillet over low heat before adding the fresh herbs, goat cheese, and eggs.

2 tablespoons extra-virgin olive oil

1 large white onion, diced

4 garlic cloves, minced

1 (28-ounce) can diced tomatoes

2 red, orange, or yellow bell peppers, or a combination, roasted (see page 57)

2 tablespoons chopped fresh thyme leaves

1 teaspoon fine sea salt, plus more to taste

¼ teaspoon freshly ground black pepper, plus more to taste

1½ teaspoons ground cumin

1 teaspoon sweet paprika

½ teaspoon ground turmeric

⅛ teaspoon cayenne pepper

1 tablespoon minced preserved lemon (optional) or 1 teaspoon fresh lemon juice

1 tablespoon chopped fresh parsley leaves

1 tablespoon chopped fresh cilantro or mint leaves, plus tender sprigs for garnish

4 ounces (1 cup) goat cheese, crumbled while still cold

6 large egg yolks, room temperature

Grilled or toasted bread, for serving

1. In a 12-inch skillet, heat the oil over medium heat. Stir in the onion and cook until it is starting to brown, 7 to 10 minutes, reducing the heat if necessary to prevent burning.

2. Stir in the garlic and cook for another minute, until fragrant. Stir in the tomatoes and their juices, the peppers and any reserved pepper juices, thyme, salt, black pepper, cumin, paprika, turmeric, and cayenne. Simmer over low heat until reduced by a third, 15 to 25 minutes.

3. Stir in the preserved lemon if using. Taste and adjust the seasoning if necessary.

4. Stir in the parsley and cilantro, and scatter the goat cheese across the sauce. Slip the yolks into the skillet. Sprinkle with salt and pepper. Cover the skillet with a lid or a baking sheet, and cook over low heat until the yolks are barely solid but still runny, 2 to 5 minutes. Serve immediately, garnished with cilantro or mint sprigs, with grilled or toasted bread alongside for dipping.

Sweet Pepper and Cheddar Clafouti

SERVES 4 TO 6

Clafoutis are custardy baked pancakes traditionally filled with sweet cherries and served for dessert. When my mother made them when we were in France, she didn't bother pitting the cherries. French cooks didn't, so why should she? She is a woman who always loves a shortcut. And my sister and I never minded—we liked having an excuse to spit out the pits, which, if we were eating outside as we often did in August, we could do straight into the garden without anyone yelling at us.

You needn't worry about pits in this savory clafouti, with its filling of sautéed bell peppers and plenty of salty sharp cheddar. It will emerge from the oven puffy and golden, then quickly deflate. Fear not, it still tastes wonderful after it flattens out, though for the most drama, seat your guests at the table and rush this out for them to admire. The oohs and ahhs are worth the jog from kitchen to dining table.

¾ cup whole milk

½ cup (4 ounces) crème fraîche

4 large eggs

2½ tablespoons (22 grams) all-purpose flour

¼ cup chopped fresh basil leaves

¾ teaspoon fine sea salt, divided, plus more as needed

½ teaspoon freshly ground black pepper

1 cup (4 ounces) coarsely grated sharp white cheddar cheese, divided

2 ounces sliced ham, chopped

2 tablespoons extra-virgin olive oil

3 sweet bell peppers, preferably different colors including red and yellow, seeded and sliced into ¼-inch-wide strips

2 garlic cloves, thinly sliced

¼ cup (1 ounce) grated Parmesan cheese

Fresh lemon juice, for serving

Crushed red pepper flakes, for serving

1. Heat the oven to 375°F.

2. In a large bowl, whisk together the milk, crème fraîche, eggs, flour, basil, ½ teaspoon of the salt, and pepper. Stir in ¾ cup of the cheddar and the ham.

3. In a 9-inch ovenproof skillet, heat the oil over medium heat. Stir in the peppers and cook until they are softened and golden at the edges, 10 to 15 minutes. Stir in the garlic and remaining ¼ teaspoon salt and cook until fragrant, about 2 minutes.

4. Scrape the egg mixture into the skillet, and top it with the remaining ¼ cup cheddar and the Parmesan. (Or, for a more elegant presentation, scrape the vegetables into a gratin or casserole dish and add the egg mixture and cheese to that.) Bake until the eggs are set, 35 to 40 minutes. Cool slightly, then top with lemon juice and red pepper flakes.

Thinking Ahead

Peppers: You can cook the peppers and garlic
up to 3 days in advance. Store the mixture,
covered, in the refrigerator. Gently rewarm it
in an ovenproof skillet before adding the egg
mixture and baking.

Twice-Baked
Cheese Soufflés

SERVES 6

Almost over-the-top rich and creamy, these cheese soufflés are double baked—once to puff them up like little clouds, then a second time covered in cheese sauce to make them all the more irresistibly gooey and browned on top. What's great about this dish is that you can prepare the whole thing the day before, then give the soufflés a final bake just before serving—a perfect brunch dish that you can do even when you're not fully caffeinated.

Thinking Ahead

Leeks: You can sauté these 2 to 3 days in advance and store them in a sealed container in the refrigerator.

Cheese soufflés: You can prepare the whole thing the day before and keep it tightly covered in the refrigerator. Before serving, bake for 10 to 15 minutes, until golden and bubbling.

4 tablespoons (½ stick / 56 grams) unsalted butter, plus more for the ramekins

2 tablespoons extra-virgin olive oil

½ cup chopped leeks (white part only) or shallots

¼ cup (32 grams) all-purpose flour

1 cup (240 milliliters) whole milk

1 teaspoon chopped fresh rosemary leaves

1 teaspoon chopped fresh thyme leaves

½ teaspoon fine sea salt

¼ teaspoon freshly ground black pepper

1 cup (240 milliliters) heavy cream

1¼ cups (5 ounces) shredded Gruyère or cheddar cheese

6 large eggs, yolks and whites separated

⅓ cup (45 grams) grated Parmesan cheese

1. Heat the oven to 350°F and butter six 8-ounce ramekins. Place the ramekins in a large baking dish.

2. Heat the oil in a medium skillet over medium-low heat. Stir in the leeks and cook until they are soft but not browned, 10 to 15 minutes. Scrape the leeks into a bowl and set aside. Return the skillet to medium heat.

3. Melt the butter in the skillet, then whisk in the flour and cook for 1 to 2 minutes, until it turns very pale gold in some spots (but not brown). Slowly add the milk in a thin stream, whisking to remove any lumps. Bring the mixture to a simmer and cook until thickened, whisking continuously, about 2 minutes. Whisk in the rosemary, thyme, salt, and pepper. This is the roux.

4. Scrape about a third of the roux into a medium bowl, then whisk in the heavy cream. Reserve until needed.

5. Over very low heat, stir the cooked leeks into the roux remaining in the skillet, then stir in the Gruyère, a handful at a time, until melted. Remove from the heat and scrape the mixture into a large bowl. Whisk in the egg yolks.

6. In the bowl of an electric mixer, beat the egg whites until they form stiff peaks. Using a spatula, fold about a third of the whites into the cheese mixture, then fold in the remaining whites until mostly incorporated, though it's okay if one or two streaks remain.

7. Divide the mixture among the prepared ramekins. Then add enough hot tap water to the baking dish to reach halfway up the sides of the ramekins. Bake until the soufflés are puffed and golden, about 20 minutes. Remove them from the oven and let them cool until you can handle them. Raise the oven temperature to 425°F.

8. Run a thin spatula around the edges of the ramekins and flip the soufflés into a large gratin dish. Pour the reserved roux/cream mixture over the soufflés and all over the bottom of the gratin dish. Sprinkle the soufflés with the Parmesan. At this point you can either cover the dish with plastic wrap and chill it overnight, or bake it straightaway until it is golden and bubbling, 10 to 15 minutes. Serve hot or warm.

Cornmeal and Harissa Soufflé

When I was a kid, if there was soufflé on offer, I ordered it. It didn't matter what flavor—to me it was all about that moment when you tapped your spoon into the fluffy whites and they deflated into a runny puddle of custardy sweetness. Even if you were a bored eight-year-old sitting through a long French meal, when the soufflé showed up, all frustrations melted into sugar-fueled joy.

This golden, puffy, cheese-filled creation is like a cross between a southern spoonbread and a savory French soufflé, with a good dose of harissa to add color and spice. Serve it for brunch, as a light supper, or as a fancy side dish.

4 tablespoons (½ stick / 56 grams) unsalted butter, plus more for the dish

3 tablespoons (30 grams) finely grated Parmesan cheese

4 scallions (white and green parts), thinly sliced

1 cup whole milk

¼ cup (35 grams) fine cornmeal

2 tablespoons harissa, plus more as needed

½ teaspoon fine sea salt, plus more as needed

4 large egg yolks

5 large egg whites

1 cup (4 ounces) grated sharp cheddar cheese

1. Position a rack in the lower third of your oven and place a baking sheet on the rack. Heat the oven to 400°F. Generously butter a 1½-quart soufflé dish. Coat the bottom and sides with the Parmesan.

2. Melt 2 tablespoons of the butter in a large skillet over medium heat. Then add the scallions and sauté until softened, about 5 minutes. Transfer them with a slotted spoon to a plate and reserve.

3. Add the remaining 2 tablespoons butter to the skillet and let it melt. Carefully pour in the milk and heat until it is simmering. Slowly stir in the cornmeal, whisking constantly; continue to cook until the mixture thickens to a sauce-like consistency, 1 to 2 minutes. Remove the skillet from the heat, and stir in the harissa and salt, adding more of each as desired. Whisk in the egg yolks, one at a time, blending fully after each addition. Transfer the cornmeal mixture to a large bowl and let it cool to lukewarm.

4. In the bowl of an electric mixer fitted with the whisk attachment, beat the egg whites on medium-high speed until they hold stiff peaks, 3 to 4 minutes; the beaten whites should have just begun to lose their sheen. Whisk a quarter of the whites into the lukewarm yolk mixture to lighten it. Then use a spatula or spoon to fold in the remaining whites in two additions while gradually sprinkling in the cheddar cheese and the sautéed scallions. Don't over-fold; the mixture should still have a few lumps. Transfer the batter to the prepared soufflé dish. Rub your thumb around the edge of the dish to create space between the dish and the soufflé mixture (this helps it rise).

5. Place the dish on the baking sheet in the oven and reduce the oven temperature to 375°F. Bake until the soufflé is puffed and golden brown on top and the center barely moves when the dish is shaken gently, 35 to 40 minutes (do not open the oven door during the first 20 minutes). Serve immediately.

Red Wine–Poached Eggs with Mushrooms and Bacon

SERVES 8

This is my somewhat simplified take on *oeufs à la meurette*, a Burgundian classic of eggs poached in a red wine sauce flavored with bacon, mushrooms, and shallots. As the wine simmers, it deepens in color, turning garishly purple—not the hue generally associated with food. But in the process it gains a heady complexity augmented by the cured pork and vegetables.

Even in my streamlined version, *oeufs à la meurette* is a bit of a production to pull off. But for lovers of velvety poached eggs and good red wine, it's worth making for a special dinner or a blow-out brunch. You don't need to use your very best wine. A pleasant but inexpensive Burgundy, Beaujolais, or Pinot Noir will do the trick for cooking. Then pull out something better for serving.

Thinking Ahead

Mushroom mixture: You can prepare the mushrooms and shallots 2 days in advance and store them, covered, in the refrigerator. Gently rewarm them in the sauté pan before adding the wine, stock, and eggs.

4 ounces (2 to 3 slices) thick-sliced bacon, diced

1 tablespoon extra-virgin olive oil, plus more for drizzling

4 ounces cremini or white mushrooms, sliced ¼ inch thick

4 large or 8 small shallots, quartered lengthwise

1 (750 ml) bottle dry red wine, preferably a Burgundy

3 cups chicken or beef stock, preferably homemade

8 large eggs, cracked into 8 small bowls, ramekins, or cups (see sidebar)

4 sprigs fresh thyme

4 sprigs fresh parsley, plus chopped fresh parsley leaves, for serving

1 bay leaf

1 celery stalk, cut in half

1 carrot, cut in half

3 garlic cloves: 2 smashed, 1 cut in half

3 tablespoons unsalted butter, cubed

Fine sea salt, as needed

Red wine vinegar, as needed (optional)

8 thick slices country bread

Turkish red pepper (*urfa biber*) or crushed red pepper flakes, for serving

Flaky sea salt, for serving

1. In a deep 10-inch sauté pan, heat the bacon and oil over medium heat. Cook, stirring occasionally, until the bacon is crisp and browned, 9 to 13 minutes. Transfer it with a slotted spoon to a paper towel–lined plate, leaving the fat in the pan.

2. Add the mushrooms and shallots to the bacon fat. Cook, without moving them too much, until they are browned and crisp, about 12 minutes. Transfer them to the plate with the bacon.

How to Poach Eggs

Crack each egg that you want to poach into a separate cup or ramekin. Bring a few inches of water to a gentle simmer in either a saucepan or a deep skillet with a lid. (I use the saucepan when I'm just doing a couple of eggs, and the skillet when I want more room to poach 6 to 8 eggs at a time.) When the water is barely simmering (a few bubbles around the edges are what you are looking for, not a boil), slip the eggs, one at a time, into the water. Stir the water gently, then cover the pan and remove from the heat. Let the pan sit for 4 minutes. If the eggs aren't done yet, cover and return them to the heat until they are, checking them at 20-second intervals. Use a slotted spoon to scoop out the eggs one by one. Pat the bottom of the spoon dry on a clean kitchen towel as you pick up each egg. This helps eliminate excess water running all over your plate or your toast.

If you want a neater-looking poached egg, you can crack it into a fine-mesh strainer before sliding it into the simmering water. This gets rid of the loose and runny parts of the egg white, which slither out into ragged wisps when they hit the water. I usually don't bother.

You can poach eggs ahead of time: Transfer the eggs from the hot water to a bowl of cold water and refrigerate until needed, up to 24 hours. To reheat, transfer the eggs to a bowl of very hot steaming (but not simmering) water for a couple of minutes.

3. Stir the wine and stock into the skillet and bring to a vigorous boil. Slip the eggs, one at a time, into the liquid, then reduce the heat to medium-low and cook until the egg whites are firm, 2 to 3 minutes (see sidebar). Transfer the poached eggs with a slotted spoon to a plate lined with a dish towel, one that you don't mind staining purple (or use paper towels).

4. Raise the heat under the skillet to bring the liquid to a simmer. Using kitchen twine, tie together the thyme sprigs, parsley sprigs, and bay leaf and toss the bundle into the broth (or skip the string and just be prepared to fish the herbs out later). Stir in the celery, carrot, and smashed garlic; continue to simmer until the liquid has reduced by half, 20 to 25 minutes.

5. While the sauce is simmering, heat the broiler.

6. When the sauce has reduced, remove and discard the herb bundle and the vegetables; then whisk in the butter and season with fine sea salt (be generous—you haven't added any salt to the sauce yet, so it will need a lot, especially if your stock was unsalted). Add a dash or two of red wine vinegar if the sauce needs verve.

7. On a rimmed baking sheet, arrange the bread in a single layer and drizzle the slices with oil. Broil until golden, about 1 minute, then flip them over and broil for another minute. Remove the toasts from the oven and immediately rub them with the cut sides of the halved garlic clove.

8. To serve, bring the broth back to a simmer. Place a slice of toast in each of eight serving bowls. Top with a poached egg, then spoon some of the piping-hot broth on top (this will reheat the egg, which will have cooled by now, and soften the toast). Sprinkle with the reserved bacon, mushrooms, and shallots, then top with Turkish red pepper, flaky sea salt, and chopped parsley.

Phyllo-Wraped Brie with Hot Honey and Anchovies, **page 56**

Cheese

Comté Cocktail Crackers

MAKES ABOUT 4 DOZEN CRACKERS

These cookie-like cocktail crackers are a bit of a tease because, if you're not expecting hot chiles and sharp cheese, you might think you are going to be biting into a vanilla shortbread. Which is to say, warn any small children in the vicinity before they are profoundly disappointed. For grown-ups, these are the perfect savory snack to serve with cocktails. They're pleasantly piquant, deeply buttery, have just the right crunch. You can serve them at room temperature, but if you really want to spoil your guests, bring them out while they're still warm from the oven, either freshly baked or briefly reheated. If you can't find Comté, substitute Gruyère or even a good extra-sharp cheddar.

Thinking Ahead

Dough: You can freeze the dough, sealed in plastic wrap, for 3 months. Let it come to room temperature for 10 minutes before rolling it out.

Crackers: You can bake them 3 days in advance and store them in an airtight container at room temperature. Before serving, reheat the crackers in a 300°F oven for 5 minutes.

1½ cups (195 grams) all-purpose flour, plus more for rolling
1½ cups (6 ounces) finely grated Comté or Gruyère cheese, divided
1 tablespoon cornstarch
1 teaspoon sugar
¼ teaspoon fine sea salt
½ teaspoon hot smoked paprika, plus more for sprinkling
10 tablespoons (1¼ sticks / 141 grams) cold unsalted butter, cubed
Flaky sea salt, to taste

1. In a food processor, pulse to combine the flour, 1 cup (4 ounces) of the Comté, the cornstarch, sugar, fine sea salt, and paprika. Add the butter and continue to process until the dough forms a ball. Or, combine everything in a large bowl and use a pastry cutter or two knives to cut the butter and cheese into the flour mixture. Be thorough so the dough is mostly smooth (though a few small butter chunks are okay).

2. Place the dough between two pieces of parchment paper or wax paper and roll it out to ¼-inch thickness. Slide the whole thing onto a baking sheet and chill until firm, 30 minutes.

3. Heat the oven to 350°F. Line two baking sheets with parchment paper.

4. Use a 1-inch round cookie cutter to cut the dough into disks, and transfer them to the prepared baking sheets. Reroll the scraps between the parchment paper and cut out more disks.

5. Sprinkle the crackers with the remaining ½ cup Comté, flaky sea salt, and paprika. Bake until golden, 15 to 18 minutes, rotating the baking sheets halfway through. Serve warm or at room temperature.

Croque Monsieur Casserole

SERVES 4 TO 6

4 tablespoons (½ stick) unsalted butter, plus more for the baking dish

¼ cup all-purpose flour

2½ cups whole milk, warmed

2½ cups (10 ounces) grated Gruyère cheese, divided

½ teaspoon herbes de Provence or dried thyme

Pinch of kosher salt

Pinch of freshly grated nutmeg

2 tablespoons Dijon mustard, preferably whole-grain, or as needed

8 slices white sandwich bread (pain de mie)

6 ounces thinly sliced ham

2 tablespoons (½ ounce) finely grated Parmesan cheese

A *croque monsieur* is a toasted ham and cheese sandwich that the French make even more decadent by showering it with a cheesy Mornay sauce and baking it until golden. I ate a lot of them when I was a college student in Paris, attempting to absorb Stendhal's *Le Rouge et Le Noir* in cafés when I was really much more interested in the sandwiches on my plate (or in anything that didn't involve looking up every third word in my unwieldy French-English dictionary, stupendously misnamed *Petit Robert*, which I heaved around with me).

Here I line up the sandwiches in a casserole dish and bake everything until the cheese melts into a gooey puddle and the ham turns soft and brawny. The mustard sharply interrupts all the richness; I like the forthright acidity and nubby texture of whole-grain mustard here, but creamy Dijon will work just as well. Be sure to buy good, firm white bread, such as French *pain de mie* or Arnold's. Soft and spongy white bread will get soggy.

Serve this for brunch, lunch, or the coziest of dinners, with a crisp green salad on the side, dressed with a shallot vinaigrette (see page 72).

1. Heat the oven to 375°F and butter a deep (1½ to 2 inches) 9 × 9-inch baking dish.

2. Melt the butter in a medium skillet over medium heat. Stir in the flour and cook, whisking, until it turns golden (but does not brown), about 3 minutes. Slowly whisk in the milk until smooth. Bring the mixture to a simmer, then remove the skillet from the heat and stir in 1 cup of the Gruyère, the herbes de Provence, salt, and nutmeg; the sauce should be thick and smooth. This is your Mornay sauce.

3. On a work surface, slather the mustard on one side of each of 4 bread slices, then top the mustard with the ham. Sprinkle 1 cup of the remaining Gruyère over the ham, and cover with the remaining bread slices. Cut each sandwich in half so you end up with two rectangles (don't cut diagonally—you don't want triangles here because they won't fit as nicely into the pan).

Thinking Ahead

Mornay sauce: You can make the sauce 4 days in advance and store it, covered, in the refrigerator.

4. Spread a little Mornay sauce on the bottom of the prepared baking dish. Spread sauce over the top of each sandwich, covering it all the way to the edges. Place the sandwiches in the dish, overlapping slightly with their cut sides facing up.

5. Spoon the remaining Mornay sauce over the sandwiches, spreading it to cover all exposed surfaces. Sprinkle the Parmesan and remaining ½ cup Gruyère over the top. Bake until puffed and golden, 35 to 40 minutes.

Sweet Potato Aligot
with Fried Sage

SERVES 4 TO 6

I first saw *pommes aligot* being whipped up tableside at a restaurant in the Auvergne. Into a well-used copper pot, the waiter beat boiled yellow potatoes with handfuls of grated nutty-tasting local *tomme fraîche* until the mixture could stretch the length of his arm as he pulled it above his head. Then he mounded the steaming elastic mix next to browned sausages, and I ate them together, spreading the *aligot* over sausage slices like a thick sauce.

In this very American version of *pommes aligot*, sweet potatoes stand in for the regular potatoes, which makes the whole thing richer and autumnal.

To create a crisp-salty garnish for all that smooth, rich purée, I strew fried sage leaves on top. Try to find the biggest sage leaves you can—they are easier to fry than small leaves, which can burn almost as soon as you add them to the oil. In any case, have everything set up before you start frying, and work quickly. Season the leaves while they are still hot so the salt sticks, and try not to gobble them all before the *aligot* is ready (this is harder than you'd think).

Serve this as a meatless main course with a snappy green salad, or on the side with grilled meats or roast chicken. Or bring it out on Thanksgiving instead of the usual sweet potato casserole.

1 pound sweet potatoes, peeled and cut into 2-inch chunks

Fine sea salt, as needed

Grapeseed, olive, or sunflower oil, as needed

1 small bunch large sage leaves

¼ cup heavy cream

1 sprig fresh thyme or lemon thyme

6 tablespoons (¾ stick) unsalted butter, cubed

1 garlic clove, finely grated or minced

Large pinch of freshly grated nutmeg

2 cups (8 ounces) grated Gruyère, Comté, or Emmentaler cheese

5 ounces Saint-Nectaire or Tomme de Savoie cheese, rind removed, cubed

Freshly ground black pepper

1. Put the sweet potatoes in a pot of heavily salted water, making sure they are covered by at least an inch of water. Bring to a boil, then reduce the heat and simmer until the potatoes are tender, 10 to 15 minutes. Drain the potatoes, but don't wash out the pot; you'll need it later.

2. While the potatoes are boiling, fry the sage leaves: Line a plate with a paper towel. In a small skillet, heat ¼ inch of oil. Add the sage leaves, a few at a time, and fry until they are golden and crisp, usually 1 minute or so. Use a slotted spoon to transfer them to the paper towel–lined plate and sprinkle with salt. Repeat with the remaining sage leaves, adding more oil to the skillet if needed.

3. In a small pot, bring the cream and thyme sprig to a simmer over medium heat. Remove the pot from the heat, cover it, and set aside until needed.

4. Transfer the cooked potatoes to a food processor and pulse until mashed. (Or you can pass the potatoes through a food mill or a large-mesh sieve to mash them.)

5. Return the potatoes to the pot and set it over low heat. Using a wooden spoon, stir in the butter, garlic, and nutmeg until the butter is melted.

6. Remove the thyme sprig from the cream. Stir the cream into the potatoes. Then stir in all the cheese, a handful at a time, until the aligot is melted and stretchy. Season with more salt if needed and serve immediately, topped with the fried sage leaves and freshly ground pepper.

Thinking Ahead

Aligot: This is most impressively served right after it's made, when the potatoes are best able to stretch to dramatic heights in front of your guests. But you can make it up to 3 days in advance. Reheat it over low heat, stirring in a little extra cream, until the mixture is melted and smooth.

VARIATION

Classic Pommes Aligot

Use russet potatoes in place of sweet potatoes, increase the cream to ½ cup, and eliminate the sage leaves.

Truffled Mac and Cheese

SERVES 10 TO 12

Adding truffles to mac and cheese may not have been a strictly French innovation, but it certainly had a moment in Paris. And with good reason: the funky mushroom earthiness of the truffle (in this case a combination of truffle oil and truffle cheese) adds depth to mac and cheese without doing anything to alter its inherent comfort factor. Try to find a truffle oil that uses real truffles rather than a synthetic flavoring; it will tell you on the bottle. You can use either white or black truffle oil here. Though their flavors are different (black truffles are more intense, white ones more ethereal), both work gorgeously with the pasta and melted cheese. If you can't find truffle cheese, you can substitute a young pecorino or a sharp white cheddar, then add a few tablespoons of chopped canned, frozen, or preserved truffles. It will be more expensive than the cheese, but more deluxe as well.

FOR THE TOPPING

2 cups panko bread crumbs

¾ cup (3 ounces) grated Gruyère cheese

¾ cup (3 ounces) grated truffle cheese (such as truffle pecorino)

2 large garlic cloves, finely grated or minced

3 tablespoons truffle oil

FOR THE MACARONI AND THE CHEESE SAUCE

4 tablespoons (½ stick) unsalted butter, plus extra for the casserole dish

1 pound elbow macaroni

¼ cup all-purpose flour

4 cups whole milk

3 cups (12 ounces) coarsely grated Gruyère cheese

1 cup (4 ounces) coarsely grated truffle cheese (such as truffled pecorino)

2 teaspoons fine sea salt, plus more for the pot

½ teaspoon Dijon mustard

Cayenne pepper, to taste

Freshly ground black pepper, to taste

1. **Make the topping:** In a large bowl, using a wooden spoon or your hands, combine the panko, Gruyère, truffle cheese, garlic, and truffle oil until uniformly mixed (make sure the garlic is well distributed).

2. Heat the oven to 400°F. Butter a large (2-quart) casserole dish or a 9 × 13-inch baking pan.

3. **Cook the macaroni:** Bring a large pot of heavily salted water to a boil, add the macaroni, and cook until 2 minutes before al dente. (It should be firmer than you'd want to eat it.) Drain and reserve.

recipe continues

Topping: You can prepare the topping 3 days in advance and store it in an airtight container in the refrigerator. Cover the macaroni mixture evenly with the topping right before baking.

Mac and cheese: You can prepare the topping and the mac and cheese (through step 4) 2 days in advance. Pour the macaroni mixture into the buttered casserole dish and keep it, well wrapped, in the refrigerator. Before serving, cover it evenly with the topping and bake.

4. **While the pasta is cooking, make the cheese sauce:** In a large saucepan, melt the butter over medium heat. Whisk in the flour, whisking until it smells nutty, 2 to 3 minutes. Whisk in the milk and bring the mixture to a boil (keep whisking). Reduce it to a simmer and continue to whisk for about 3 minutes, until slightly thickened. Stir in the Gruyère, truffle cheese, salt, mustard, cayenne, and black pepper. Then stir the drained pasta into the cheese sauce, taste, and adjust the seasonings if needed. The mixture will be very, very loose, but don't worry—the sauce will get absorbed as the macaroni bakes.

5. Pour the macaroni mixture into the buttered casserole dish and cover it evenly with the topping. Place the dish on a baking pan (to catch drips), and bake until the mac and cheese is golden and bubbly, 30 to 35 minutes. Let it sit for 5 to 10 minutes before serving.

VARIATION

Mac and Cheese with Roquefort and Gruyère

This golden-topped dish has a lot more oomph than your average mac and cheese, partly due to the piquancy of the Roquefort and Gruyère, and partly because of all the garlic I grate into the crunchy bread-crumb topping. It's still got all the gooey allure of the more classic casserole, but with an added French panache.

For the topping, substitute ¾ cup extra-sharp cheddar for the truffle cheese and 4 tablespoons melted butter for the truffle oil.

For the mac and cheese, substitute 2 cups (8 ounces) Roquefort cheese for the truffle cheese.

Fromage Blanc and Smoked Trout Dip

MAKES 1½ CUPS

Fromage blanc gives this herbed smoked trout dip a creamy texture and pronounced tang. The dip is perfect to serve with crackers or crudités alongside cocktails, but it also works well smeared on a bagel, should you want to introduce a French accent to your usual Sunday brunch. And although it might be fishy overkill to some, I wouldn't object to a little lox draped over the top. If you don't have smoked trout on hand, other smoked fish—salmon, tuna, or mackerel—can be substituted.

1 cup fromage blanc or plain Greek yogurt

4 ounces smoked trout, bones and skin removed

⅓ cup thinly sliced scallions (white and green parts)

2 tablespoons (1 ounce) cream cheese, at room temperature

1 tablespoon chopped fresh dill fronds or parsley leaves

1 tablespoon chopped fresh tarragon leaves

½ teaspoon finely grated lime zest

1 teaspoon fresh lime juice, plus more to taste

¼ teaspoon freshly ground black pepper

¼ teaspoon fine sea salt, plus more to taste

Cut-up vegetables, sliced bread, or crackers, for serving

1. In the bowl of a food processor or blender, combine the fromage blanc with the trout, scallions, cream cheese, dill, tarragon, lime zest and juice, and pepper and salt. Pulse until almost smooth. Taste, and add more lime juice and/or salt, as needed.

2. Spoon the mixture into a serving bowl or crock, and serve with the vegetables, bread, and/or crackers.

Thinking Ahead

You can make the dip 1 to 2 days in advance and store it, covered, in the refrigerator. The dip will get stronger in flavor as it sits. Bring it to room temperature before serving.

Classic Fromage Fort with Chives

MAKES ABOUT 1 CUP

French cooks whip up *fromage fort*—a creamy, heady cheese spread spiked with garlic and wine—when they want to use all the little bits of cheese left over in their fridges (those lonely pieces just a tad too small to put out on the cheese plate). And because they are French, these cooks just happen to have a great variety of excellent cheese bits on hand, which makes for a richly flavored spread. But even two or three different varieties will make a delicious *fromage fort*, especially if you've got at least one pungent, stinky piece (a blue cheese or a runny Camembert, for example) to give the spread some soul. Serve with crackers or thin slices of bread. I especially like a bread studded with dried fruit for a bit of sweetness to contrast with the saltiness of the cheese.

8 ounces mixed cheese bits (remove any rinds you don't want to eat before weighing), such as blue cheese, feta, goat cheese, Gruyère, cheddar, Brie, or whatever you've got on hand—the more the merrier

4 tablespoons (½ stick) unsalted butter, room temperature

1 small garlic clove, finely grated or minced

¼ cup dry rosé or white wine

2 tablespoons chopped fresh chives

½ teaspoon freshly ground black pepper, or more to taste

⅛ teaspoon fine sea salt, or more to taste

Crackers, sliced bread, and/or sliced radishes, for serving

1. In the bowl of a food processor or blender, combine the cheeses with the butter, garlic, wine, chives, pepper, and salt. Blend until smooth. Taste, and adjust the seasonings as needed.

2. Scoop the mixture into a pretty crock or small serving bowl, cover, and let it rest at room temperature for at least 2 hours. Serve with crackers, bread, and/or sliced radishes.

Thinking Ahead

Cheese mixture: You can make the fromage fort and store it, covered, in the refrigerator for up to 1 week. Bring it to room temperature before serving.

Jalapeño Fromage Fort

MAKES ABOUT 1 CUP

If *fromage fort* went to Texas on vacation, it might come back looking like this: a rich, cheese-filled spread speckled with cilantro and pickled jalapeño and spiked with tequila. It's only slightly spicy to allow the flavors of the cheeses to come through, but if you want more of a punch, use the whole fresh jalapeño, including its fiery seeds.

4 ounces mixed cheese bits (whatever you have in the fridge; cut off any rinds that you don't want to eat before weighing)

½ cup (2 ounces) coarsely grated cheddar cheese

2 ounces (½ cup) fresh goat cheese

⅓ cup fresh cilantro leaves and tender stems, packed

2 tablespoons unsalted butter

2 tablespoons dry white wine

2 tablespoons chopped pickled jalapeño

2 teaspoons tequila (optional, or use more white wine)

1 garlic clove, finely grated or minced

½ fresh jalapeño, seeded if you like, chopped

Fine sea salt and freshly ground black pepper, to taste

Ritz or other crackers, for serving

1. In the bowl of a food processor or blender, combine all the cheeses with the cilantro, butter, wine, pickled jalapeño, tequila if using, garlic, fresh jalapeño, and a pinch of salt and pepper. Blend until smooth. Taste, and adjust the seasonings as needed.

2. Scoop the mixture into a pretty crock or small serving bowl, cover, and let it rest at room temperature for at least 2 hours. Serve with Ritz or other crackers.

Thinking Ahead

Cheese mixture: You can make the *fromage fort* and store it, covered, in the refrigerator for up to 1 week. Bring it to room temperature before serving.

Stuffing a layer of grated Gruyère cheese into latkes is not at all traditional, but it is extremely good. Most of the cheese melts into the potatoes, giving the latkes a soft and runny center, while the little bit that escapes mingles with the grated potatoes frying in the oil, adding extra crunch to the already brittle golden shards. Scallions replace the usual onion here, giving the whole thing a slightly sweeter flavor and a bit of color. Serve these as you would regular latkes, smothered in sour cream (or crème fraîche) and topped with either applesauce or salmon roe.

Gruyère Latkes

MAKES ABOUT 12 LATKES

1 pound (about 2 large) russet potatoes, cut lengthwise into quarters

6 scallions (white and green parts)

2 large eggs

1¼ cups (5 ounces) grated Gruyère cheese, divided

½ cup all-purpose flour

1½ teaspoons fine sea salt, plus more as needed

1 teaspoon baking powder

½ teaspoon freshly ground black pepper

Olive or grapeseed oil, or duck fat, for frying

Chopped fresh chives, for serving (optional)

Crème fraîche or sour cream, for serving (optional)

Applesauce or salmon roe, for serving (optional)

1. Use the coarse grating disk of a food processor to grate the potatoes and scallions; you can grate them together. (Or you can grate the potatoes by hand on a box grater and finely chop the scallions.) Transfer the potatoes and scallions to a clean dish towel and squeeze out as much liquid as possible. Be thorough; the drier your mixture, the crisper the latkes.

2. Transfer the potato mixture to a large bowl and stir in the eggs, 1 cup of the cheese, and the flour, salt, baking powder, and pepper. Scoop out a golf ball–size mound (about 3 tablespoons), and flatten it to about ¼ inch thick on a cutting board. Top it with 1 teaspoon of the remaining cheese, then scoop another golf ball–size mound on top and squish it down over the first mound to make a ¾-inch-thick patty with cheese in the middle. Repeat with the remaining batter and cheese.

3. Heat ¼ inch of oil in a large heavy-bottomed skillet over medium heat. Once the oil is hot, carefully drop the patties into the skillet, leaving generous space around each one. Use a spatula to flatten them into disks. Cook until the edges are brown and crispy, about 5 minutes. Then carefully flip them over and cook until very brown on the second side, about another 5 minutes. Reduce the heat if the potatoes start to burn, or raise the heat if they don't turn golden brown. If some of the cheese leaks out, this is a good thing; it will turn crunchy as it hits the hot pan. As they are finished, transfer the latkes to a paper towel–lined plate and immediately sprinkle them with a little salt. Repeat until all the latkes are fried, adding more oil as needed. Serve hot, with chives, crème fraîche, and applesauce or salmon roe, if you like.

Savory Gruyère Bread with Ham

MAKES 1 LOAF

In France, savory loaf breads like this one are called *cakes salés*. They are the kind of thing someone might bake up to serve as an hors d'oeuvre, thinly sliced and served either naked or topped with even more cheese or ham, crostini-style. These *cakes* feel a bit like *gougères* in their deep cheesiness, except they're easier and can be made entirely in advance without losing anything by being served at room temperature. Leftovers are great for breakfast the next day— I love my slices toasted, buttered, and topped with slices of ripe tomatoes. If you'd like to skip the meat, substitute ⅔ cup sliced pitted olives for the ham.

Thinking Ahead

Bread: You can bake the loaf up to 3 days in advance. Store it, well wrapped, in the refrigerator and bring it to room temperature before serving. Or freeze it for up to 2 months. After freezing, this is best sliced and served toasted and warm— and spread with butter if you like.

4 tablespoons (½ stick / 56 grams) unsalted butter, melted and cooled, plus more for the pan

2½ cups (325 grams) all-purpose flour, plus more for the pan

1½ teaspoons baking powder

1 teaspoon fine sea salt

½ teaspoon baking soda

1 cup (180 grams) coarsely chopped ham

3 tablespoons thinly sliced scallions, white and green parts (optional)

1 tablespoon chopped fresh thyme leaves

2 cups (8 ounces / 198 grams) grated Gruyère or sharp cheddar cheese

2 large eggs

1 cup (240 milliliters) buttermilk

1. Heat the oven to 350°F. Butter and flour a metal 9 × 5-inch loaf pan and set it aside.

2. In a large bowl, whisk together the flour, baking powder, salt, and baking soda. Stir in the chopped ham, scallions if using, thyme, and 1¾ cups (7 ounces) of the Gruyère (reserving the rest for topping). In a separate bowl, whisk together the melted butter, eggs, and buttermilk. Add the wet mixture to the flour mixture and stir to combine. The batter will be thick.

3. Transfer the batter to the prepared loaf pan and spread it out evenly, smoothing the top. Sprinkle the remaining ¼ cup (1 ounce) cheese over the top. Bake until the top springs back when lightly pressed and a skewer inserted in the center comes out with some moist crumbs attached, 45 to 55 minutes.

4. Transfer the pan to a wire rack and let it cool for 10 minutes. Then remove the bread from the pan and let it cool completely on the wire rack.

Phyllo-Wrapped Brie with Hot Honey and Anchovies

SERVES 10 TO 12

I have an unhealthy relationship with baked Brie. I cannot resist its gorgeous melted siren song, usually eating far more than my fair share of a dish that is, in theory, put out as a party snack for everyone to enjoy. Of course the obvious solution is just to bake up more of it. So whenever I make baked Brie, I go straight for the large hubcap-size rounds. They're harder to find than little six-inch wheels, but they make a more impressive presentation, and you rarely have to worry about running out (though you may need an extra set of hands to help you maneuver the bigger cheese).

While most baked Bries are on the sweet side, with layers of jam or chutney under the crust, here I go savory with anchovies, garlic, and roasted bell peppers. A drizzle of hot or regular honey adds complexity without making it cloying, and a pinch of lemon zest brightens things up. Serve this straight from the oven when it's at its runniest, with crisp crackers or crusty bread for crunch.

NOTE: If you don't have hot honey but want the spice here, you can make your own by stirring a pinch or two of cayenne into mild honey, such as clover or orange blossom.

¼ cup chopped roasted red bell pepper (from a jar or homemade; see sidebar)

3 oil-packed anchovy fillets, minced

1 garlic clove, finely grated or minced

¾ teaspoon finely grated lemon zest

1 pound phyllo dough, thawed if frozen

10 tablespoons (1¼ sticks) unsalted butter, melted

1 large (about 26 ounces) wheel of Brie

Hot honey (see note) or regular honey, for serving

Crackers and/or sliced bread, for serving

1. Heat the oven to 425°F.

2. In a small bowl, stir together the roasted bell pepper, anchovies, garlic, and lemon zest. Set aside.

3. On a clean work surface, lay out the phyllo dough and cover it with a barely damp kitchen towel to keep it from drying out. Take 2 phyllo sheets and lay them in an 11 × 17-inch rimmed baking sheet. Brush the top sheet generously with melted butter, then lay another 2 phyllo sheets on top the opposite way, so they cross in the center and are perpendicular to the first two (like making a plus sign). Brush the top sheet with butter. Repeat the layers, reserving 4 sheets of phyllo.

4. Using a long sharp kitchen knife, halve the Brie horizontally and lay one half, cut-side up, in the center of the phyllo (you will probably need another set of hands to help lift off the top layer of cheese). Then spread the red pepper mixture all over the top. Cover with the other half of Brie, cut-side down, and then fold the phyllo pieces up around the Brie. There will be a space in the center on top where the Brie is uncovered, and that's okay.

How to Roast Bell Peppers

Over an open flame on your stovetop, on your grill, or under the broiler, roast the bell peppers, turning them often, until the skins are black and blistered all over, 10 to 15 minutes. Transfer the peppers to a heatproof bowl, cover it with a plate, and let them sit for 15 minutes to steam and cool. Using paper towels or your fingers, rub off the skins. Peppers can be roasted up to 2 days in advance and stored, with any juices, in the refrigerator.

5. Lightly crumple one of the remaining sheets of phyllo and place it on top of the phyllo/Brie package to cover up that space. Drizzle a little butter on top, then repeat with the remaining phyllo sheets, scattering them over the top of the pastry and drizzling a little butter each time. It may look messy but will bake up into gorgeous golden waves of pastry, so fear not.

6. Bake until the phyllo is golden, 20 to 25 minutes. Remove it from the oven and let it rest for about 15 minutes before drizzling it with the hot honey. Slice (it will be runny) and serve with crackers or bread, and with more hot honey as needed.

Lillet Fondue

SERVES 8

A dash of Lillet, the aromatic aperitif from Bordeaux, adds a touch of sweetness to this otherwise very traditional cheese fondue. But feel free to use this basic recipe as the template for your own experimentation, substituting other alcohols—whiskey, Amaro, tequila—for the Lillet. This spirited fondue is open to suggestion. Or to make things perfectly classic, just use a little more white wine.

Note that you don't need a fondue set here—a Dutch oven or other thick, heavy pot will work perfectly well; just bring it back to the stove to reheat if the cheese gets cold and starts to harden. Regular forks (and chopsticks!) do as well as fondue forks—as long as everyone keeps track of which one is theirs.

1 small garlic clove, halved

1 cup dry white wine

2 tablespoons Lillet (or sweet sherry or other liquor)

3 cups (12 ounces) grated Gruyère cheese

3 cups (12 ounces) grated Emmentaler cheese

1½ tablespoons cornstarch

Fine sea salt and freshly ground black pepper, to taste

Freshly grated nutmeg, to taste (optional)

Cubes of sturdy country bread and cut-up vegetables (such as raw carrots, mushrooms, cherry tomatoes, zucchini, or romaine hearts; or steamed broccoli, cauliflower, fennel, or potatoes), for serving

1. Rub the cut side of the garlic halves over the inside of a large Dutch oven, heavy-bottomed saucepan, or fondue pot, covering the bottom and halfway up the sides. Add the wine and Lillet and bring to a simmer over medium-high heat.

2. Meanwhile, in a large bowl, toss the cheeses with the cornstarch.

3. A handful at a time, add the cheese mixture to the simmering wine, stirring until each handful melts before adding the next. Reduce the heat to medium and stir constantly until the cheese is completely melted. Season with salt, pepper, and nutmeg if desired. Serve at once, with the bread cubes and cut-up vegetables for dipping. (If the fondue cools and starts to congeal, just put it back over low heat for a minute or two, stirring, to loosen it up again.)

Burrata with Brown Butter, Lemon, and Cherries

SERVES 4

This gorgeously scarlet-dappled dish is the thing to serve at the height of summer cherry season, when you need a stunning appetizer but you don't feel like turning on the oven. The lemon zest–spiked brown butter is the French connection to the Italian cheese, adding a bright, nutty flavor to the rich, soft burrata. If you want to make this at other times of the year, substitute another juicy fruit for the cherries, such as diced blood oranges in winter or grapes or plums in fall.

Thinking Ahead

Cherries: You can halve and pit the cherries 5 days in advance and store them, covered, in the refrigerator.

3 cups (about 11 ounces) whole fresh cherries

1 tablespoon balsamic vinegar, plus more for serving

4 tablespoons (½ stick) unsalted butter

¼ teaspoon finely grated lemon zest

8 ounces burrata or fresh mozzarella cheese

Torn fresh mint leaves, for serving

Flaky sea salt, for serving

Sliced baguette or other crusty bread, for serving (optional)

1. Using a paring knife, halve and pit the cherries. In a medium bowl, toss together the cherries and vinegar. Let them sit while you make the brown butter.

2. Melt the butter in a small saucepan over medium heat. Continue to cook until it smells nutty and is browned, about 5 minutes. Remove the pan from the heat and stir in the lemon zest.

3. To serve, place the burrata in the center of a serving dish. Spoon the cherries around it, then drizzle the brown butter on top. Top with the mint, flaky sea salt, and more balsamic vinegar to taste.

4. Serve with bread, if you like, or with spoons for catching the milky juices of the cheese.

Salads

Caesar Salad au Frisée

SERVES 4

1 large egg

2 tablespoons (½ ounce) grated Parmesan cheese, plus more for serving

2 to 4 oil-packed anchovy fillets, minced

1 fat garlic clove, finely grated or minced

½ teaspoon fresh lemon juice, plus more to taste

¼ teaspoon freshly ground black pepper

Fine sea salt, to taste

Dash of Worcestershire sauce

Dash of Tabasco sauce

3 to 4 tablespoons extra-virgin olive oil

2 heads frisée, washed, dried, and torn into bite-size pieces

Using curly frisée in place of romaine lettuce in a Caesar salad is a textural delight. The frisée is still crisp enough to stand up to all the egg, Parmesan, and anchovies in the dressing, and it offers far more nooks and crannies into which that dressing can seep. If you can't find frisée, you can certainly make this with romaine—it will be more traditional but just as delicious. That's how I make it for my ten-year-old daughter, who loves nothing more than eating Caesar salad with her fingers, straight from the bowl, rubbing the lettuce pieces all over the bottom and sides to get every last garlicky drop. I can't say I blame her.

You'll notice two other unusual things about this salad. One is that I simmer the egg for a few minutes, just to firm up the white slightly and thicken the yolk—it adds a bit of texture and keeps the egg from totally disappearing into the dressing. Also, I don't add croutons, which makes this a bit less filling than other Caesars. But feel free to add them if you're looking for something more substantial.

1. Fill a small bowl with cold water and ice.

2. Place the egg in a small pot and add cold water to cover it by 1 inch. Bring the water to a boil, then reduce the heat and simmer for 3 minutes. Remove the egg with a slotted spoon and submerge it in the ice bath. Let it cool slightly, then peel while it is still warm.

3. In a small bowl, combine the Parmesan, anchovies, garlic, lemon juice, pepper, pinch of salt, Worcestershire, Tabasco, and egg. Use a whisk to break apart the egg, then whisk everything together. In a slow, steady stream, pour in the oil, whisking constantly. Taste, and add more salt and/or lemon juice if needed.

4. In a large bowl, toss the frisée with the dressing to taste. Then transfer the salad to serving plates, top it with more Parmesan to taste, and serve.

Thinking Ahead

Dressing: The dressing will keep for 1 week in an airtight container in the refrigerator. Bring it to room temperature and whisk together before dressing the salad.

I can get hardy dark green dandelion greens at my farmers' market in sweater season—usually spring and fall. And I love to use them in salads next to rich ingredients that contrast with their wild bitterness, which is happily still not bred out of these assertively flavored greens. Here, soft sweet confited garlic, crisp pancetta, and crumbled creamy blue cheese tame the dandelion, and the poached eggs make this satisfying enough if you want to serve it for lunch or a light dinner. If you can't get dandelion greens, mature arugula or spinach or escarole make good substitutes. Just avoid delicate lettuces or baby greens, which will wilt too quickly when they make contact with the hot oil.

Dandelion Salad with Sweet Garlic Confit, Pancetta, and Blue Cheese

SERVES 4

4 tablespoons extra-virgin olive oil, divided, plus more as needed

1 head garlic, broken into cloves and peeled, divided

8 ounces pancetta, cut into ¾-inch pieces

6 ounces dandelion or other bitter greens, washed, dried, and torn into bite-size pieces

½ large head radicchio or 2 heads red endive, cut into bite-size pieces

1 tablespoon sherry vinegar, plus more to taste

Fine sea salt, to taste

¼ teaspoon freshly ground black pepper

½ teaspoon Dijon mustard

½ cup (2 ounces) crumbled blue cheese (use a sweeter blue cheese, such as Bleu d'Auvergne, or Gorgonzola dolce)

4 poached eggs (optional; see sidebar, page 37)

1. Heat 2 tablespoons of the oil in a medium skillet over medium-low heat. Reserving 1 garlic clove for the dressing, add the remaining cloves to the skillet. Cook until they are pale golden all over, 7 to 10 minutes. Raise the heat to medium and stir in the pancetta. Cook until the pork is crisp and the garlic is deep golden and soft, 15 to 20 minutes. If the mixture starts to dry out, drizzle it with a little more oil. If the garlic starts to turn dark brown in spots, reduce the heat. Using a slotted spoon, transfer the garlic and pancetta to a paper towel–lined plate (reserve the oil in the skillet).

2. Place the dandelion greens in a large heat-proof bowl. Scatter the radicchio on top. Pour the hot oil from the skillet over the greens and toss well.

3. Grate or press the reserved garlic clove into a small bowl, and add the vinegar, salt, and pepper. Let the mixture sit for 1 minute. Then whisk in the mustard and finally the remaining 2 tablespoons oil.

4. Drizzle the dressing over the greens and radicchio and toss to coat, adding more oil, vinegar, and/or salt to taste. Fold in the pancetta lardons, garlic, and blue cheese. Transfer the salad to individual plates and top each serving with a poached egg if you like.

Thinking Ahead

Garlic-pancetta mixture: You can make this up to 3 weeks in advance. Let it cool to room temperature, then place it in an airtight container and refrigerate. Bring it to room temperature before serving.

Dressing: You can make this up to 7 days in advance and refrigerate it in an airtight container. Bring the dressing to room temperature and whisk it together before drizzling over the salad.

Roasted Beet, Caraway, and Crème Fraîche Salad with Arugula

SERVES 6

Most recipes for roasted beets call for cooking them still in their skins, then peeling after they're soft and supple. But I prefer peeling first, then roasting. This allows the beet flesh to take on a slight char, and it condenses their honeyed juices. Plus, I find it easier to slip off their skins with a vegetable peeler while they are still quite firm, rather than maneuvering a paring knife over their slick, slippery flesh after they're cooked (I've ruined many a T-shirt that way). And, since you don't have to wait for them to cool in order to peel them, you can toss the hot-from-the-oven beets directly into your waiting bowl of vinaigrette, which helps them absorb the maximum amount of dressing.

In this very colorful recipe, the roasted beets are paired with caraway-scented crème fraîche, arugula, and toasted nuts for crunch. It's a substantial salad that works as first course to a lighter dinner or as a side dish to grilled meats or pasta.

2½ pounds beets, peeled and cut into ½-inch-thick wedges

4 tablespoons extra-virgin olive oil, divided, plus more as needed

½ teaspoon fine sea salt, plus more as needed

½ teaspoon freshly ground black pepper, plus more as needed

2 tablespoons white wine vinegar

¼ teaspoon Dijon mustard

1 teaspoon caraway seeds

1 cup (8 ounces) crème fraîche

2 tablespoons chopped fresh dill, plus more for garnish

1 small garlic clove, finely grated or minced

3 cups (3 ounces) baby arugula, washed and dried

⅓ cup hazelnuts or walnuts, toasted and coarsely chopped

Flaky sea salt, for serving

1. Heat the oven to 400°F.

2. **Prepare the beets:** On a rimmed baking sheet, toss the beets with 2 tablespoons of the oil, the salt, and the pepper. Roast until tender, 45 to 60 minutes, tossing them halfway through.

3. **Meanwhile, make the vinaigrette:** In a large bowl, whisk together the white wine vinegar, mustard, and a large pinch of salt and pepper. In a slow steady stream, whisk in the remaining 2 tablespoons oil until emulsified. Pour half of the vinaigrette into a medium bowl and set it aside.

4. In the large bowl, toss the warm beets with the remaining vinaigrette and let them cool.

recipe continues

5. **Make the caraway crème fraîche:** In a small dry skillet over medium heat, toast the caraway seeds until fragrant, 1 to 2 minutes. Transfer them to a mortar and pestle and pound until coarsely crushed, or crush them on a cutting board with the flat side of a knife. In a small bowl, stir together the crushed caraway, crème fraîche, dill, garlic, and a big pinch of salt.

6. Toss the arugula with the reserved vinaigrette in the medium bowl; if the mixture seems a bit dry, drizzle with a little more olive oil.

7. To serve, spread the caraway crème fraîche over the bottom of a large serving platter and mound the beets, and then the arugula, on top. Scatter the hazelnuts over the arugula. Garnish with some dill and flaky sea salt, and finish with a drizzle of oil. Serve immediately.

Thinking Ahead

Beets: You can roast the beets and toss them in the vinaigrette up to 1 week ahead; store, covered, in the fridge. Bring to room temperature before using.

Vinaigrette: You can make this up to 7 days in advance and refrigerate it in an airtight container. Bring it to room temperature and whisk it together before using.

Caraway crème fraîche: You can make the mixture and refrigerate it, covered, up to 8 hours in advance. Drain off any excess moisture before spreading it on the platter.

Grated Carrot Salad with Preserved Lemon and Coriander

SERVES 4

1½ teaspoons coriander seeds

2 tablespoons fresh lemon juice, plus more to taste

2 tablespoons chopped preserved lemon

¼ teaspoon fine sea salt, plus more to taste

½ teaspoon honey, or to taste

5 tablespoons extra-virgin olive oil, plus more as needed

1 pound carrots

¼ cup fresh cilantro leaves and tender stems, chopped

2 tablespoons fresh mint leaves, chopped

Coarsely ground black pepper, for serving

During my student days in Paris, if I wasn't hanging out in cafés devouring croque monsieurs, it was only because I was having momentary qualms about my prodigious cheese consumption and was cooling it for a few days by ordering plates of crudités. It wasn't at all a sad alternative—the mix of colorful vegetable salads, each individually dressed and arranged on a plate, was always fantastic, even without any cheese within reach. Nowadays I order crudités for lunch before a big Parisian restaurant dinner, just to keep the whole day at least somewhat balanced (which means I can still have *pains au chocolate* for breakfast). Grated carrot salad inevitably shows up in the crudités mix, and it's always the one I devour first, before tucking into the mayonnaise-y celery root rémoulade. This salad recalls that ruddy tangle of carrots, but with the added pizzazz of preserved lemon and coriander—both seeds and leaves. It holds up well in the fridge if you want to make it in advance.

1. Heat a small skillet over medium heat. Toast the coriander, shaking the pan once or twice, until fragrant, 1 to 2 minutes. Transfer the seeds to a mortar and pestle and crush them. Scrape them into a large bowl. Add the lemon juice, preserved lemon, salt, and honey and stir together. In a slow, steady stream, whisk in the oil. Taste and, if necessary, add more salt or honey or lemon juice (or all three).

2. Grate the carrots on the largest holes of a box grater or in a food processor using the grating disk. Toss the carrots into the vinaigrette, along with the cilantro and mint. Add more salt and lemon juice if needed. Serve with a drizzle of olive oil and a sprinkling of pepper.

Thinking Ahead

Dressing: You can make the dressing 3 days in advance. Store it in an airtight container in the refrigerator and bring it to room temperature before using.

Salad: The salad can be made 24 hours ahead and stored, covered, in the fridge.

Baby Lettuce Salad with Shallot Vinaigrette

SERVES 6

As classic as can be, this salad is a perennial favorite. I serve it all year round, varying the lettuces to reflect what's in season. The shallot gives the dressing a little sweetness, while the mustard and vinegar (or lemon juice) add the necessary acid. I usually whisk lemon juice into my dressings because I like its freshness. But wine vinegar or, for that matter, rice vinegar, sherry vinegar, or cider vinegar, can all add their individual characters to the mix. I always toss salad with my hands. It's really the gentlest way to distribute the dressing on the greens without bruising them.

Thinking Ahead

Dressing: The vinaigrette will keep for 1 week in an airtight container in the refrigerator. Bring it to room temperature and whisk (or shake) it together before dressing the salad.

FOR THE GREENS

8 cups (8 ounces) baby lettuces or other salad greens (any kind you like is fine), washed and dried

FOR THE VINAIGRETTE

1 shallot, minced

2 tablespoons fresh lemon juice or white wine vinegar

2 teaspoons Dijon mustard

¼ teaspoon fine sea salt, plus more to taste

½ teaspoon coarsely ground black pepper, plus more to taste

1 cup extra-virgin olive oil, plus more to taste

1. **Clean the greens:** Rinse the leaves in cold water. Spin them dry in a salad spinner or let them air-dry, spread out over a towel, and pat them with paper towels.

2. **Prepare the vinaigrette:** In a small bowl, whisk together the shallot, lemon juice, and mustard. Add the salt and pepper and whisk again to dissolve the salt. Continue whisking while adding the oil in a slow stream. (Working slowly will give you a smooth and emulsified dressing.) Taste as you go, adding more salt and pepper and/or lemon juice or vinegar to balance the flavors. You can also do the whole process in a lidded jar, shaking the contents instead of whisking them (add the oil ⅓ cup at a time for this method, shaking vigorously after each addition). The jar technique makes it easy to store any excess dressing.

3. Place your greens in a large serving bowl. Just before you are ready to serve the salad, dress it (if you let the dressed salad sit for too long, the greens will become droopy). Drizzle the dressing over the greens a little at a time, tossing the leaves with your hands until they are just coated, or you can use salad tossers or tongs if you prefer. (You probably won't use all of the dressing.) Serve immediately.

Spinach and Grape Salad with Roquefort Dressing

SERVES 3 TO 4

As much as I adore the convenience and tenderness of the baby spinach that you can find just about anywhere these days, there's much to be said for mature spinach, with its crinkly, crunchy texture and deep mineral flavor. You can use either type here; mature spinach will give you a firmer, more pronounced bite than the floppy baby leaves, some of which will wilt when meeting the warm pancetta. The grapes, sautéed in pancetta fat for a few minutes until they turn slightly syrupy, add a gentle sweetness to the salty, tangy mix.

Thinking Ahead

Dressing: You can make the dressing 3 days in advance and store it in an airtight container in the refrigerator. Bring it to room temperature before adding it to the salad.

2 teaspoons fresh lemon juice

1 garlic clove, finely grated or minced

¼ teaspoon fine sea salt

2 tablespoons extra-virgin olive oil, plus more as needed

½ cup (2 ounces) Roquefort or other blue cheese, crumbled

⅓ cup (3 ounces) crème fraîche or sour cream

8 cups (8 ounces) spinach leaves (preferably mature spinach), washed, dried, and torn into bite-size pieces if large

3 ounces pancetta or bacon, cubed

1 cup seedless red grapes

Sherry vinegar, as needed

1. In a small bowl, combine the lemon juice, garlic, and salt; let it sit for a few minutes. Then whisk in the oil, and fold in the Roquefort and crème fraîche.

2. Place the spinach in a large serving bowl.

3. Heat a large skillet over medium heat. Add the pancetta and cook until it is golden and crispy, 7 to 12 minutes, adding a little oil if the pan looks dry. Transfer it with a slotted spoon to a paper towel–lined plate (keep the skillet over medium heat).

4. Add the grapes to the pancetta fat in the warm skillet. Stir in a splash of sherry vinegar and cook until the grape skins start to split, 2 to 3 minutes. Spoon the grapes, including any juices left in the skillet, over the spinach. Add the Roquefort dressing a little at a time, to taste, and toss to combine. Serve with the pancetta scattered on top and a sprinkling of more sherry vinegar, to taste.

Fennel Salad with Grapefruit and Warm Goat Cheese

SERVES 4

---

1 large fennel bulb with fronds

3 ounces watercress, washed, dried, and torn into bite-size pieces (about 2 cups)

2 large grapefruits

2 teaspoons white wine vinegar

½ teaspoon fine sea salt, plus more to taste

3 tablespoons extra-virgin olive oil, plus more as needed

Freshly ground black pepper, as needed

1 (4- to 5-ounce) goat cheese log, cold

½ cup finely ground hazelnuts

Baked goat cheese salads were once the darling of California cuisine for good reason. Coated in crushed nuts, then baked until velvety in the center and a little melted at the edges, warm goat cheese disks bring creamy verve to a plate of dressed salad greens. In this incarnation, spicy watercress is mixed with shaved fennel and grapefruit segments for a juicy, sweet, and tangy salad beneath the rounds of warm, hazelnut-coated cheese. Although the recipe is simple to put together, it does require the use of four bowls (sorry!). But this rich and retro salad is well worth it.

1. Heat the oven to 400°F.

2. Remove the fronds of the fennel bulb; chop them coarsely and reserve them. Peel away and discard the tough outer layers of the bulb. Halve the fennel bulb lengthwise and shave each half on a mandoline or thinly slice them with a knife. Transfer the slices to a large bowl and add the watercress.

3. Slice away the top and bottom of each grapefruit, so that they stand flat on a work surface. Following the curve of the fruit, cut off the peel, including all the white pith, with a sharp knife. Holding the fruit over a small bowl, cut the citrus segments away from the membranes, allowing the fruit to drop into the bowl.

4. **In a separate small bowl, make the vinaigrette:** Whisk together the vinegar, salt, and reserved chopped fennel fronds. Whisk in the oil and black pepper.

5. Slice the goat cheese into four ½-inch-thick rounds (dip a knife in warm water between slices to prevent the cheese from crumbling). Place the hazelnuts in a bowl and dip the goat cheese rounds in the nuts, coating them evenly. Transfer the cheese rounds to a small baking sheet, drizzle them with a little oil, and bake until they are warm and golden, about 10 minutes.

6. Toss the fennel and watercress with enough of the vinaigrette to coat everything. Gently toss in the grapefruit segments. Taste, and adjust the seasoning if necessary. Transfer the salad to individual serving plates and arrange the warm goat cheese rounds alongside. Serve immediately.

Thinking Ahead

Dressing: You can make the dressing 1 week in advance and store it in an airtight container in the refrigerator.

Grapefruit: You can segment the grapefruits 3 days in advance, cover the bowl, and store it in the refrigerator.

Radicchio and Baked Camembert Salad

SERVES 4

Unlike warm goat cheese salads, baked Camembert salads never had their moment of glory in restaurants all over California and beyond. And while I adore warm goat cheese, I might like warm Camembert even better. After a brief stint in the oven, the heady cheese will gush all over the plate, coating the greens (or, in this case, reds and greens since I use both radicchio and parsley) with its mushroomy creaminess. It's an easy salad to make once you get your hands on a small wheel of Camembert, but it offers maximum sexiness—as sexy as salad gets, if you ask me. Serve it with crusty bread to mop up all the bits that you'd otherwise have to lick off the plate. There's only so much a salad course can take.

Thinking Ahead

Dressing: You can make this 1 week in advance. Store it in an airtight container in the refrigerator and bring it to room temperature, whisking if needed, before tossing it with the greens.

1 (8-ounce) wheel Camembert, cut into 4 wedges

1 large head (about 8 ounces) radicchio, sliced or torn into bite-size pieces (4 cups)

2 cups fresh Italian parsley leaves

1 packed cup (1 ounce) spinach leaves (preferably hearty, mature leaves rather than the baby ones), washed, dried, and torn into pieces if large

¼ cup very thinly sliced spring onion or sweet onion (or shallots)

1 tablespoon white wine vinegar, plus more to taste

¼ teaspoon fine sea salt, plus more to taste

Freshly ground black pepper, as needed

¼ cup extra-virgin olive oil

Crusty bread, for serving (optional)

1. Heat the oven to 450°F.

2. Place the cheese pieces about 1 inch apart on a small parchment-lined baking sheet. Bake until the cheese is soft and brown around the edges, 5 to 10 minutes.

3. Meanwhile, in a large bowl, toss together the radicchio, parsley, spinach, and onion.

4. In a small bowl, whisk together the vinegar, salt, and pepper; then whisk in the oil. Toss the dressing with the greens. Taste and adjust the salt and vinegar if desired. Serve the salad with the hot cheese wedges alongside, and crusty bread, if you like.

Endive, Ham, and Walnut Salad

SERVES 4

This brawny wintry salad is richer and more complex than most, with toasted walnuts for crunch and a mustard dressing for brightness. If you can find a mix of red and pale-green-tipped endive, it will be gorgeous as well. Serve it with more of the same ham you've used in the salad, which can be either a mild pink ham such as *jambon de Paris* (or any of the other dozens of varieties of cooked ham) or a drier, saltier cured ham, smoked or unsmoked. *Jambon de Bayonne* would be your French pick here, but prosciutto and Serrano ham are also excellent.

Thinking Ahead

Walnuts: You can toast the nuts 1 week ahead and store them in an airtight container at room temperature.

Dressing: You can make the dressing 1 week in advance. Store it in an airtight container in the refrigerator and bring it to room temperature, whisking if needed, before tossing the salad.

½ cup walnut halves

2 tablespoons white wine vinegar, plus more to taste

1 tablespoon Dijon mustard

½ teaspoon fine sea salt, plus more to taste

Freshly ground black pepper, to taste

¾ cup walnut oil (or extra-virgin olive oil), plus more to taste

4 heads Belgian endive

1 packed cup fresh parsley leaves

4 ounces sliced ham, diced

1. Heat the oven to 350°F.

2. Spread the walnuts on a small rimmed baking sheet and bake until they are golden, 5 to 10 minutes. Transfer them to a plate to cool.

3. While the nuts are baking, in a small bowl, whisk together the vinegar, mustard, salt, and pepper. Slowly whisk in the walnut oil until the mixture is well combined.

4. Remove a few nice-looking outer leaves from the endives, and reserve them. Slice the inner endive leaves crosswise into ½-inch-thick rounds, and transfer them to a large bowl. Add the parsley, ham, and enough dressing to coat; toss to combine. Taste, and add more salt, pepper, and/or vinegar if needed.

5. To serve, arrange the reserved whole endive leaves around the edge of a platter, heap the salad in the middle, and top it with the toasted walnuts.

Classic Salade Niçoise

SERVES 4

The Niçoise salads I ate in France when I was a kid all featured good canned tuna, the kind so richly infused with olive oil it was the ocean equivalent of butter. Then one day, fresh tuna—seared but still rare—started replacing the canned fish. The novelty was thrilling, making the whole dish heartier and more main course–like, without the bagged-lunch stigma the words *tuna fish* can convey. French traditionalists, however, were less impressed, insisting that in a true *salade Niçoise*, the fish must be preserved in oil and cooked through and through, without any of the sushi-centered, charred-edged frippery of the seared kind. (Also of note: Those same traditionalists, including *Larousse Gastronomique*, eschew adding cooked vegetables like green beans and potatoes to a *salade Niçoise*.)

While I say that there's room for all kinds of *salade Niçoise* interpretations, my heart is with the canned tuna version, as long as the tuna is of really good quality. Look for tuna packed in olive oil in cans or jars, rather than anything packed in soybean oil or water.

2 tablespoons minced shallots

2 teaspoons Dijon mustard

2 teaspoons red wine vinegar

4 oil-packed anchovy fillets, finely chopped

Fine sea salt and freshly ground black pepper, as needed

⅓ cup extra-virgin olive oil, plus more as needed

1 pound baby or very small red potatoes

1 pound haricots verts, trimmed

2 large ripe tomatoes, cut into chunks

4 large eggs

10 ounces good-quality olive oil–packed tuna, drained

½ cup Niçoise olives

Chopped fresh basil leaves, to taste

1. In a small bowl, whisk together the shallots, mustard, vinegar, anchovies, a pinch of salt, and pepper to taste. Slowly whisk in the oil until the dressing is emulsified. Taste, and add more salt if needed.

2. In a pot of salted boiling water, cook the potatoes until tender, 10 to 15 minutes. Use a slotted spoon to transfer the potatoes to a large bowl (save the water in the pot); pat the potatoes dry and toss with enough of the dressing to thoroughly coat them. Taste and add more salt if needed.

3. Bring the potato water back to a boil and add the green beans. Cook until crisp, 2 to 3 minutes. Drain, pat the beans dry, and add them to the bowl containing the potatoes, tossing with a little more of the dressing.

4. In a separate bowl, combine the tomatoes and more of the dressing. Taste and add more salt if needed.

5. While the vegetables marinate, cook the eggs: Place the eggs in a medium pot and add water to cover by 1 inch. Bring to a boil. Immediately remove the pot from the heat, cover it, and set it aside for 8 minutes.

6. Meanwhile, fill a medium bowl with ice and cold water.

7. Transfer the eggs with a slotted spoon to the bowl of ice water. Once they are cool enough to handle, peel and halve the eggs lengthwise. Sprinkle lightly with salt.

8. Arrange the potatoes, green beans, tomatoes, egg halves, and tuna on a large platter. Scatter the olives over all. Spoon the remaining dressing over the salad. Drizzle the salad with oil and sprinkle with basil.

Thinking Ahead

Dressing: You can make the dressing 1 week in advance. Store it in an airtight container in the refrigerator and bring it to room temperature, whisking if needed, before using it.

Eggs: You can cook the eggs up to 3 days in advance. Peel them, and store them in a covered container in the refrigerator.

Shaved Zucchini and Melon Salad with Mint and Almonds

SERVES 6 TO 8

The zucchini and olive oil make this savory, the mint and melon make it sweet, and the almonds add a gentle crunch to this supremely summery salad. I often serve this with some soft goat cheese and a baguette alongside, but it's also nice as a side dish with simply grilled or sautéed fish. You can use any kind of melon here, as long as you make sure the ratio of zucchini to melon is approximately equal, without one overpowering the other.

2 medium zucchini, ends trimmed

Fine sea salt, as needed

1 cup fresh mint leaves, torn

2 tablespoons extra-virgin olive oil, plus more for drizzling

2 tablespoons white balsamic vinegar or fresh lemon juice

1 small sweet melon (or half a large melon), halved, seeded, and thinly sliced into half-moons, then skins removed

Flaky sea salt

⅓ cup sliced almonds, toasted

Shaved Parmesan cheese

Freshly ground black pepper, to taste

1. Use a mandoline or a sharp knife to slice zucchini lengthwise into very thin ribbons. Place the ribbons in a colander, sprinkle them lightly with fine sea salt, and toss. Let the zucchini sit for 5 minutes to drain. Then pat it dry with a clean dish towel and place it in a bowl.

2. Add the mint, oil, vinegar, and a pinch of fine sea salt to the zucchini and mix gently but thoroughly.

3. Fan the melon slices on individual serving plates and sprinkle them with flaky sea salt. Heap the zucchini ribbons in a mound on top of the melon. Scatter the almonds, Parmesan, more flaky sea salt, and black pepper to taste over the salad, drizzle with olive oil, and serve.

Asparagus Salad with Herbed Crème Fraîche

SERVES 4

This delicate salad allows the sprightly, grassy green flavor of asparagus to sparkle, highlighted with just a touch of herb-flecked crème fraîche, a little lemon zest for tang, and capers for brininess. It's light but deeply flavored and works as either a first course or a side dish. I like to pair it with roast chicken and polenta for a cozy supper with friends, the kind of thing you'd serve in spring when tender asparagus is just coming into season but the nights are still chilly enough to turn on the oven.

Thinking Ahead

Herbed crème fraîche: You can make the crème fraîche mixture up to 8 hours in advance; cover and refrigerate it. Drain off any excess moisture before drizzling it over the asparagus.

1 pound asparagus, woody ends snapped off

1 cup (8 ounces) crème fraîche

½ teaspoon finely grated lemon zest

1 tablespoon fresh lemon juice, plus more to taste

1 tablespoon fresh tarragon or dill leaves, chopped

1 tablespoon drained capers, coarsely chopped

1 garlic clove, finely grated or minced

Fine sea salt, to taste

Extra-virgin olive oil, for serving

Freshly ground black pepper, for serving

¼ cup mixed chopped soft fresh herbs, such as parsley, dill, and/or tarragon, for serving

1. Fill a large pot with 1 inch of water. Set a steamer rack in the pot and bring the water to a boil. Arrange the asparagus evenly on the steamer, cover the pot, and simmer until the spears are fork-tender, 2 to 4 minutes for skinny asparagus, 3 to 6 minutes for fatter stalks. Transfer the asparagus to a serving platter.

2. While the asparagus is steaming, in a small bowl, stir together the crème fraîche, lemon zest and juice, tarragon, capers, and garlic. Season with salt to taste.

3. To serve, drizzle the sauce over the asparagus. Top with a drizzle of oil, some black pepper, and the chopped herbs.

Watercress, Avocado, and Feta Salad

SERVES 4

Watercress is not as popular a salad green—either here in North America or in France—as I think the spicy leaves deserve to be. In France, when it appears at all, it's mostly used in soups, and it's only occasionally available at my local supermarket (and almost never at the farmers' market except in early spring). But peppery and mineral-flavored, the curling, succulent shoots can hold their own next to both salty and creamy ingredients. In this salad they get a chance to do both, with feta and avocado layered into the mix. Watercress wilts quickly after being dressed, so make sure to serve this immediately after tossing.

Thinking Ahead

Dressing: You can make the dressing 1 week in advance. Store it in an airtight container in the refrigerator and bring it to room temperature, whisking if needed, before using it in the salad.

2½ tablespoons rice vinegar or white wine vinegar, plus more to taste

1 garlic clove, finely grated or minced

¼ teaspoon fine sea salt, plus more as needed

¼ teaspoon dried oregano

¼ cup extra-virgin olive oil

2 ripe Hass avocados

4 cups (6 ounces) watercress (or substitute baby arugula)

½ to ¾ cup (2 to 3 ounces) feta cheese, crumbled

1. In a small bowl, combine the vinegar, garlic, and salt. Let it sit for 1 minute, then whisk in the oregano and drizzle in the oil, a little at a time, until the dressing is thick and emulsified.

2. Peel, pit, and slice the avocados. Leave the slices on a cutting board and sprinkle them with salt to taste.

3. In a large bowl, toss the watercress with enough of the dressing to lightly coat the leaves, then taste and add more salt if needed. Transfer the salad to a serving platter. Top it with the avocado and feta to taste, and drizzle with more dressing if you like.

Fresh Corn and Tomato Salad with Tapenade

SERVES 4

This salad is all about the contrast between the sugar-sweet corn and the salty olive tapenade. Since many commercial tapenades shamefully neglect to include anchovies along with the olives and capers, I like to make my own. But if you have a favorite brand (with or without anchovies—I won't judge), feel free to use it. It will make this salad ridiculously easy to throw together, which is exactly what you want at the height of summer corn season.

Thinking Ahead

Tapenade: You can make the tapenade 5 days in advance. Keep it, covered, in the refrigerator. Bring it to room temperature before tossing it with the salad.

NOTE: My favorite way to quickly cook corn on the cob is to microwave on high the ears in their husks. Four ears of corn will take about 5 minutes. Let them cool completely, then remove the husks and silk (which is much easier to do after it's all cooked). To cut the kernels off the cob, I find it easiest to lay the corn flat on a cutting board and cut the kernels from there rather than trying to hold the cob over a bowl. It makes less of a mess, too.

FOR THE TAPENADE DRESSING

1¼ cups pitted Kalamata olives

½ cup fresh basil leaves, coarsely chopped

¼ cup fresh parsley leaves

2 tablespoons capers, drained

⅓ cup extra-virgin olive oil

Grated zest of ½ lemon

Juice of 1 lemon, plus more as needed

2 oil-packed anchovy fillets, chopped

1 garlic clove, finely grated or minced

½ teaspoon freshly ground black pepper

FOR THE SALAD

4 ears fresh corn, cooked (see note), kernels sliced off and reserved

1 pint golden or red cherry tomatoes, halved

½ small red onion, thinly sliced

¾ cup fresh basil leaves, torn

¾ cup fresh parsley leaves

Flaky sea salt, for serving

Sliced baguette or crusty bread, for serving

1. **Prepare the tapenade:** Combine the olives, basil, parsley, capers, oil, lemon zest and juice, anchovies, garlic, and pepper in a food processor or blender, and pulse to form a coarse paste. Taste, and add more lemon juice if it tastes flat.

2. **Make the salad:** Toss the corn kernels, tomatoes, red onion, basil, and parsley together in a large bowl. Fold in just enough tapenade to coat the vegetables. Sprinkle the salad lightly with flaky sea salt, and serve it with the remaining tapenade and some bread alongside.

French Onion Soup with Grilled Gruyère Sandwiches, **page 102**

Soups

Whether served chilled in the summer or steaming hot to warm the brisk nights of spring, velvety pea and lettuce soup (*potage Saint-Germain*) is a French classic, wonderfully rich with butter and sometimes cream. This is a great place to use up all those large, torn, or wilted lettuce leaves that are not pristine enough for a salad. I like to add dollops of lemon zest–spiked fresh ricotta to the bowl, some of which melts into the soup and some of which floats on top like little lemony clouds. It's decadent but not devastating, with the pure flavors of sweet green peas and gentle lettuces shining through. Serve it as a first course before a simple grilled fish, or as a main course in its own right.

Delicate Pea and Lettuce Soup with Ricotta and Tarragon

SERVES 6

---

5 tablespoons unsalted butter, divided

1 large white onion or 1 large leek (white and light green parts only, cleaned), diced

2 garlic cloves, chopped

6 cups (6 ounces) coarsely chopped lettuce, such as romaine, green leaf, Boston, or Little Gem

2½ pounds fresh peas, shelled to make about 3 cups peas (or use frozen peas)

2 cups chicken or vegetable stock, preferably homemade

2 teaspoons fine sea salt, plus more to taste

¼ teaspoon freshly ground black pepper

1 tablespoon chopped fresh tarragon leaves, plus more for garnish

½ cup heavy cream

1 cup (8 ounces) fresh ricotta cheese

Finely grated zest of ½ lemon

1. Melt 3 tablespoons of the butter in a large Dutch oven or heavy soup pot over medium heat. Stir in the onion and cook until it is soft and translucent, about 7 minutes (if the onion starts to brown, reduce the heat). Stir in the garlic and cook for another 2 minutes. Stir in the lettuce and sauté until the leaves are wilted, about 7 minutes.

2. Stir in the peas, stock, 1 cup of water, the remaining 2 tablespoons butter, and the salt and pepper, and bring to a simmer. Continue to simmer until the peas are soft, 2 to 5 minutes. Use a slotted spoon to scoop about ½ cup of the peas out of the stock and transfer them to a small bowl; reserve.

3. Add the tarragon and cream to the pot, then purée the mixture until smooth, using either an immersion blender or a standard blender (in batches, if necessary). Taste and adjust the seasoning if necessary.

4. In a medium bowl, fold together the ricotta, lemon zest, and salt to taste.

5. To serve hot, reheat the soup and ladle into bowls; dollop each serving with lemony ricotta, then top with the reserved peas and a sprinkling of chopped tarragon. Serve immediately. For a cold soup, let the soup cool, then chill for at least 2 to 3 hours before garnishing and serving.

Thinking Ahead

Soup: You can make the soup 5 days in advance. Store it in a covered container in the refrigerator. If serving hot, gently rewarm the soup on the stove and then top it with the ricotta, peas, and tarragon.

Pea garnish: Place the peas in a small container and keep them, covered, in the refrigerator for up to 5 days.

Ricotta: You can make the ricotta topping 2 days in advance. Store it in the refrigerator in an airtight container. Drain off any excess moisture before garnishing the soup.

Fish and Mussel Soup with Rouille

MAKES 6 TO 8 MAIN COURSE SERVINGS OR
10 TO 12 APPETIZER SERVINGS

If there's Provençal fish soup (*soupe de poisson*) on the menu, my mother will always order it, just so she can float croutons topped with garlicky *rouille* (red pepper mayonnaise) all over the surface. She learned in France that it's perfectly acceptable to spoon the hot soup over the croutons until they absorb the liquid and sink to the bottom of the bowl. That's when you dig in. The *rouille* makes the soup extra spicy and the cheese sprinkled on top makes it rich, while the croutons lose some, but not all, of their crunch.

This is a somewhat complicated, multi-step recipe that should not be entered into lightly. Save it for a special dinner party of seafood lovers, where it can serve as a starter or as the main course. With its deep ocean flavor (not to mention all those cheesy, garlicky croutons), it's worth the time spent.

FOR THE SOUP

¼ cup extra-virgin olive oil

2 leeks (white and light green parts only), cleaned and coarsely chopped

1 large onion, coarsely chopped

1 fennel bulb, tough outer layer removed, coarsely chopped (reserve the fennel fronds for serving)

3 teaspoons fine sea salt, divided, plus more to taste

½ teaspoon freshly ground black pepper, or to taste

5 garlic cloves, minced

1 (28-ounce) can diced tomatoes

1 pound mild (non-oily) fish fillets, such as cod, hake, flounder, porgy, or skate

1½ pounds fish bones (optional)

4 cups fish stock, preferably homemade

1½ cups dry white wine

2 sprigs fresh thyme

2 bay leaves

1 large sprig fresh basil

1 large sprig fresh parsley

4 strips orange zest

Small pinch of saffron threads

3 tablespoons pastis, such as Pernod

2 pounds mussels, scrubbed

FOR THE ROUILLE

1 large garlic clove, sliced

1½ teaspoons fresh lemon juice

¾ teaspoon fine sea salt

⅛ teaspoon freshly ground black pepper

Pinch of saffron threads

1 egg yolk

1 red bell pepper, roasted, peeled, and diced (see page 57)

1 cup extra-virgin olive oil

1 small baguette, preferably a day old, cut into ¼-inch-thick slices

Olive oil, for brushing

1 cup (4 ounces) coarsely grated Gruyère or Parmesan cheese, for serving

1. **Make the soup:** Heat the oil in a large Dutch oven or heavy soup pot over medium heat. Stir in the leeks, onion, fennel, 1 teaspoon of the salt, and the pepper, and cook until the vegetables have softened, about 8 minutes (if the onion starts to brown, reduce the heat). Stir in the garlic and cook for another 2 minutes.

2. Stir in the tomatoes, fish, fish bones, if using, stock, 1 cup of the wine, and 1 cup of water. Using kitchen twine, tie the thyme sprigs, bay leaves, basil sprig, parsley sprig, and orange zest together into a bundle; then stir it into the pot (or just throw the herbs and orange zest directly into the pot, though you'll have to fish them out later). Stir in the saffron, pastis, and remaining 2 teaspoons salt. Bring to a simmer, skim off any foam that forms on top of the soup, then cover and reduce the heat to maintain a simmer. Simmer for 1 hour, stirring occasionally and skimming off more foam as needed.

3. Meanwhile, in another large pot, bring the remaining ½ cup wine to a simmer. Add the mussels and cover the pot. Cook until the mussels open, 5 to 10 minutes, transferring the mussels as they open to a bowl (use tongs to do this). Discard any mussels that have not opened. When they are cool enough to handle, pluck the mussels out of their shells and place them in a small bowl; reserve until ready to serve. Strain the mussel broth and reserve it as well.

4. **Make the rouille while the soup is still simmering:** In the bowl of a food processor or blender, combine the garlic, lemon juice, salt, pepper, and saffron. Let the ingredients sit for a few minutes, then add the egg yolk

recipe continues

Soup: You can make the soup base, without adding the mussels, up to 3 days in advance. Store it, covered, in the refrigerator.

Rouille: You can make the rouille up to 1 week in advance. Store it in a covered container in the refrigerator.

and half the roasted bell pepper, and pulse to combine. With the motor running, slowly pour in the oil until the rouille is thick and emulsified. Chill until ready to use, reserving the remaining chopped bell pepper.

5. When the soup is done simmering, remove the fish bones (if used) and the herb bundle (or loose herbs and orange zest) and discard them. Add the reserved strained mussel broth and then use an immersion blender to blend the soup until it is thick and still a little chunky. (Or you can pass the soup through a food mill set with a coarse disk.) Strain the soup through a coarse-mesh strainer into a saucepan, pressing down hard on the solids to extract as much liquid as possible. Discard the solids.

6. **Make the croutons:** Heat your broiler. Spread the baguette slices out on a baking sheet and brush both sides with oil. Broil until toasted on both sides, 1 to 3 minutes per side, depending on your broiler. Watch them carefully.

7. To serve, reheat the soup as needed, adding the mussels and reserved diced red bell pepper. Ladle the soup into bowls and serve them with the rouille, croutons, and cheese on the side for guests to add as they like. To eat, top the croutons with the rouille, then float them on the soup and sprinkle them with the cheese. If they like, your guests can then spoon the soup over the croutons until they sink.

Vegetable Soup
au Pistou

SERVES 6 TO 8

Pistou is France's answer to pesto: a basil-based paste that's heavy on the garlic, though smoother and silkier than its Italian incarnation because it is made without pine nuts. Like *pesto*, the word *pistou* is derived from the Italian *pestare*, meaning "to pound." Some *pistou* recipes include a little tomato pulp, and I really like the sweetness that it adds.

Pistou is usually spooned into vegetable soups as a powerful seasoning, but you can also use it as a condiment with grilled fish or meat. I love this soup in fall, when the late-season zucchini are so big and fat that you don't mind simmering them until they practically collapse into plush little pillows. Combined with soft white beans and bits of pasta, the soup is both brothy and hearty, as well as deeply warming.

FOR THE SOUP

¼ cup extra-virgin olive oil, plus more for drizzling

6 garlic cloves, finely grated or minced

2 medium carrots, diced into ¼-inch pieces

2 large celery stalks, diced into ¼-inch pieces

1 large white onion, coarsely chopped

2 teaspoons fine sea salt, divided, plus more as needed

1 bay leaf

4 sprigs fresh thyme

4 sprigs fresh parsley

8 ounces green beans, trimmed and cut into 1-inch pieces (about 2⅓ cups)

1 medium zucchini, diced into ½-inch pieces

1 (15-ounce) can cannellini beans, drained and rinsed

1 (14.5-ounce) can diced tomatoes (do not drain)

1 cup small-size pasta, such as shells, ditalini, or elbows

FOR THE PISTOU

2 cups (about 2 ounces) fresh basil leaves and tender stems

½ cup extra-virgin olive oil

2 garlic cloves, finely grated or minced

¼ teaspoon fine sea salt, plus more as needed

Freshly ground black pepper, as needed

1 ripe plum tomato, seeded and chopped

½ cup (2 ounces) grated Parmesan cheese

1. **Prepare the soup:** Heat the oil in a large heavy soup pot or Dutch oven over medium-high heat. Add the garlic, carrots, celery, onion, and ½ teaspoon of the salt. Cook, stirring, until the onions are just starting to brown at the edges, about 7 minutes.

Soup: You can make the soup up to 1 week in advance. Keep it, covered, in the refrigerator. You can also freeze the soup for up to 3 months in advance. In both cases, omit the pasta and add it when the soup is simmering before you serve it.

Pistou: You can make the pistou 3 days in advance. Store it, topped with a thin layer of olive oil to help preserve it, in an airtight container in the refrigerator. Or freeze it for up to 3 months.

2. Use kitchen twine to tie the bay leaf, thyme sprigs, and parsley sprigs together and add the bundle to the pot (or you can skip the twine and just throw the herbs directly in the pot, though you'll have to fish them out later).

3. Stir in the green beans, zucchini, and another ½ teaspoon salt; cover and cook, stirring occasionally, until everything is just tender, about 6 minutes. Stir in the cannellini beans, tomatoes and their juices, 4 cups of water, the pasta, and another 1 teaspoon salt.

4. Bring the mixture to a boil, then reduce the heat and simmer until the pasta is just al dente (this will vary from 5 to 12 minutes depending on your pasta, so check it often). Remove from the heat.

5. **Meanwhile, make the pistou:** In a food processor or blender, blend together the basil, oil, garlic, salt, and a large pinch of pepper. Scrape the sides of the container and blend in the tomato and Parmesan. Taste, and add more salt if needed.

6. To serve, remove the bouquet garni (or loose herbs), ladle the soup into bowls, and top them with dollops of the pistou and a drizzle of olive oil.

Gazpacho by Way of Provence

SERVES 4 TO 6

Gazpacho may not have originated in France, but the French have adopted it so fully that almost all summer menus feature at least some version of the cold tomato-based soup. I like to purée watermelon into mine; it makes the chilled soup sweeter and also a little lighter—a quality that I quickly mitigate by topping it with buttery brioche croutons. The jalapeño adds a touch of spice to the mix, but not so much that you really feel it on your tongue—it stays in the background, adding vibrant complexity. Leave in the seeds if you want more heat.

Thinking Ahead

Because gazpacho is served cold, you must prepare it in advance and chill it in the refrigerator for 4 hours or as long as overnight.

2 pounds ripe tomatoes, cored and cut into chunks

2 cups (about 1 pound) cubed seeded watermelon

½ jalapeño, seeded if you want to mitigate the heat

1 shallot, sliced

1 garlic clove, sliced

3 tablespoons chopped fresh basil leaves, plus more for garnish

1¾ teaspoons fine sea salt, plus more as needed

1 teaspoon champagne vinegar or sherry vinegar, plus more to taste

2 teaspoons chopped fresh mint leaves

⅓ cup plus 3 tablespoons extra-virgin olive oil, plus more as needed

1 large or 2 small brioche rolls, preferably a day old

¼ teaspoon herbes de Provence (optional)

1. In a blender, combine the tomatoes, watermelon, jalapeño, shallot, and garlic. Blend until very smooth, about 2 minutes. Add the basil, salt, vinegar, and mint; blend to combine. With the motor running, drizzle in ⅓ cup oil and blend until emulsified, adding more oil if needed—the gazpacho will turn bright pink or orange.

2. Strain the mixture through a fine-mesh sieve into a bowl, discarding the solids. Chill it for at least 4 hours or overnight. Before serving, taste the soup and add more salt and/or vinegar if needed.

3. **Make the croutons:** When you are ready to serve the gazpacho, slice the brioche rolls into ½-inch-wide strips, then use your fingers to tear off ½-inch cubes, to make about 1 cup of cubes.

4. Heat the remaining 3 tablespoons oil in a medium skillet over medium-high heat. Stir in the bread cubes and the herbes de Provence, if using, and cook, tossing the croutons often, until they are golden brown, about 3 minutes. Transfer the croutons to a paper towel–lined plate and let them cool.

5. Serve the gazpacho topped with the croutons and chopped basil, and drizzled with a little more oil, if you like.

French Onion Soup with Grilled Gruyère Sandwiches

SERVES 4 TO 6

The French may have their gratinéed onion soup with croutons and Gruyère melted on top, but our American tradition of tomato soup with grilled cheese sandwiches for dunking offers similar warming, cheese-oozing pleasures. This recipe merges elements from each dish. The broth (preferably homemade) is full of deeply caramelized onions, but the Gruyère is layered, along with more caramelized onions, onto bread and fried into sandwiches to serve on the side. This hybrid is a bit easier to serve than classic French onion soup because you don't need to broil the individual bowls just before serving. And with all that dunking, I think it's a lot more fun to eat, too.

See photograph on **page 90.**

FOR THE SOUP

- 1 bay leaf
- 6 sprigs fresh thyme
- 8 tablespoons (1 stick) unsalted butter
- 3 pounds onions, thinly sliced
- 2 teaspoons fine sea salt, divided
- ¾ cup brandy
- 2 tablespoons Port, Madeira, or sweet Marsala
- 2 cups dry white wine
- 4 cups beef stock, preferably homemade
- 4 cups chicken stock, preferably homemade
- ½ teaspoon freshly ground black pepper
- Chopped fresh parsley leaves, for serving

FOR THE GRILLED CHEESE

- 1 tablespoon unsalted butter, plus more for the bread, room temperature
- 4 slices white or whole-wheat sandwich bread
- Dijon mustard, for spreading (optional)
- 1 cup (4 ounces) grated Gruyère cheese

1. **Make the soup:** Make a bouquet garni by tying the bay leaf and thyme sprigs together with kitchen twine (or skip this step and just throw the herbs directly into the pot with the onions in step 2, though you'll have to fish them out later).

2. In a large heavy soup pot or Dutch oven, melt the butter over low heat. Stir in the onions and bouquet garni and cover the pot. Cook for 30 minutes, then uncover the pot and raise the heat to medium-high. Cook, sautéing,

Soup: You can make the soup 1 week in advance. Store it, covered, in the refrigerator.

Onions: You can store the reserved cooked onions for the sandwiches, covered, in the refrigerator for up to 1 week.

until the onions are caramelized and golden, 25 to 35 minutes longer. If the onions start to burn, reduce the heat. You are looking for soft, evenly golden onions without dark brown spots.

3. Stir in 1 teaspoon of the salt, the brandy, and Port (be careful, it may flame up). Scrape up any browned bits stuck to the bottom of the pot, and cook until the liquid has been absorbed, 3 to 5 minutes. Remove ⅓ cup of the cooked onions and reserve it for the sandwiches.

4. Stir the wine, beef stock, chicken stock, and pepper into the soup pot. Simmer for 1 hour, skimming off any large pockets of foam that form from time to time. Remove the bouquet garni or loose herbs, taste the soup, and add 1 more teaspoon salt, or to taste (this will depend on how salty your stock was to start).

5. **Make the grilled cheese:** In the last 10 minutes of the soup's cooking time, butter both sides of each slice of bread. Then, if you are using it, spread the mustard over the butter on one side of each slice. Heap half of the reserved onions, and then half of the Gruyère, on the mustard side of 2 bread pieces. Top with the remaining 2 pieces of bread (mustard side facing the cheese) and press down firmly with a spatula. The plain buttered sides should be on the outside of the sandwiches.

6. Heat the 1 tablespoon butter in a large nonstick skillet over medium-low heat. When the butter is hot, place both sandwiches in the skillet, cover, and cook for 3 to 4 minutes, until the underside is golden. Flip them over and cook the other side for about another 3 minutes, until the bread is golden and the cheese is molten.

7. To serve, ladle the soup into serving bowls and sprinkle each serving with parsley. Cut the sandwiches in fourths and serve them alongside the soup for dunking, or float the sandwiches on top of the soup.

Chilled Melon Soup with Spiced Yogurt

SERVES 4

1 cup whole-milk plain yogurt

2 garlic cloves, finely grated or minced, divided

½ teaspoon ground garam masala

1¼ teaspoons fine sea salt, divided, plus more as needed

2½ pounds sweet orange-fleshed melons, peeled and cubed (2 pounds cubed)

2 scallions (white and green parts) or 1 shallot, coarsely chopped

½ jalapeño, seeded if you like, chopped

2 teaspoons fresh lemon juice, plus more as needed

2 tablespoons extra-virgin olive oil

Flaky sea salt, for serving

Although it's rare to have a glut of bursting, nectar-filled melons on one's hands, I found myself in that lucky predicament in Provence one July after a farmers' market shopping spree. Who can resist four Cavaillon melons for ten euros? And then, who can eat them fast enough when they all ripen at the exact same moment? Hence this quickly whirled-together soup, which is juicier and sweeter than gazpacho but has a similar cooling effect. It's a soup worth making, even without a melon glut on your hands. Just plan ahead, buying your fruit enough in advance so it ripens before you start puréeing. Semi-ripe melons will also work in a pinch, though you might want to add a teensy drizzle of honey to bring out their sweetest side.

Thinking Ahead

Yogurt: You can make the spiced yogurt 2 days in advance. Keep it in a covered container in the refrigerator. Drain off any excess moisture before serving.

Soup: You can make and chill the soup up to 1 day in advance.

1. In a small bowl, stir together the yogurt, half of the garlic, the garam masala, and ¼ teaspoon of the fine sea salt. Cover and refrigerate until serving.

2. In a blender, combine the melon cubes, scallions, jalapeño, lemon juice, the remaining garlic, and the remaining 1 teaspoon fine sea salt, blending until very smooth, about 2 minutes. Don't be alarmed by the glaring color—it will turn a prettier shade when you add the olive oil. Pour in the oil and blend until smooth. Chill for at least 1 hour in the fridge.

3. To serve, taste the soup and add more lemon juice or salt if needed. Ladle the soup into bowls, and top each serving with a dollop of the spiced yogurt and a sprinkling of flaky sea salt.

Brandied Chestnut Soup

SERVES 4

Before jars of peeled roasted chestnuts became supermarket-available—at least around Thanksgiving—making chestnut soup was a laborious job. Not only did the chestnuts have to be roasted, but each one also needed to be painstakingly peeled while still hot, before the husks cooled and glued themselves to the chestnut meats. It was slow, finger-burning work. Compared to all that, this ultra-creamy autumnal soup is a cinch to make. But it's fancy, too, scented with brandy and dotted with crunchy brioche croutons toasted in butter. If you love chestnut soups (and desserts!), stock up on the jars of peeled roasted chestnuts in November so you can use them all winter long.

3 tablespoons unsalted butter, divided

2 tablespoons extra-virgin olive oil

1 leek (white and light green parts only), halved lengthwise, cleaned, and thinly sliced

1 celery stalk, coarsely chopped

1 medium carrot, coarsely chopped

1 bay leaf

1⅛ teaspoons fine sea salt, divided, plus more as needed

4 cups chicken or vegetable stock, preferably homemade

10 ounces whole peeled roasted chestnuts, diced

2 slices brioche, cut into ¾-inch cubes

½ cup half-and-half (or use ¼ cup heavy cream plus ¼ cup whole milk)

2 tablespoons brandy

Chopped fresh chives, for serving

Flaky sea salt, for serving

1. Melt 2 tablespoons of the butter and the oil together in a large Dutch oven or heavy soup pot over medium-high heat. Stir in the leek, celery, carrot, bay leaf, and ⅛ teaspoon fine sea salt. Sauté until the vegetables have softened and their edges are lightly browned, 10 to 15 minutes.

2. Stir in the stock, 1 cup of water, the chestnuts, and the remaining 1 teaspoon fine sea salt. Partially cover the pot, bring the liquid to a simmer, then reduce the heat to medium and let everything simmer gently until the vegetables and chestnuts are thoroughly soft, 45 minutes to 1 hour.

3. **While the soup is cooking, make the croutons:** Melt the remaining 1 tablespoon butter in a large skillet over medium heat. Stir in the bread cubes and cook, tossing them occasionally, until they are golden brown, 6 to 10 minutes. Transfer the croutons to a paper towel–lined plate and reserve.

4. Discard the bay leaf and purée the soup using an immersion blender; or transfer it to a blender, in batches if necessary, and purée. Taste it and see if it's smooth enough for you. If you want an ultra-silky soup, pass it through a fine-mesh sieve after puréeing. Return the soup to the pot if you've taken it out.

5. Stir the half-and-half and brandy into the soup and simmer for 2 more minutes. Taste, and add more fine sea salt if needed. Ladle the soup into individual bowls and top each serving with croutons, chives, and flaky sea salt.

Thinking Ahead

Soup: You can make the soup through step 4 up to 5 days in advance. Store it in a covered container in the refrigerator or freeze it for up to 3 months. Gently rewarm the soup on the stove, and stir in the half-and-half and brandy before serving.

Croutons: You can make the croutons 2 days in advance. Store them in an airtight container at room temperature.

Savory Mushroom Soup

SERVES 4

Chickpea flour, toasted until golden and fragrant, is the surprise ingredient in this complex and lightly spiced mushroom soup. It's not something that your guests will be able to identify unless you tell them, but it adds body and a warm, toasty character to the broth. If you can't get it, you can leave it out. The soup will be a little thinner and not quite as deeply flavored, but still filled with mushrooms, shallots, and plenty of herbs. Make sure to use a really good broth here—either homemade or purchased. With or without the chickpea flour, the flavor of the broth will really come through.

Thinking Ahead

Soup: You can make the soup up to 1 week in advance. Store it, covered, in the refrigerator. Or you can freeze it for up to 3 months. Bring it to a simmer before adding the garnish.

4 tablespoons (½ stick) unsalted butter, divided

2 tablespoons extra-virgin olive oil, divided

1½ pounds mixed fresh mushrooms (such as cremini, white mushrooms, shiitake, oyster, chanterelles, portabellas), chopped

4 large shallots, diced

2 garlic cloves, finely grated or minced

1 tablespoon tomato paste

1 teaspoon chopped fresh thyme leaves

1 teaspoon chopped fresh rosemary leaves

2 teaspoons fine sea salt, plus more to taste

½ teaspoon ground coriander

½ teaspoon sweet paprika, plus more for serving

¼ cup chickpea flour

4 cups chicken or vegetable stock, preferably homemade

¼ cup chopped fresh cilantro or parsley leaves, for serving

1. Melt 2 tablespoons of the butter and 1 tablespoon of the oil in a large Dutch oven or heavy soup pot over medium-high heat. Stir in half of the mushrooms and half of the shallots, and cook, stirring occasionally, until browned, 10 to 12 minutes. Use a slotted spoon to transfer the mushrooms and shallots to a large bowl. Repeat with the remaining 2 tablespoons butter, 1 tablespoon oil, and mushrooms and shallots.

2. Pour all the mushrooms back into the pot, stir in the garlic and tomato paste, and cook until the garlic is fragrant, about 1 minute. Then stir in the thyme, rosemary, 1 teaspoon of the salt, coriander, and paprika, and cook for another minute.

3. Stir the chickpea flour into the pot and cook, stirring, for 1 minute. Stir in the stock, 1 cup of water, and the remaining 1 teaspoon salt. Let simmer for 20 minutes. Taste and add salt if needed. Garnish with a sprinkling of paprika and chopped herbs.

Roasted Tomato and Zucchini Tarts, **page 128**

Quiches, Tarts
& Savory Pies

Asparagus, Goat Cheese, and Tarragon Tart

SERVES 6 TO 8

Because you don't have to make your own crust, this gorgeous asparagus-striped tart is so easy it almost feels like cheating. But it's not—it's just one of those perfectly simple yet stunning recipes that every French cook has in their repertoire: effortlessly chic, company-ready.

Be sure to buy a good all-butter brand of puff pastry. There are so few ingredients in this recipe that each one makes an impact. If you can manage to serve this tart warm, within an hour of baking, it will be at its absolute best, with crisp pastry that shatters into buttery bits when you bite down and still-runny cheese. But it's also excellent a few hours later, should you want to get all your baking done before your guests arrive.

If tarragon isn't your favorite herb, you can use chives, basil, or mint instead. And if you can manage to trim all the asparagus to the same length, this tart will be especially neat and orderly looking.

4 ounces (1 cup) fresh goat cheese, room temperature

1 large egg, lightly beaten, room temperature

1 large garlic clove, finely grated or minced

1½ tablespoons chopped fresh tarragon leaves, plus more for serving

½ tablespoon finely grated lemon zest

½ teaspoon fine sea salt, plus more for sprinkling

Pinch of freshly grated nutmeg

1 cup (8 ounces) crème fraîche, room temperature

All-purpose flour, for dusting the work surface

1 sheet or square all-butter puff pastry, thawed if frozen (about 9 to 14 ounces; brands vary)

8 ounces thin asparagus, woody ends trimmed

Extra-virgin olive oil, as needed

2 tablespoons grated Parmesan cheese

Freshly ground black pepper, to taste

Crushed red pepper flakes, to taste (optional)

1½ ounces Parmesan cheese, shaved with a vegetable peeler (about ½ cup)

1. Heat the oven to 425°F.

2. In a medium bowl, use a wooden spoon or a fork to mash together the goat cheese, egg, garlic, tarragon, lemon zest, salt, and nutmeg until smooth. Switch to a whisk and beat in the crème fraîche until smooth.

3. On a lightly floured surface, roll the puff pastry out to form a 13 × 11-inch rectangle about ⅛ inch thick. Transfer the dough to a parchment-lined cookie sheet. With a sharp knife, lightly score a ½-inch border around the edges of the puff pastry.

4. Spread the crème fraîche mixture evenly inside the scored border. Line up the asparagus spears on top, and brush them with olive oil. Sprinkle some salt and the grated Parmesan over the asparagus.

Tart: You can assemble the tart 1 day in advance; but reserve the sprinkling of salt and grated Parmesan until right before baking. Loosely cover the tart and store it in the refrigerator.

5. Bake until the pastry is puffed and golden, 25 to 30 minutes. Let it cool on the cookie sheet for at least 15 minutes before serving (or for up to 4 hours). Then sprinkle black pepper, red pepper flakes (if using), the shaved Parmesan, tarragon leaves, and a drizzle of oil on top.

Herbed Tomato and Gruyère Pie

SERVES 8

This gooey, cheesy, slightly messy-looking pastry is my Frenchified version of a Southern tomato pie. In the classic recipe, sliced raw tomatoes and scallions are layered with cheddar and mayo in an unbaked pie crust, then the whole thing is baked until burnished on top and custardy at heart. In this slightly fussier incarnation, Gruyère steps in for the cheddar, and instead of using raw vegetables, I roast some of the tomatoes and brown the onions, adding their caramelized, condensed flavors to the mix. I also prebake the crust, which, once it becomes truly golden and crunchy, is better able to stand up to its molten filling. It's a bit more work than the original recipe but worth every minute.

There are very few situations in which I'd recommend using purchased rather than homemade mayonnaise, but this is one of them. You need the sweetness of Hellmann's to meld with the tomatoes. Homemade mayonnaise is too savory in this context—though, if you insist on using your own, just add a pinch or two of sugar or a drizzle of honey to balance things out.

FOR THE CRUST

1¼ cups (162 grams) all-purpose flour, plus more for the work surface

½ teaspoon fine sea salt

Pinch of sugar

8 tablespoons (1 stick / 113 grams) cold unsalted butter, cut into cubes, plus more for greasing

⅓ cup ice water, plus more if needed

FOR THE FILLING

1 large or 2 small tomatoes, sliced crosswise into ¼-inch-thick rounds

¾ teaspoon fine sea salt, divided, plus as needed

1 pint cherry tomatoes, cut in half

3 tablespoons extra-virgin olive oil, divided

1 teaspoon fresh thyme leaves

1 tablespoon unsalted butter

1 large onion, thinly sliced

2 garlic cloves, minced

1 large egg

1 cup (4 ounces) grated Gruyère or Swiss cheese

⅓ cup (3 ounces) crème fraîche or sour cream

⅓ cup plus 2 tablespoons (about 2 ounces total) grated Parmesan cheese, divided

⅓ cup (3 ounces) mayonnaise, preferably Hellmann's

¼ teaspoon freshly ground black pepper, plus more as needed

½ cup fresh basil leaves, chopped

1. **Make the crust:** Using the ingredients listed above, make the dough, either by hand or in a food processor (see page 117).

recipe continues

2. On a lightly floured surface, roll out the chilled dough to form a 12-inch round, rolling from the center toward the edges and trimming the edges as needed. Drape the dough over a 9-inch pie pan and press it onto the bottom and up the sides. Crimp the edges to make a decorative crust. Use a fork to poke evenly spaced holes in the dough (including the sides), and chill it for at least 30 minutes and up to 24 hours (don't worry about covering the dough).

3. Heat the oven to 425°F.

4. Butter a piece of foil or spray it with nonstick cooking spray. Line the chilled dough with the buttered foil, butter-side down, and fill the foil with pie weights. Place the pie pan on a rimmed baking sheet and bake for 15 minutes. Then remove it from the oven, carefully lift off the foil and pie weights, and return the pan to the oven to continue baking until the dough is just baked through and barely turning golden on the edges, 5 to 7 minutes. Transfer to a wire rack and let it cool to room temperature.

5. **Make the filling:** Raise the oven temperature to 500°F.

6. Sprinkle the tomato slices with ¼ teaspoon of the salt, then place them in a colander set over a bowl; let them drain while you prepare the rest of the filling.

7. On a rimmed baking sheet, toss the cherry tomatoes with 2 tablespoons of the oil, the thyme, and ½ teaspoon of the salt. Roast until the tomatoes are browned and the juices have evaporated, 12 to 15 minutes.

8. While the tomatoes are roasting, heat the remaining 1 tablespoon oil and the butter in a skillet over medium-high heat. Stir in the onion and a pinch of salt, and cook until lightly browned in spots, 7 to 10 minutes, reducing the heat if necessary to prevent burning. Stir in the garlic and cook for another minute, then scrape the mixture into a medium bowl.

9. In a large bowl, beat the egg until well mixed, and then fold in the Gruyère, crème fraîche, ⅓ cup Parmesan, the mayonnaise, a pinch of salt, and the pepper.

10. Add the roasted cherry tomatoes and the basil to the onion mixture, and toss until mixed. Add a big pinch each of salt and pepper. Scrape the mixture into the baked pie shell and top it with the cheese mixture. Pat the tomato slices dry and arrange them on top of the cheese. Sprinkle the top with the remaining 2 tablespoons Parmesan.

11. Reduce the oven temperature to 375°F. Bake the pie until the filling is lightly golden, about 30 minutes. Let it cool slightly, then serve it warm or at room temperature.

Directions for Making Any Pie or Tart Dough

In a food processor: Pulse the flour, salt, and sugar to combine. Add the cubed butter and pulse until the mixture has formed lima bean–size pieces. Drizzle in the water and pulse just to combine, taking care not over-process the dough.

By hand: In a large bowl, mix together the flour, salt, and sugar. Add the cubed butter and mix it in with your hands, pinching and squeezing the butter cubes with your fingers (or using a pastry blender) until the largest pieces are the size of lima beans. Drizzle in the water a little at a time, mixing until the dough starts to come together.

With either method, you may not need all the water, or you may need to add more water if the dough doesn't come together.

Transfer the dough to a lightly floured surface and press it together into a ball. You should see bits of butter in the dough; those will bake up into delectable flakes. Flatten the dough to form a disk, wrap it in plastic wrap, and chill it for 1 hour or as long as 2 days.

Sweet Potato and Bacon Quiche with Parsley

SERVES 8

When people think of French pâtisserie, they generally think sweet. But buttery, flaky pastries are just as much a savory tradition, and none is as thoroughly entrenched in the rhythms of French daily life as the elegant quiche.

Although the quiche has gone international, the French are the ones who perfected it. Make it once, and it's easy to master, becoming something you can throw together with ingredients you probably already have in the fridge (or at least you do if you're French): butter, cream, and eggs.

This combination of sweet potato and bacon takes quichedom to a whole new dimension. The sweet potato, roasted and caramelized before it meets the crust, turns into burnished velvet as it nearly melts into the custard. Brawny nuggets of bacon and salty strands of Gruyère and cheddar provide the savory notes, while lemon zest adds necessary freshness.

Use this recipe as a template for your own combinations; you'll need 3 cups of any cooked vegetables and other tidbits (olives, herbs, capers, meats) to replace the sweet potatoes and bacon.

You'll need a 10-inch tart pan. Or you can use a 9-inch tart pan and add a few minutes to the baking time.

FOR THE CRUST

- 2 cups (260 grams) all-purpose flour, plus more as needed
- ¾ teaspoon fine sea salt
- ¼ teaspoon sugar
- 1 cup (2 sticks / 225 grams) unsalted butter, cut into ½-inch cubes, plus more at room temperature for greasing
- Scant ½ cup ice water

FOR THE FILLING

- 1 pound sweet potatoes, peeled and cut into ½-inch cubes (about 3½ cups)
- 2 ounces bacon (2 slices), diced into ½-inch cubes
- 1 tablespoon extra-virgin olive oil
- 1¼ teaspoons fine sea salt, divided
- 3 large eggs
- 1 cup heavy cream
- ¾ teaspoon finely grated lemon zest
- ⅛ teaspoon freshly ground black pepper
- ⅛ teaspoon freshly grated nutmeg
- ¾ cup chopped fresh parsley leaves
- ½ cup (2 ounces) grated cheddar cheese
- ¼ cup (1 ounce) grated Parmesan cheese

1. **Make the tart crust:** Make the dough using the ingredients above, according to the directions on page 117.

2. Butter a 10-inch tart pan with removable bottom and place it on a rimmed baking sheet. On a lightly floured surface, roll the dough out to form a 12-inch round, rolling from the center toward the edges and trimming the edges as needed. Drape the dough over the tart pan and press it onto the bottom and up the sides, folding the excess down to bulk up the thickness of the sides of

recipe continues

Dough: You can make the dough and chill it in the refrigerator up to 2 days in advance. Flatten it into a disk and wrap it in plastic wrap before chilling.

Pastry shell: You can bake the pastry shell up to 1 day in advance and store it, uncovered, at room temperature. You can also store the unbaked shell, covered, in the refrigerator for up to 1 day.

Sweet potatoes and bacon: You can roast the potatoes and bacon up to 1 day in advance, then store the mixture in an airtight container in the refrigerator.

Quiche: You can make the quiche and store it at room temperature for up to 8 hours in advance of serving.

the tart shell. Then use your fingers to push the dough ¼ inch up past the rim. Use a fork to poke evenly spaced holes in the bottom and sides of the dough. Chill the tart shell for 30 minutes or up to 24 hours, uncovered.

3. Arrange the racks in the top and lower thirds of the oven, then heat the oven to 425°F.

4. Butter a piece of foil or spray it with nonstick cooking spray. Line the chilled dough with the buttered foil, butter-side down, and fill the foil with pie weights. Place the rimmed baking sheet on the upper rack in the oven, and bake for 15 minutes. Then remove the baking sheet from the oven, carefully lift the foil and pie weights off the tart shell, and return the baking sheet to the oven. Continue baking until the tart shell is barely turning golden on the edges, 5 to 7 minutes. Transfer to a wire rack and let it cool slightly.

5. **While the tart shell is baking, make the filling:** On a rimmed baking sheet, toss together the sweet potatoes, bacon, oil, and ¼ teaspoon of the salt. Place the baking sheet on the lower rack in the oven along with the tart shell and roast until the potatoes and bacon are golden brown, about 20 minutes, stirring halfway through. Remove the baking sheet from the oven and let the mixture cool. (The tart shell and the potatoes will come out of the oven at about the same time.) Reduce the oven temperature to 375°F.

6. In a large bowl, whisk together the eggs, cream, lemon zest, remaining 1 teaspoon salt, the pepper, and nutmeg. Fold in the parsley.

7. Scatter the roasted potato-bacon mixture and the grated cheddar into the tart shell. Scrape the egg mixture into the shell, smoothing the top, and then sprinkle the Parmesan on top. Bake on the lower oven rack until the tart is puffed and browned, 30 to 35 minutes. Let the tart cool slightly, then remove the ring from the tart pan and slide the quiche from the tart pan bottom onto a wire rack. Serve it warm or at room temperature.

Pissaladière with Tomato, Olives, and Anchovies

SERVES 6 TO 8

There are myriad versions of this thin, pizza-like Provençal tart. While all have a blanket of softly simmered onions covering the crust, the other ingredients can vary, including some combination of anchovies, sardines, tomatoes, herbs, and olives—but never cheese or cream. The name, *pissaladière*, is derived from *pissala*, an anchovy and sardine purée from the South of France that classically was layered under the onions. In this version, I simmer the onions with some of the anchovies so their briny flavor permeates the mix, and then layer even more anchovies on top. I use a yeast-risen pizza-like crust here—I like the way its breadiness and chew contrasts with the silky onion filling. But puff pastry is just as traditional and if you want to substitute it, use a 9- to 12-ounce sheet or square, rolled out thin, in place of the homemade dough and jump from step 1 to step 5.

FOR THE TOPPING

18 oil-packed anchovy fillets (from about two 2-ounce tins)

3 tablespoons olive oil

2 pounds onions, halved root to stem and thinly sliced into half moons

2 garlic cloves, finely grated or minced

1 teaspoon fresh thyme leaves, chopped

½ teaspoon fine sea salt

1 large or 2 small ripe tomatoes, halved, seeded, and thinly sliced

¼ cup Niçoise olives, pitted or not, or to taste

FOR THE DOUGH

1½ teaspoons active dry yeast

⅔ cup warm water

2 tablespoons olive oil, plus more for the bowl and the baking sheet

2 cups (260 grams) all-purpose flour, plus more for kneading

1½ teaspoons fine sea salt

1. **Make the topping:** Mince 2 of the anchovies. Heat the oil in a large skillet over medium heat, then stir in the onions, garlic, thyme, and minced anchovies. Cook, covered, for 20 minutes, stirring occasionally. Then uncover and continue to cook until the onions are pale golden, another 25 to 35 minutes, stirring frequently. Don't let the onions caramelize; you want to cook the liquid out of the onions without browning them very much. Remove the skillet from the heat and stir in the salt.

recipe continues

Onion mixture: You can make the onion mixture up to 3 days in advance and store it in an airtight container in the refrigerator.

Dough: You can mix the dough as described in step 3 up to 12 hours ahead and let it rise in the refrigerator. Bring it to room temperature before proceeding to step 4.

Pissaladière: You can bake this up to 1 day in advance, store it loosely covered in the refrigerator, and then reheat it in a 350°F oven until warm (or bring it to room temperature).

2. **Make the dough:** In a small bowl, combine the yeast and warm water, and let the mixture sit until it is foamy, about 5 minutes. Then stir in the oil.

3. In a large bowl, stir together the flour and salt. Pour the yeast mixture into the flour and mix with a wooden spoon until the dough is shaggy. Turn it out onto a floured surface and knead until the dough is uniform and elastic, about 5 minutes. Place the dough in an oiled bowl, turning it so the oil coats the dough, cover the bowl, and let the dough rise for 1 hour in a draft-free place. It won't rise much.

4. Lightly oil an 11 × 17-inch rimmed baking sheet. On a floured surface, roll the dough out to form an 11 × 16-inch rectangle. Transfer the dough to the baking sheet, pressing it onto the bottom and slightly up the sides. Cover the dough with a damp kitchen towel and let it rest for 30 minutes.

5. Heat the oven to 400°F.

6. Spread the onion topping evenly over the dough, and then top it with the tomato slices. Arrange the remaining 16 or so anchovies in a crosshatch pattern (or any other pattern) over the tomatoes, and dot the top with the olives. Bake until golden brown, 25 to 35 minutes. Serve warm or at room temperature.

Classic Tarte Flambée, page 126

Classic Tarte Flambée

SERVES 6 TO 8

Tarte flambée, also known as *flammekueche,* hails from northern France—Alsace and the surrounding regions. Traditionally this onion and bacon pastry was a baker's treat made from the scraps of dough left over from bread baking. They were rolled out, topped with raw onion, bacon, and *fromage blanc* (a soft, yogurt-like cheese), and baked until the dough puffed up and the onions were singed at the edges.

Here I use a combination of ricotta and crème fraîche in place of *fromage blanc* (which can be hard to find), and I cook the onions with the bacon for just a few minutes to give them a head start before they hit the oven. They end up more tender and golden that way. Using a pizza stone can make the crust a little crunchier, but it's not a huge difference and you can skip it if you don't have one. Serve this warm if you can, as an appetizer, a lunch, or a light dinner with a big green salad. And if you can get *fromage blanc,* use ¾ cup of it here instead of the ricotta–crème fraîche combination.

See photograph on **page 125.**

FOR THE DOUGH

- ⅓ cup warm water
- ¾ teaspoon active dry yeast
- 1½ tablespoons olive oil, plus more for greasing the bowl
- 1 cup (130 grams) all-purpose flour, plus more for kneading
- ½ teaspoon fine sea salt

FOR THE TOPPINGS

- 3.5 ounces (2 strips) thick-sliced smoked bacon, finely chopped
- ½ cup thinly sliced red or white onion
- ½ cup (4 ounces) crème fraîche
- ¼ cup (2 ounces) whole-milk ricotta cheese
- Pinch of freshly grated nutmeg
- ½ teaspoon fine sea salt, plus more to taste
- Freshly ground white pepper, to taste

1. Place a pizza stone, if you have one, or a cookie sheet (overturned if it's a rimmed pan so the flat side is facing up) on the middle rack of the oven and heat the oven to 475°F. Line another cookie sheet with parchment paper.

2. **Make the dough:** Pour the warm water into a medium bowl and sprinkle the dry yeast over the water. Let it stand until it foams a bit, about 5 minutes, then whisk in the oil.

3. Oil a large bowl and set aside. In another large bowl, whisk together the flour and salt; then add the yeast mixture, stirring with a wooden spoon until the dough is shaggy. Turn the dough out onto a floured surface and knead until it is uniform and elastic, 3 to 5 minutes (flour your hands if necessary to keep the dough from sticking). Transfer the dough to the oiled bowl, turn it

Dough: After resting the dough for 1 hour in step 3, you can cover the bowl with plastic wrap and store it in the refrigerator for up to 1 day. Bring it to room temperature before rolling it out in step 4.

to cover it with oil, cover the bowl with a damp kitchen towel, and let the dough rest in a draft-free place for 1 hour.

4. Roll the dough out on a floured surface to form a 12-inch round, and transfer the round to the lined cookie sheet. Cover it with a clean damp kitchen towel and let it rest for 30 minutes.

5. **Prepare the toppings:** Meanwhile, heat a medium skillet over medium heat. Add the bacon and cook until it starts rendering its fat but doesn't really brown much, about 4 minutes. Stir in the onion and cook until it has wilted, about 2 minutes longer. Remove the skillet from the heat.

6. In a medium bowl, whisk together the crème fraîche, ricotta, nutmeg, salt, and white pepper.

7. Remove the damp cloth from the dough and spread the crème fraîche mixture evenly over it, leaving a ½-inch border around the edges. Sprinkle the bacon-onion mixture on top and transfer the dough, still on the parchment-lined cookie sheet, either to the pizza stone or to the heated cookie sheet in the oven. Bake until the top is beginning to brown and the sides are golden and crispy, 9 to 18 minutes. Serve warm.

VARIATION

Tarte Flambée with Swiss Chard

Leaves of fresh Swiss chard can stand in for the onions in a *tarte flambée*. Simply slice enough Swiss chard leaves (stems removed) into thin ribbons to make 1½ cups (this will take 3 to 5 large leaves). Add the Swiss chard ribbons to the bacon in the skillet in place of the onions in step 5. Cook, stirring occasionally, until the chard is wilted and all its liquid has cooked off, 3 to 5 minutes (you'll know it's ready when it starts to stick to the pan). Proceed with the rest of the recipe.

Roasted Tomato and Zucchini Tarts

SERVES 8

These vivid little tarts, baked in individual muffin cups, are filled with roasted summer vegetables and herbed ricotta cheese. Despite their buttery whole-wheat crusts, with their abundant vegetables and relatively small size, the tarts are still fairly light—and perfect to serve as a first course at an elegant meal. Or serve them for brunch with poached eggs (see page 37) perched on top of the filling; add them just before serving. They are adorable, unexpected, and surprisingly perfect with mimosas.

See photograph on **page 110.**

FOR THE CRUSTS

¾ cup (97 grams) all-purpose flour

½ cup (77 grams) whole-wheat flour

¼ teaspoon fine sea salt

10 tablespoons (1¼ sticks / 141 grams) unsalted butter, cold, cut into cubes, plus more for greasing

1 large egg yolk

2 tablespoons ice water, plus more as needed

FOR THE FILLING

1 pound zucchini, trimmed and cut into ½-inch cubes

1 cup halved cherry tomatoes

1½ teaspoons finely chopped fresh rosemary leaves

¾ teaspoon fine sea salt, plus more as needed

Freshly ground black pepper, as needed

2 tablespoons extra-virgin olive oil

½ cup (4 ounces) fresh whole-milk ricotta cheese

1 egg

2 tablespoons mixed chopped fresh herbs, such as parsley, thyme, and chives

1 small garlic clove, finely grated or minced

5 tablespoons (1¼ ounces) finely grated Parmesan cheese

1. **Make the crusts:** Using the ingredients listed above, prepare the crust according to the directions on page 117, adding the egg yolk along with the ice water. Gather the dough into a ball and then form it into a disk. Wrap the disk in plastic wrap and refrigerate it for at least 1 hour. (Note that this sticky dough comes together best in the food processor—which distributes the butter and egg more evenly—but you can do it by hand.)

2. Heat the oven to 375°F.

Dough: You can make the tart dough and chill it in the refrigerator up to 2 days in advance. Flatten it into a disk and wrap it in plastic wrap before chilling.

Tart shells: You can bake the shells up to 1 day in advance before filling them. Store them, uncovered, at room temperature.

3. Grease 8 cups of a standard 12-cup muffin tin, leaving the other 4 cups ungreased (or use two 6-cup pans). Divide the dough into 8 equal pieces, shape each one into a golf ball–size sphere, and roll each ball out to form a ⅛-inch-thick round. Press each round into a greased muffin cup and lightly crimp the edges. Nestle a second muffin pan on top of the first to help weight down the crusts. (If you don't have a second muffin tin, crumple up balls of foil and place them in each dough-lined muffin cup instead; the goal here is to keep the pastry from shrinking too much.) Transfer the muffin tin(s) to the oven and bake for 15 minutes. Remove the top tin (or foil balls) and continue to bake until the bottom of each crust is just dry to the touch, about 5 minutes more. Transfer the muffin tin to a wire rack to cool.

4. **Prepare the filling:** While crusts cool, raise the oven temperature to 400°F.

5. In a bowl, toss the zucchini and tomatoes with the rosemary, salt, pepper, and oil. Spread the mixture out on a rimmed baking sheet and roast it, tossing the vegetables occasionally, until they are tender and light golden, about 25 minutes.

6. In a small bowl, whisk together the ricotta, egg, mixed herbs, and garlic. Season with a large pinch each of salt and pepper.

7. Spoon an equal amount of the ricotta mixture (about a heaping tablespoon) into each cooled crust. Top the ricotta with the roasted vegetables. Sprinkle the Parmesan over the top. Transfer the muffin tin to the oven and bake until the tarts are bubbling and golden, about 25 minutes. Cool slightly before serving. I like to pop these out of the tins with a small offset spatula, but a butter knife also works.

Salmon Confit with Lime, Juniper, and Fennel, **page 156**

Fish & Shellfish

Classic Brandade

MAKES ABOUT 4 CUPS; 12 TO 20 APPETIZER SERVINGS

1 pound salt cod

1 large medium white potato (about 6 ounces), unpeeled, pierced all over with a fork

1 bay leaf

1 whole clove

1 medium onion, peeled but left whole

¾ cup extra-virgin olive oil

½ cup heavy cream, plus more as needed

3 garlic cloves, finely grated or minced

Fine sea salt and freshly ground black pepper, to taste

Fresh lemon juice, to taste

Chopped fresh chives, for garnish (optional)

Crackers, toasted bread, and/or crudités, for serving

The first time I sampled brandade, as a kid in France, it reminded me of lox and cream cheese spread—briny, rich, and fishy in a good way, though without the marked flavor of the smoked salmon that was familiar to me. The biggest difference between the two was the texture. The stuff I smear on a bagel is thick and dense. Brandade, a mix of salt cod, olive oil, potatoes, and cream, is fluffy and cloudlike, like extra-savory mashed potatoes that taste a little like the sea. In France (and parts of Spain, for that matter), brandade can be served either hot and gratinéed as a main course (think: a fishy shepherd's pie) or at room temperature as a dip or spread for bread, crackers, and crudités. I prefer the dip version, which I like to offer with aperitifs as a festive way to start a dinner party.

This recipe makes a lot of brandade—enough for a pretty big gathering—but you can halve it if you're cooking for a small group. If you can only find a 1-pound piece of salt cod at the market (it's available at Mediterranean specialty markets and some fish stores), after soaking it, you can freeze half for another time (straight out of the package and rock hard, it can be difficult to cut before it's softened). Look for a thick center-cut piece of salt cod. It will be less salty than the thinner pieces at the ends.

1. Rinse the salt cod well, then place it in a bowl and add enough water to cover it by at least 1 inch. Cover the bowl, put it in the fridge, and let the salt cod soak overnight, changing the water a few times to reduce the saltiness.

2. Heat the oven to 450°F (or use a microwave; see next step).

3. Place the potato on a baking pan and bake it in the oven until it is tender, about 45 minutes. (Alternatively, microwave the potato for 5 minutes, turn it over, and microwave for another 3 to 5 minutes, until tender.) Let the potato cool, and then peel off the skin with your fingers or a paring knife.

4. Drain the soaked cod and transfer it to a medium pot. Add cold water to cover, and then add the bay leaf. Stick the clove into the onion and add it to the pot. Bring the water to a simmer and simmer for 5 minutes. Remove the pot from the heat and let the cod cool in the water. Then drain, skin, and remove the bones from the cod; discard the onion and bay leaf.

Cod: You can let the cod soak for up to 2 days, covered, in the refrigerator, periodically changing the water.

Potato: You can bake or microwave the potato 3 days in advance. Store it, loosely covered, in the refrigerator. Peel it when you're ready to add it to the processor.

Brandade: You can make this up to 2 days in advance; store it in an airtight container in the refrigerator. Before serving, drain off any excess moisture and bring it to room temperature.

5. Return the cod to the pot, stir in ¼ cup of the oil, and heat it over medium heat, breaking up the fish as you stir. Once it's hot, remove the pot from the heat.

6. Meanwhile, in a small pot, bring the remaining ½ cup oil and the cream to a simmer. Remove that pot from the heat.

7. In the bowl of a food processor, combine the cod, potato, and garlic, and pulse until the mixture is chunky. Add the cream mixture and pulse until the brandade reaches a fluffy consistency, adding more cream if necessary. Taste, and season with salt, pepper, and lemon juice as needed. Transfer the brandade to a serving bowl and top it with chopped chives. Serve crackers, bread, or crudités alongside for dipping.

Sardine and Tomato Toasts

MAKES 2 MAIN COURSE SERVINGS OR 4 APPETIZER SERVINGS

Canned sardines on toast is one of my favorite "I have nothing in the house for dinner" dinners. Although the dish couldn't be any simpler, there are a few details that will make it truly shine. The toast needs to be hot when you rub it with the garlic, the oil needs to be lush and herbal, and the onion should be crisp and juicy. This sardine toast also has the guts of a ripe tomato rubbed into the bread, kind of like a Catalan *pan con tomate* (tomato bread with olive oil and salt), which adds a wonderful sweetness to the fish. If you can't get a perfectly ripe tomato that's about to burst, just skip it entirely. It's nice to have but not essential. Just make sure to splurge on really good canned sardines—their quality makes all the difference.

When I eat this by myself, I usually devour it leaning over my counter within seconds of assembling it, while the toast is at its crunchiest before the olive oil has a chance to soak in. The walk to the table can seem so long when there's hot sardine toast within reach, though it's good a few minutes later, too.

1 (10-inch) baguette, halved lengthwise and then cut crosswise into 4 pieces

1 fat garlic clove, halved

1 ripe juicy tomato, halved through the equator (not through the stem end)

Extra-virgin olive oil, for drizzling

Flaky sea salt, to taste

1 (6- to 7-ounce) tin very good sardines, deboned if you like

Thinly sliced red onion or shallot

Fresh lime juice, to taste

Coarsely ground black pepper, to taste

Fresh basil leaves, torn, for garnish

1. Heat the broiler.

2. Place the baguette pieces, cut-side up, on a rimmed baking sheet and broil them until lightly toasted, 30 seconds to 2 minutes; watch them carefully so they don't burn. (Or you can toast the bread in a toaster oven if that's more convenient for you—any way you can toast the bread will work.)

3. Immediately rub the cut sides (aggressively!) with the cut sides of the garlic halves, and then with the cut sides of the tomato. You want the garlic and tomato flesh to nearly disappear as they get smooshed into the bread.

4. Drizzle the bread generously with oil and sprinkle it with salt, then top it with the sardines and onion. Sprinkle with lime juice, more salt, and pepper. Garnish with fresh basil and serve immediately.

Giant Prawns with Preserved Lemon, Herbs, and Brandy

SERVES 4

Giant prawns—those enormous leggy crustaceans, still in their shells, that you can sometimes find at the fishmonger's—are always wonderful to cook and eat. But the real star of this recipe is the fragrant herb sauce, so irresistible you'll want to spread it on everything. Verdant with scallions, basil, and parsley, funky and bright from preserved lemon, hot from jalapeño, it all gets puréed with really good olive oil until the mix becomes smoothly rich and emerald green. And yes, the sauce tastes fantastic on fat pink shrimp as big as cannoli. But if you can't find them, buy regular shrimp (preferably wild) still in their shells, and use those instead. Cooked in the sauce along with lots of sliced garlic, then flambéed dramatically in brandy and finished with butter, this makes a stunning, company-worthy dish—just as long as your company doesn't mind eating messy green sauce–covered shrimp with their fingers. To me, gnawing on the shrimp shells is part of the fun, so invite guests who agree.

If you can't find preserved lemon, leave it out of the sauce and add a couple of anchovies and some extra lemon juice instead. It won't be the exact same sauce, but it will still be utterly delicious.

FOR THE SAUCE

- 6 tablespoons extra-virgin olive oil
- ¼ cup packed fresh parsley leaves
- ¼ cup packed fresh basil leaves
- 2 garlic cloves, finely grated or minced
- 2 tablespoons chopped scallions (greens only)
- 1½ tablespoons chopped preserved lemon (seed it first if necessary)
- 1 jalapeño, seeded (or not if you want more heat)
- 1 teaspoon fresh lemon juice, plus more to taste
- ½ teaspoon fine sea salt, plus more to taste

FOR THE SHRIMP

- ¼ cup extra-virgin olive oil
- 6 garlic cloves, very thinly sliced
- 1½ pounds giant shrimp, the largest you can find, in the shell
- ½ teaspoon fine sea salt, plus more as needed
- 2 tablespoons brandy or pastis
- 2 tablespoons unsalted butter

1. **Make the sauce:** In a blender, combine the oil, herbs, garlic, scallions, preserved lemon, jalapeño, lemon juice, and salt with 1 tablespoon water until the sauce is well blended and smooth. Taste, and add more salt and/or lemon if you like.

2. **Cook the shrimp:** Heat the oil in a large skillet over low heat, then stir in the garlic slices. Cook slowly until the garlic is golden and fragrant, 3 to 6 minutes. Don't rush this—you want evenly cooked, lightly golden garlic slices here.

recipe continues

3. Stir the shrimp into the skillet, sprinkle with the salt, and cook until the shrimp just turn opaque but are not cooked through, 2 to 3 minutes (or less for smaller shrimp). Remove the skillet from the heat.

4. Pour the brandy into the skillet (still off the heat) and use either a long lighter or a long match to (carefully!) ignite the brandy. Once the flames have died (there might not be a lot), return the skillet to medium heat and whisk in the butter and ¼ cup herb sauce. Continue to cook until the shrimp are cooked through, 3 to 5 minutes. (If you'd rather not ignite the brandy, you can skip that step and just cook the mixture for an extra minute or two.) Taste the sauce; when the raw sting of the brandy has mellowed and the sauce has condensed slightly, it's ready.

5. Serve the shrimp with more of the sauce on the side.

Thinking Ahead

Sauce: You can make the sauce up to 1 day ahead and keep it refrigerated in a sealed container. Bring it to room temperature before adding it to the shrimp.

Roasted Tarragon Shrimp and Onions

SERVES 4 TO 6

With its mix of caramelized onions, fresh tarragon, and roasted shrimp, this is about as elegant as sheet-pan suppers get, but it is still weeknight-easy and very fast. The only chopping involved is one onion and some tarragon—a small grater or press will take care of the garlic. The sherry vinegar is an important element here. Without it, the sweetness of the onions can dominate. Add the vinegar gradually, sprinkling it lightly over the browned onions and tasting as you go.

Thinking Ahead

Onions: You can roast the onions up to 3 days in advance and keep them, covered, in the refrigerator. When you are ready to roast the shrimp, toss them with the onions on a rimmed baking sheet.

⅓ cup finely chopped fresh tarragon leaves and tender stems, plus 4 whole sprigs

2 garlic cloves, finely grated or minced

4 tablespoons extra-virgin olive oil, divided, plus more for drizzling

½ teaspoon fine sea salt, plus more as needed

¼ teaspoon freshly ground black pepper, plus more as needed

2 pounds large shrimp, peeled

1 large white onion, cut into ¼-inch-thick slices (about 2 cups)

4 sprigs fresh thyme

Sherry vinegar, to taste

1. Heat the oven to 425°F.

2. In a large bowl, combine the chopped tarragon, garlic, 2 tablespoons of the oil, salt, and pepper. Stir in the shrimp and let them sit at room temperature while you roast the onions.

3. On a large rimmed baking sheet, toss the onion slices with the remaining 2 tablespoons oil, the thyme sprigs, and the tarragon sprigs. Roast, tossing the onions halfway through, until they are lightly browned all over, 20 to 25 minutes.

4. Thoroughly toss the shrimp with the onions on the baking sheet, then return the baking sheet to the oven and roast until the shrimp are cooked through, 5 to 7 minutes. Sprinkle with sherry vinegar and serve immediately.

The best part about a pan full of sizzling escargots is the garlic and parsley butter bubbling up inside the snail shells. When I was a kid, even before I would consider noshing on one of the curled gastropods my parents had ordered, I'd dab a morsel of baguette across the pan, letting the pungent herbal butter soak in. Eventually I started eating the snails, too, but my first and deepest love is that green-speckled butter.

It took a long time for me to agree to taste a snail, but that was my parents' fault. When I was about seven, we spent the summer in a house in Burgundy, where fat garden snails overran the tomatoes. My mother got the idea to cook the intruders. She paid my sister and me ten centimes for each one we collected. Then, under instruction from the neighbor, she packed them into a crate with a screen on top, set it on the porch, and attempted to starve them, which was a necessary purge before cooking. My sister and I felt so bad for the snails that we snuck leaves and flowers into the crate when no one was around. They did eventually end up in the pot, and I probably still ate the garlic butter, though to be honest no one in my family remembers all the details of the meal.

In this dish, I keep the snail butter—spiked with Pernod—but ditch the snails, substituting shrimp and mushrooms. To my mind, the combination is sort of what snails taste like, anyway.

Shrimp and Mushrooms with Garlicky Herb Butter

SERVES 4 TO 6

FOR THE HERB BUTTER

2 tablespoons chopped fresh parsley leaves, plus more for garnish

1 tablespoon chopped fresh chives, plus more for garnish

1 tablespoon chopped fresh tarragon or basil leaves

1 tablespoon pastis, such as Pernod

2 fat garlic cloves, finely grated or minced

1 teaspoon fine sea salt, plus more as needed

1 teaspoon freshly ground black pepper

½ teaspoon finely grated lemon zest

6 tablespoons (¾ stick) unsalted butter, room temperature

TO FINISH

12 ounces oyster mushrooms, chopped into 1-inch pieces

¼ teaspoon fine sea salt, plus more as needed

¼ teaspoon freshly ground black pepper, plus more as needed

2 large shallots, thinly sliced

2 pounds shelled large shrimp

2 tablespoons dry white wine

2 tablespoons pastis, such as Pernod

2 tablespoons chopped fresh parsley leaves, plus more for garnish

2 tablespoons chopped fresh chives, plus more for garnish

2 tablespoons chopped fresh tarragon or basil leaves

Fresh lemon juice, to taste

Torn baguettes or cooked rice, for serving

1. **Prepare the herb butter:** In a mini food processor or a blender, combine the parsley, chives, tarragon, pastis, garlic, salt, pepper, and lemon zest and pulse until well mixed. Add the butter and process until you have a smooth, green-flecked paste.

2. **To finish:** In a large skillet, heat 2 tablespoons of the herb butter over medium-high heat. Stir in the mushrooms and cook until their liquid has cooked off and the mushrooms are browned and crispy, 8 to 12 minutes. Try not to disturb the mushrooms as they cook—the less stirring here means the browner they will get. Season the mushrooms with the salt and pepper. Add the shallots and cook until they are tender and translucent, 3 to 5 minutes. Reduce the heat to medium.

3. Add the shrimp to the skillet and season them generously with salt and pepper. Add the wine, pastis, and another 2 tablespoons of the herb butter and cook, stirring, until the shrimp are just pink, 3 to 7 minutes. Stir in another tablespoon or two of the herb butter and more salt to taste. (Any extra herb butter can be frozen.) Transfer the mixture to a platter and scatter the parsley, chives, and tarragon on top. Drizzle with lemon juice, and serve with baguette chunks or rice to soak up the sauce.

Lemony Spanish Mackerel

SERVES 4

Poor misunderstood mackerel—it has such an undeservedly fishy reputation. When very fresh, its pale fillets are sweet and delicate. Mackerel may have more character than your average mild whitefish like flounder, but it's far gentler and less oily than the ever-popular salmon, and more sustainable, too. Here I roast mackerel with red onions perfumed with minced preserved lemon (which you can leave out in a pinch) and a topping of garlic-thyme butter. If you can't get really good thick pieces of mackerel (usually about ½-inch thick), use thinner fillets and roast them for a few minutes less. Or substitute salmon; the dish will be a bit richer and sweeter, but that's not necessarily a bad thing.

Thinking Ahead

Onions: You can roast the onions up to 3 days in advance and store them, covered, in the refrigerator. When you are ready to roast the fish, arrange the onions around the fillets on the baking sheet.

Lemon butter: You can make the butter up to 1 week ahead. Wrap it well with plastic wrap and refrigerate it. Or you can freeze it for up to 3 months.

2 medium red onions, thinly sliced

¼ cup extra-virgin olive oil

1 tablespoon plus 1 teaspoon minced preserved lemon, divided (seed it first if necessary)

¼ teaspoon fine sea salt, plus more as needed

6 tablespoons (¾ stick) unsalted butter, room temperature

1 garlic clove, finely grated or minced

1 teaspoon minced fresh lemon thyme or regular thyme leaves

Pinch of Turkish red pepper (*urfa biber*) or chile powder such as ancho

4 (6-ounce) fillets mackerel, preferably thick and center cut, patted dry

Freshly ground black pepper, as needed

Chopped fresh parsley leaves, for serving

Chopped fresh chives, for serving

Lemon wedges, for serving

1. Heat the oven to 425°F. On a rimmed baking sheet, toss the onions with the oil, 1 teaspoon of the preserved lemon, and the salt. Roast for 10 minutes.

2. Meanwhile, prepare the lemon-thyme butter: In a medium bowl, use a fork to mash together the butter, remaining 1 tablespoon preserved lemon, garlic, thyme, a large pinch of salt, and the Turkish pepper.

3. Season the mackerel lightly with salt and pepper, and then coat it with all but 1 tablespoon of the lemon butter. Toss the onions on the baking sheet and use a spatula to clear a space in the middle for the fish. Place the fish, skin-side down, in the cleared space and roast it along with the onions until cooked through, 10 to 15 minutes.

4. Remove the baking sheet from the oven and dot the mackerel and onions with the remaining 1 tablespoon lemon-thyme butter. Serve the mackerel topped with the parsley and chives, with the onions and lemon wedges on the side.

Hake with Herb Butter en Papillote

Cooking anything *en papillote* is both dramatic and practical. The drama comes from the presentation: Individual parchment-wrapped packets, in this case stuffed with pearly hake fillets dotted with herb butter and nestled in spinach, are brought to the table for your guests to open. When they do, fragrant, herby steam pours forth—white and heady and scenting the air. It's very impressive. The practical part is that since you throw away the parchment afterward, there's not a lot of cleanup.

Since baby spinach can turn mushy, try to use mature, crinkly spinach leaves here. Or use baby kale, which has a sturdier and more robust texture.

4 tablespoons (½ stick)
unsalted butter, room
temperature

2 tablespoons chopped
mixed fresh herbs, such as
dill, tarragon, parsley,
and/or chives

2 teaspoons minced shallot
or scallion whites

1 teaspoon fresh lemon juice

¼ teaspoon fine sea salt,
plus more as needed

Freshly ground black pepper,
as needed

Pinch of freshly grated
nutmeg

4 (6- to 7-ounce) hake or
flounder fillets

4 ounces (5 loosely packed
cups) mature spinach
leaves, stems removed and
discarded

Lemon wedges, for serving

Flaky sea salt, for serving

1. Heat the oven to 450°F.

2. In a small bowl, use a fork to mash together the butter, herbs, shallot, lemon juice, salt, several grinds of black pepper, and the nutmeg until the butter has absorbed the lemon juice.

3. Season the fish with salt and pepper. Cut 4 large sheets of parchment paper, each about 12 × 15 inches. Place each fillet on a parchment sheet. Top each fillet with a quarter of the butter mixture and a quarter of the spinach leaves. Season the spinach lightly with salt and pepper.

4. Fold the parchment over the fish and spinach. Crimp and tightly fold the edges of the parchment to create a sealed packet. (It doesn't matter exactly how you crimp or fold the parchment—the aim is just to seal the packet. Sometimes I staple the packets closed instead of folding them, which is easier if not quite as elegant.)

5. Arrange the packets on two large rimmed baking sheets and bake for 8 to 12 minutes, depending on the thickness of the fish. You can check one for doneness by opening a corner of the packet and poking the fish with a fork (it should slide in easily)—then make sure to serve that opened packet to yourself. Transfer the packets to serving plates. Allow your guests to tear or cut open the parchment themselves (watching out for a sudden waft of steam), and serve the lemon wedges and flaky sea salt on the side.

Thinking Ahead

Herb butter: You can make the butter up to 1 week ahead and store it, wrapped in plastic wrap, in the refrigerator. You can also freeze it for up to 3 months.

Packets: You can fill and seal the packets up to an hour before baking. Store them in the refrigerator.

Buttery Crab Pasta with Golden Tomatoes and Chervil

MAKES 2 MAIN COURSE SERVINGS OR 4 APPETIZER SERVINGS

Most crab pastas don't have enough crab—just a few unsatisfying flakes scattered here and there amidst far too many noodles. Not this one! Filled with big chunks of buttery lump crabmeat, along with cherry tomatoes and chervil, it's highly decadent and perfectly crabby. Save it for a special occasion—an appetizer for an intimate dinner party or a main course for a cozy meal for two. If you can't find chervil—which, outside of France, isn't as popular as the delicate, mildly licorice-y herb should be—use basil, mint, or cilantro instead. This dish needs a soft fresh herb to counter the richness of the copious amounts of butter and crab.

Fine sea salt, as needed

8 ounces bucatini or linguine

4 tablespoons (½ stick) unsalted butter

¼ cup grated Parmesan cheese, plus more for serving

2 cups halved golden or red cherry tomatoes

1 scallion (white and green parts), thinly sliced

⅛ teaspoon red pepper flakes, plus more to taste

½ cup fresh chervil leaves, divided

Finely grated zest of 1 lemon

Juice of ½ lemon

Freshly ground black pepper, to taste

8 ounces lump crabmeat, picked over to remove any stray shells

Extra-virgin olive oil, for serving

Flaky sea salt, for serving

1. Bring a large pot of heavily salted water to a boil. Add the pasta and cook until al dente (usually a minute or two less than the package directs). Reserve 1 cup of the pasta water and drain the pasta.

2. Melt the butter in a large skillet over medium heat. Whisk in ½ cup of the pasta water and the Parmesan. Then stir in the tomatoes, scallion, red pepper flakes, and a large pinch of salt and simmer for 1 minute.

3. Stir in the pasta, ¼ cup of the chervil, the lemon zest and juice, and black pepper to taste; toss until warmed through. Gently fold in the crabmeat. Remove the skillet from the heat and serve the crab pasta sprinkled with Parmesan, the remaining ¼ cup chervil, a drizzle of olive oil, and flaky sea salt to taste.

Swordfish Brochettes with Basil and Harissa

SERVES 4

One summer when I was on vacation with my parents and sister in Brittany, there was an old, neglected charcoal grill in the backyard. My parents—longtime barbecue enthusiasts who thought nothing of grilling burgers under a golf umbrella in a November rainstorm—made good use of the rickety thing. They tossed local oysters on the fire in the pinkish Brittany dusk, and we ate them burning hot, with lemon juice and melted butter drizzled on top while the neighborhood cats vamped for handouts. We grilled a lot of fish brochettes, too, sometimes brushing them with spices like the ones in this harissa-laced marinade and stuffing the fish chunks with herbs plucked straight from the garden. The local seafood was so pristine in that coastal region that we went a little nuts with it all.

Swordfish cubes are particularly well suited to brochettes, but any thick chunks of firm, meaty fish will do. As long as the pieces are thick enough not to tear or fall off the skewers, they will be happy here. And any fish that does escape can be saved for the cats—and then they'll be happy, too.

2 teaspoons fennel seeds

3 tablespoons extra-virgin olive oil, plus more as needed

2 tablespoons harissa

Finely grated zest of 1 lemon

¼ teaspoon finely grated lime zest

1 fat garlic clove, finely grated or minced

¾ teaspoon fine sea salt, plus more to taste

½ teaspoon freshly ground black pepper

2 (10- to 12-ounce) swordfish steaks, skinned and cut into 1½-inch cubes

1 small bunch fresh basil (the kind with large leaves is preferable)

Lime wedges, for serving

1. Heat a small skillet over medium heat. Add the fennel seeds and toast them in the dry skillet until they are fragrant, 1 to 2 minutes. Grind them with a mortar and pestle or a spice grinder.

2. Transfer the fennel seeds to a medium bowl and add the oil, harissa, lemon zest, lime zest, garlic, salt, and pepper. Gently fold in the swordfish, cover the bowl, and refrigerate for 20 minutes or up to 1 hour.

3. Heat a grill to medium-high or heat the broiler.

4. Remove the fish from the fridge. Cut a slit halfway into a swordfish cube, then swipe 1 basil leaf through the marinade and stuff it inside the cube. Repeat with the remaining fish and more basil, reserving extra basil leaves for serving. Thread the fish cubes onto metal skewers, keeping a little space between the cubes.

5. Grill or broil the fish until it has just turned opaque on the outside, about 2 minutes per side (8 minutes total). Transfer to a platter and serve immediately, with the reserved basil and lime wedges alongside.

Brown Butter Scallops with Parsley and Lemon

MAKES 4 MAIN COURSE SERVINGS OR 8 APPETIZER SERVINGS

For restaurants, the holy grail of sea scallop cooking is a crunchy browned exterior surrounding a soft, slippery center. This is a fine thing for chefs, but at home, I can never quite get it right. Usually, by the time the scallops brown to that mahogany degree, they are also overcooked in their middles. The whole fast-moving, risky endeavor makes me anxious, especially when hungry guests are waiting.

Much less stressful and also just as delicious is poaching scallops in brown butter. You don't get the crispness of the sear, but the butter takes on the caramelized flavors of the browning and the scallops turn positively velvety and luscious in their buttery bath. A little lemon (both zest and juice), some garlic, and some coriander seeds add a subtle perfume, which is all the scallops really need. But if you want to wow those waiting guests, a spoonful of salmon roe adds a deep brininess to the rich mollusks and a stunning reddish color to the plate.

8 tablespoons (1 stick) unsalted butter

¼ cup minced fresh parsley leaves, plus more for serving

1 teaspoon finely grated lemon zest

1 to 2 garlic cloves, finely grated or minced

¾ teaspoon coriander seeds, lightly crushed

1½ pounds sea scallops, patted dry

Kosher salt, as needed

Freshly ground black pepper, as needed

½ teaspoon fresh lemon juice, or to taste

Salmon roe, for serving (optional)

1. In a large skillet, melt the butter over medium heat and let it cook until it turns lightly browned and nutty, about 5 minutes. Stir in the parsley, lemon zest, garlic, and coriander, and cook until fragrant, about another 30 seconds.

2. Meanwhile, season the scallops with salt and pepper to taste.

3. Slip the scallops into the brown butter and sauté until they are cooked through, 2 to 4 minutes, flipping them over halfway through. Transfer the scallops to a serving platter, reserving the butter in the skillet.

4. Stir the lemon juice into the skillet, taste, and adjust the seasoning if necessary. Spoon the butter over the scallops and sprinkle with parsley. Serve immediately, topped with salmon roe if you like.

Cod with Aioli and Heirloom Tomatoes

SERVES 4

Mild whitefish like cod cry out for garlicky aioli. Or at least they do in my mind whenever I see the milky fillets lined up at the fish counter, just waiting to be coated in a pungent, creamy sauce. In this dead-simple recipe, they get their wish. After a quick stint roasting in a hot oven, the opaque fillets are piled onto a fresh tomato salad, then dolloped with homemade aioli. Since there's nothing else to it, be sure to seek out the very freshest fish, the greenest and most herbal olive oil, and the ripest, prettiest heirloom tomatoes available. Then consider serving this in soup plates, with both forks and spoons at the ready. All that sweet tomato nectar mingled with aioli and cod makes for a delightfully juicy meal.

2 to 3 heirloom tomatoes (about 1¼ pounds), cored and cut into ½-inch-thick wedges

½ teaspoon fine sea salt, plus more as needed

Extra-virgin olive oil, as needed

4 cod fillets (about 6 ounces each), patted dry

½ teaspoon freshly ground black pepper, plus more for garnish

8 sprigs fresh thyme

1 lemon, thinly sliced

Aioli (page 19)

Torn fresh basil leaves, for serving

Flaky sea salt, for serving

1. In a small bowl, toss the tomato wedges with ¼ teaspoon of the salt and drizzle them with olive oil to taste. Let the tomatoes sit while you prepare the fish.

2. Heat the oven to 400°F.

3. Place the cod fillets on a rimmed baking sheet, drizzle them with olive oil, and season them with the remaining ¼ teaspoon salt and the black pepper. Top the fish with the thyme sprigs, and then cover them with the lemon slices. Roast until the fish is cooked through, 10 to 15 minutes depending on the size. Remove the lemon slices and thyme sprigs.

4. Use a slotted spoon to transfer the tomatoes to a serving platter, and top them with the cod. Dollop the aioli on top of the fish, and drizzle it with the tomato juices and more olive oil. Sprinkle everything with basil, flaky sea salt, and lots of freshly ground black pepper.

Mustard Seed–Cured Salmon

MAKES 16 OR MORE APPETIZER SERVINGS

Homemade gravlax has to be one of the best party snacks out there. It's far less expensive than buying the best-quality smoked salmon, and it's even more impressive *because you've cured it yourself!* You don't even really need a recipe; as long as you maintain the proportions for the salmon, salt, and sugar, you can use whatever fresh herbs you've got on hand. Dill is the classic choice, and I combine it here with tarragon, mint, and cilantro for a more nuanced flavor. I also add a small amount of brown mustard seeds to the curing mix; they have a spicy, musky bite that goes well with the buttery fish.

I like to serve my gravlax with something creamy (crème fraîche or sour cream), and something tangy and a little sweet (honey mustard does the trick), along with bread or crackers on which to drape the soft slices of fish. But I've seen plenty of my party guests just eat gravlax with their fingers, spreading crème fraîche and/or mustard directly on the slices before devouring them in one bite. (Eating less bread can mean eating more fish, appetite-wise.) If you think your guests may be similarly inclined, be sure to have lots of cocktail napkins at the ready.

FOR THE FISH

2 tablespoons brown mustard seeds, lightly crushed

½ cup Diamond Crystal kosher salt or ⅓ cup fine sea salt

½ cup sugar

1 (3½- to 4-pound) side of salmon, halved crosswise

¼ cup packed fresh dill fronds

¼ cup packed fresh tarragon sprigs

¼ cup packed fresh cilantro sprigs

1 small bunch fresh mint, divided

FOR SERVING

1 cup (8 ounces) crème fraîche or sour cream

2 tablespoons minced mixed fresh herbs (such as chives, tarragon, mint, and/or parsley)

Fresh lemon juice, to taste

Fine sea salt and freshly ground black pepper, to taste

Brown bread or baguette slices, for serving

Honey mustard, for serving (optional)

1. **Cure the fish:** Stir together the mustard seeds, salt, and sugar in a medium bowl. Rub the mixture all over the flesh of the salmon pieces (not the skin). Then arrange the dill, tarragon, cilantro, and half of the mint sprigs on top of one piece of the salmon. Place the other salmon piece on top, flesh-side down, to sandwich the herbs. Arrange the remaining mint sprigs around the salmon, place the stuffed fish in a resealable plastic or silicone bag, and seal the bag, squeezing out any excess air.

Salmon: You must cure the salmon for 2 to 3 days in the refrigerator, turning the bag over every 12 hours.

Crème fraîche mixture: You can make the mixture up to 8 hours in advance. Cover it loosely and refrigerate. Drain off any excess moisture and bring it to room temperature before serving.

2. Place the plastic bag on a rimmed baking sheet or plate, and top it with another rimmed baking sheet or plate (I use quarter sheet pans for this). Place a heavy pan or pot or a large can of something (I use tomatoes) on top to weight it down.

3. Refrigerate the salmon for 2 to 3 days, turning the bag over every 12 hours.

4. **To serve:** In a small bowl, mix together the crème fraîche, herbs, a squeeze of lemon juice, and salt and pepper to taste. Remove the salmon from the bag and discard the herbs. Rinse the fish and pat it dry. Thinly slice the salmon, discarding the skin. Serve the fish with bread, the crème fraîche sauce, and honey mustard on the side, if you like.

Salmon Confit with Lime, Juniper, and Fennel

SERVES 4

Confiting salmon fillets in olive oil makes their flesh extravagantly tender and silky. Most fish confiting takes place over low heat on the stovetop, but here I use the oven, which makes the recipe relatively hands-off once you've got everything arranged in the pan.

You can season the cooking oil for a confit with practically anything aromatic. I particularly like the combination of floral lime, piney juniper, and both fennel seeds and the bulb for their licorice notes. It's a very complex-tasting dish given the scant amount of work it takes to make it. You can reuse the infused oil, too: Store it in the fridge and then drizzle it on salads or use it to sauté other fish or seafood. Or try tossing it with boiled potatoes and chopped dill; it adds richness without any obvious fishiness, and you can serve the potato salad alongside the salmon if you're looking to round out the plate.

Thinking Ahead

Salmon: You can place the seasoned fish in the baking dish, cover it with the herbs and oil, and refrigerate it, covered, up to 4 hours ahead. Add the lime slices just before roasting.

2 limes

½ teaspoon fine sea salt, plus more as needed

½ teaspoon freshly ground black pepper

4 dried juniper berries, lightly crushed with a mortar and pestle or the side of a heavy knife

½ teaspoon fennel seeds, lightly crushed with a mortar and pestle or the side of a heavy knife

4 (6- to 8-ounce) skinless salmon fillets

6 sprigs fresh marjoram or thyme

Extra-virgin olive oil, as needed

1 large fennel bulb, with fronds

Flaky sea salt, for serving

1. Heat the oven to 325°F. Finely grate the zest from 1 of the limes and place the zest in a bowl (reserve the lime for later). Stir in the salt, pepper, and crushed juniper berries and fennel seeds. Sprinkle the mixture all over the salmon fillets and place them, packed close together, in a small baking dish (a large loaf pan or an 8-inch cake pan will work).

2. Thinly slice the remaining lime and lay the slices on the fish. Tuck the marjoram sprigs around the fish. Cover the fish with olive oil—you'll need at least ½ cup, possibly even 1 cup, to submerge it. Bake the fish until it's just cooked through, 15 to 20 minutes. (Thinner fillets may take less time—start checking at 10 minutes.)

3. Remove the fennel fronds from the bulb and chop enough to make ½ cup. Trim the fennel bulb and thinly slice it on a mandoline or with a very sharp knife. In a bowl, toss the fennel fronds and slices with a pinch of fine sea salt. Juice the zested lime and add juice, to taste, to the fennel. Drizzle the fennel with oil. Serve the salmon and fennel sprinkled with flaky sea salt.

Sautéed Salmon with Fennel Beurre Blanc

SERVES 6

6 (8-ounce) salmon fillets, skin on

1 teaspoon fine sea salt, divided, plus more to taste

1 teaspoon fennel pollen or ground fennel seeds

Freshly ground black pepper, as needed

2 tablespoons extra-virgin olive oil

2 tablespoons dry white wine

2 tablespoons white wine vinegar

2 tablespoons finely chopped fennel bulb (reserve the fronds for serving)

1 tablespoon finely chopped shallot

1 tablespoon pastis, such as Pernod

12 tablespoons (1½ sticks) unsalted butter, cut into cubes, room temperature

½ teaspoon fresh lemon juice, or to taste

Beurre blanc is a smooth and satiny mix of shallots, wine and/or vinegar, and lots of butter. This zippy sauce came into being in the early 1900s when a Loire Valley cook forgot to add the egg to a béarnaise sauce. My parents learned how to make it from Julia Child, and it was a staple at fancy dinner parties at our house, where the rich elixir was drizzled over fish, shellfish, even potatoes. I liked swabbing the saucepan with bread to get every last buttery drop.

Like all emulsified sauces—mayonnaise, hollandaise—temperature is the key to success here. You don't want to heat the mixture until it simmers, which will break the sauce, but it shouldn't get too cold either, or it won't thicken. If at any point the sauce starts steaming as if it's on the verge of a simmer, pull the pan off the heat and whisk it furiously to cool it down. As long as you don't walk away from the pot, you should be okay. Also make sure you start with room-temperature butter.

I've flavored this *beurre blanc* with fennel and a little Pernod to give it a licorice kick. It goes beautifully with salmon fillets, though any fish fillets can be substituted. This dish is all about the savory, silky sauce—and the fish is a mere excuse to get it onto the plate.

1. Season the fish with ½ teaspoon of the salt, the fennel pollen, and pepper to taste. Coat it with the oil and let it sit at room temperature while you make the sauce.

2. In a small saucepan, combine the white wine, white wine vinegar, fennel, shallot, pastis, remaining ½ teaspoon salt, and pepper to taste. Simmer over medium-high heat until the mixture reduces by about two-thirds, 3 to 5 minutes. Meanwhile, pour hot water into a bowl to warm it (to hold the finished sauce). Before using it, pour out the water from the warmed bowl and dry it.

3. Reduce the heat under the saucepan to low. Whisk in a few cubes of butter until smooth. Continue whisking in the butter, a few cubes at a time, until all of the butter has been incorporated and melted into the sauce—it should be thick and emulsified (go low and slow here). Do not allow the mixture to come to a boil while cooking, which will break the emulsification. Whisk in the lemon juice, then taste and add more lemon juice

recipe continues

Beurre blanc: You can combine the white wine mixture (step 2) and reduce it 1 hour in advance. Immediately before serving, warm it gently before adding and emulsifying the butter.

The emulsified sauce will keep for 30 minutes if you put the pan in a bain-marie (a vessel of hot water). But it doesn't stay quite as hot as when freshly made, and the texture can thin out.

and/or salt if needed. Immediately strain the sauce into it. Cover the bowl with foil or plastic wrap to keep the sauce warm while you cook the salmon.

4. Place a large skillet over high heat until it is very hot. Add the fish, skin-side down, in batches if necessary, so you don't overcrowd the pan. Cook without moving the fish for 2 to 3 minutes, until the skin turns golden. Flip the fillets over and continue to cook until the fish reaches your desired doneness, about 3 minutes more for medium. Transfer the fillets to a platter or serving plates.

5. Spoon the beurre blanc over the fish and garnish it with the reserved fennel fronds. Serve immediately.

Spaghetti with Anchovies, Tomatoes, and Basil

SERVES 4

I probably cook a version of this simple pasta every other week. It's one of my favorite meals, and I even put up with sub-par tomatoes in the middle of winter to satisfy my craving for its deep umami flavor. I used to make my pasta with anchovies the classic way: just garlic, olive oil, red pepper flakes, and anchovies. But then a few years ago, while on vacation in Provence, when ripe tomatoes were everywhere in the market, I added a handful to the anchovies and garlic simmering away in the pan. Fresh tomatoes have since become essential to the mix, adding a wonderful sweetness and tang. It's not really a French-inspired recipe, per se, so much as a Brooklyn recipe that blossomed in a kitchen in France.

Salt, as needed

12 oil-packed anchovy fillets

6 garlic cloves

¼ cup fresh parsley leaves, plus more for serving

2 tablespoons fresh basil or mint leaves, plus more for serving

¼ teaspoon crushed red pepper flakes

2 tablespoons extra-virgin olive oil, plus more for serving

1½ cups chopped fresh plum tomatoes (2 to 3 plum tomatoes, or use cherry tomatoes)

12 ounces spaghetti

2 tablespoons unsalted butter, cubed

½ teaspoon finely grated lemon zest

1. Bring a large pot of heavily salted water to a boil.

2. While the water is heating, chop the anchovies, garlic, parsley, basil, and red pepper flakes together on a large cutting board. Heat the oil in a large skillet over medium heat, and cook the anchovy mixture until the garlic starts to turn golden, about 5 minutes.

3. Stir the tomatoes into the skillet, cover, and cook until they are soft and release their liquid, stirring occasionally, 7 to 10 minutes. Uncover and cook for 3 minutes longer to condense the juices slightly.

4. While the sauce is cooking, add the spaghetti to the boiling water and cook until it is just al dente (usually a minute or two less than the package directs). Reserve 1 cup of the pasta water, then drain the pasta.

5. Stir the spaghetti, butter, and lemon zest into the skillet, tossing to coat the pasta well. Stir in a little of the reserved pasta water if the mixture seems dry. Serve immediately, topped with chopped parsley and basil and drizzled with olive oil.

Provençal Tuna with Sweet Onions, Peppers, and Capers

SERVES 4

My parents loved to tell the story of the time my sister and I rebelled at a seafood restaurant in Marseille.

"Girls, just try one bite of tuna. You can dunk it in mayonnaise," my mother cajoled, pushing a plate of braised tuna steaks with onions and peppers across the tablecloth.

My sister and I pushed it right back. With arms crossed and brows knitted, we refused even a bite.

"You like fish," we told our parents, our little-girl voices quavering with indignation. "We don't like fish. We will never like fish. And you can't make us!"

My parents found this fit of pique hilarious, and told the story over and over for years—until I made them stop when I was in college and thought I'd die of embarrassment.

The punch line is that, after stamping my feet and hiding under the table for what seemed like forever but might have been about six minutes, eventually I was hungry enough to dunk a forkful of pink tuna into some mayonnaise. I dunked another, and another, until I ate almost the entire thing all by myself, then proceeded to demand tuna fish sandwiches for my school lunch for the next five years. *We will never like fish!*

½ cup extra-virgin olive oil, divided

1 red bell pepper, halved, seeded, and sliced ¼ inch thick

1 yellow or orange bell pepper, halved, seeded, and sliced ¼ inch thick

1 large white onion, peeled, halved, and sliced ¼ inch thick

½ jalapeño, seeded and finely chopped

1 tablespoon chopped fresh thyme leaves

2 tablespoons drained capers

½ teaspoon fine sea salt, plus more as needed

½ teaspoon freshly ground black pepper, plus more as needed

4 (6- to 8-ounce) tuna steaks

¼ cup dry white wine

Chopped fresh basil or parsley leaves, as needed

1. Heat the oven to 350°F.

2. Heat ¼ cup of the oil in a 12-inch ovenproof skillet over medium-high heat. Add the bell peppers, onion, jalapeño, and thyme. Cook, stirring frequently, until the vegetables begin to soften, about 5 minutes. Reduce the heat to medium and cook, stirring occasionally, until the vegetables are very soft and lightly caramelized, 20 to 25 minutes. Stir in the capers, salt, and black pepper.

3. Season the fish all over with salt and several grinds of black pepper. Push the vegetables to the side of the skillet, place the fish in the center of the skillet, and top it with the vegetables. Drizzle the wine and the remaining ¼ cup oil over the vegetables.

Pepper mixture: You can sauté the bell pepper mixture up to 3 days in advance. Let it cool and then store it in an airtight container in the fridge. When you are ready to cook the fish, add the bell pepper mixture to a skillet and gently reheat it before adding the fish.

4. Transfer the skillet to the oven and cook, uncovered, until the fish is opaque at the edges but rosy in the center, 5 to 10 minutes. Transfer the fish to a platter or individual plates, and top it with the vegetables and some of the pan juices. Scatter the basil or parsley over the top and serve.

Basque Squid with Pancetta, Espelette, and Garlic

SERVES 2 TO 3

The trick to cooking squid, the old chestnut goes, is to cook it for either two minutes or two hours; anything in between will leave the squid tough. I've heard this over and over through the years but have never had the patience to try two-hour squid. Why should I keep the heat on when the floppy rings turn opaque and tender just about as soon as they land in the pan? Allowing them to pass through all the intermediary stages of cardboard and leather before they return to silky seems unnecessarily risky to me.

And so it goes with this speedy recipe. The longest part is cooking the pancetta, which does need nearly ten minutes to render its fat and crisp up through its middle. Once you toss in the squid, the dish is done.

Squid loves strong flavors, and here I don't stint on them, adding garlic and Espelette pepper, which is a fiery chile from the Basque region of France. Make sure the table is set and your wine is poured before you switch on your stove. You'll have no time for multitasking once the fire is on.

1 pound squid

3 tablespoons extra-virgin olive oil, divided

2 ounces pancetta, diced small

¼ teaspoon Espelette chile powder or hot paprika, plus more to taste

Salt, as needed

2 garlic cloves, finely chopped, divided

Fresh lemon juice, as needed

¼ cup chopped fresh parsley leaves

Crusty bread, for serving (optional)

1. Rinse the squid under cool running water. Drain them and then transfer them to a paper towel to dry completely. Cut the bodies into ½-inch-thick rings and leave the tentacles whole (or halve if large). Pat the squid dry again with paper towels; transfer them to a large bowl.

2. Place a 12-inch skillet over medium heat. Add 1 tablespoon of the oil and the pancetta, and cook until the pancetta is crisp and golden, 7 to 12 minutes. Transfer the pancetta to a paper towel–lined plate, leaving the fat in the pan.

3. Raise the heat to high and let the skillet get very hot. Add 1 tablespoon of the oil to the skillet.

4. Toss the squid with the Espelette powder and a pinch of salt. Slide half the squid into the hot skillet and cook, stirring frequently, until they are cooked through, 1 to 2 minutes, adding half of the garlic for the last 20 seconds or so of cooking. Transfer the squid and garlic to a platter.

5. Repeat with the remaining 1 tablespoon oil, the squid, and the garlic. Make sure not to overcrowd the skillet; if it doesn't hold the squid comfortably, cook them in smaller batches.

6. Drizzle lemon juice all over the squid and then sprinkle the parsley, pancetta, and more Espelette powder on top. Serve at once, with crusty bread if you like.

Trout Meunière with Thyme and Pine Nuts

SERVES 2 TO 4

An anchor of French cuisine, the term *meunière* means "in the style of the miller's wife" and refers to the flour the fish is dredged in before frying, which helps it turn gorgeously crisp and brown. Although sole is the most traditional, any fish can be *meunièred*, and here I use trout. I keep the same lemony, buttery essence of the dish, but also add a handful of pine nuts for crunch and a little thyme to zip things up.

One thing that may raise an eyebrow or two is the clarified butter. Yes, it's an extra step, but I think it's worth doing, and it takes less than 15 minutes. Once the moisture is cooked out of the butter and the milk solids are removed, the resulting golden oil has a higher smoke point and is more stable in the pan. Clarified butter also gives a deeper, richer flavor than regular butter, and the leftovers will keep for months in the fridge for any future fish frying you may desire. If you really don't want to make your own, you can substitute all-butter ghee, which is basically clarified butter in which the milk solids have been allowed to brown before being removed, lending a lightly caramelized flavor. Or you can just use all regular butter here, but watch it carefully, turning the heat down if it starts to burn.

½ cup all-purpose flour

2 (12-ounce) rainbow trout, butterflied, patted dry

Kosher salt

Freshly ground white or black pepper

4 tablespoons clarified butter (recipe follows) or all-butter ghee, divided

Chopped fresh parsley leaves, for serving

4 tablespoons (½ stick) unsalted butter (regular butter, not clarified)

1 tablespoon fresh thyme leaves

¼ cup pine nuts or slivered almonds

1 lemon, cut into wedges, for serving

1. Heat the oven to 200°F and place a large oven-safe plate or baking sheet inside.

2. Place the flour in a large shallow plate. Open the fish like a book and season it all over with salt and pepper. Dredge the fish in the flour, shaking off the excess.

3. In a 12-inch (preferably nonstick) skillet over medium-high heat, heat 2 tablespoons of the clarified butter until bubbling. Lay one of the fish, still open like a book, skin-side down in the skillet and cook until golden, about 3 minutes. Flip the fish over and cook until the flesh is flaky and cooked through, about another 3 minutes. Transfer the fish to the warmed plate and hold it in the warm oven while you cook the other fish, using the remaining 2 tablespoons clarified butter. Wipe out the skillet and reserve it.

4. Arrange the cooked fish on a serving platter and top them with the parsley. In the reserved skillet, heat the 4 tablespoons regular butter, thyme leaves, and pine nuts until bubbling, then pour the sauce evenly over the fillets. Serve immediately, with the lemon wedges on the side.

Clarified Butter

MAKES 12 TABLESPOONS

1 cup (2 sticks) unsalted butter, preferably European high-fat butter

Thinking Ahead

   Clarified butter: Stored in an airtight container, clarified butter will keep for up to 6 months in the fridge.

1. In a small pot, melt the butter over low heat, then cook it until the bubbling and foaming subsides, 5 to 8 minutes. Remove the pot from the heat and let the butter cool slightly (but don't let it solidify), then skim any foam off the top.

2. Leaving the white milk solids in the bottom of the pot, slowly pour (or spoon) the yellow liquid portion into a heat-safe container. Discard the solids left at the bottom of the pot (or swab some bread in them and eat it).

Poule au Pot Pie, **page 185**

Chicken &
Other Meats

Chicken Paillards with Endive-Parsley Salad

Chicken *paillards* sounds much sexier than "cutlets," but the thinly pounded pieces of white meat are exactly the same thing (as are the Italian-termed *scallopini*—a word shimmering with its own air of seduction). No matter what you call them, these quick-cooking chicken breasts are the staples of the weeknight kitchen: fast, easy, and completely adaptable. Because the meat is so lean, it doesn't have a lot of inherent flavor. But a thirty-minute stint in a garlicky, lemony marinade seasons the flesh through and through. Then, all they need is a quick sauté in a pan of hot butter and a crisp garnish of mustardy salad greens. Dinner, elegantly solved.

1. **Marinate the chicken:** Place a chicken breast between two pieces of parchment paper and use a mallet or a rolling pin to pound it to a thickness of about ½ inch. Repeat with the remaining breasts.

2. Season the chicken breasts all over with the salt and pepper. In a bowl, combine the lemon zest, garlic, and olive oil. Add the chicken and toss to coat. Cover the bowl and let the chicken marinate at room temperature for 30 minutes.

3. **Prepare the salad dressing:** In a small bowl, whisk together the mustard, garlic, lemon juice, salt, and olive oil. Season with pepper and more salt if needed.

4. **Prepare the salad:** In a medium bowl, toss together the endive and parsley. Set aside.

5. **Finish the chicken:** Melt half the butter in a large skillet over medium-high heat. Add half the chicken breasts, including half the garlic slices, and cook until the meat is golden brown and tender, about 3 minutes per side. Transfer the chicken to warm serving plates and tent with foil to keep warm; repeat with the remaining butter and chicken.

6. Toss the dressing with the salad greens and serve the salad with the chicken and the lemon wedges alongside.

FOR THE CHICKEN

4 (6- to 8-ounce) boneless skinless chicken breast halves

1¼ teaspoons fine sea salt

1 teaspoon freshly ground black pepper

2 teaspoons finely grated lemon zest

4 garlic cloves, thinly sliced

2 tablespoons extra-virgin olive oil

3 tablespoons unsalted butter, divided

FOR THE SALAD DRESSING

1 tablespoon whole-grain mustard

1 garlic clove, finely grated or minced

1½ tablespoons fresh lemon juice

¼ teaspoon fine sea salt, plus more to taste

¼ cup extra-virgin olive oil

Freshly ground black pepper

FOR THE SALAD

4 heads Belgian endive, leaves torn into bite-size pieces (about 6 cups)

1 cup packed fresh flat-leaf parsley leaves

Lemon wedges, for serving

Thinking Ahead

Chicken: You can marinate the chicken, covered, up to overnight in the refrigerator.

Dressing: The dressing will keep for 1 week in an airtight container in the refrigerator. Bring it to room temperature and whisk it together before dressing the salad.

Chicken Salad with Rouille

SERVES 4 TO 6

In southern France you can usually find little jars of *rouille*—a garlic-flecked, red pepper–spiced mayonnaise—in the supermarket. Traditionally served with Provençal fish soup, the *rouille* is piled on croutons to be floated on top of the broth. But I think the pungent sauce deserves a wider audience beyond the soup pot, and I like to pair it with chicken salad. It's used here in two ways—once to gloss the chicken as it roasts, helping to crisp its skin, and again whisked into the dressing to coat the greens. If you have any *rouille* left over, and you probably will, you can smear it on bread to serve alongside. When it comes to creamy, garlicky *rouille*, it's hard to stop eating until the bowl is empty.

Thinking Ahead

Chicken: You can refrigerate the chicken in the marinade, uncovered, for as long as overnight.

Homemade rouille: You can make the rouille up to 1 week in advance. Store it in an airtight container in the refrigerator.

Chicken salad: You can make the chicken salad up to 3 days in advance. Store it in an airtight container in the refrigerator.

2 tablespoons chopped fresh rosemary leaves

2 teaspoons fine sea salt, plus more as needed

1 teaspoon finely grated lemon zest

1 teaspoon sweet paprika

¼ teaspoon hot smoked paprika

½ teaspoon freshly ground black pepper

3½ to 4 pounds bone-in skin-on chicken parts, patted dry

1 cup rouille (purchased or homemade; see page 94)

2 to 3 tablespoons extra-virgin olive oil, plus more as needed

Fresh lemon juice, as needed

1 head radicchio, leaves torn into bite-size pieces

1 head frisée, torn into bite-size pieces

½ cup sliced radishes

1. In a large bowl, mix together the rosemary, salt, lemon zest, sweet paprika, hot smoked paprika, and pepper. Add the chicken and rub the mixture evenly into the pieces. Spread out the chicken, skin side up, on a rimmed baking sheet and refrigerate it, uncovered, for at least 2 hours and up to overnight.

2. Heat the oven to 425°F.

3. Scrape ⅓ cup of the rouille into a small bowl, and then brush it all over the chicken. Roast until the skin is golden, 25 to 35 minutes for breast meat and 35 to 45 minutes for dark meat. As they finish roasting, remove the chicken pieces from the oven. Let them sit until they are cool enough to handle but still warm, and then remove the bones and shred the meat along with the skin if you like.

4. Transfer the shredded chicken to a medium bowl, and toss it with 2 to 3 tablespoons of the remaining rouille (enough to coat it).

5. To make the salad dressing, whisk 2 tablespoons of the olive oil and a squeeze of lemon juice into the remaining rouille to make it pourable. Taste, and add more oil, salt, and/or lemon juice if needed.

6. In a large bowl, toss the radicchio, frisée, and radishes with just enough of the dressing to coat.

7. To serve, heap the salad onto individual plates and top it with the chicken. Drizzle the chicken with more rouille dressing, if desired.

This is a classic roast chicken—herb-scented and bronze-skinned—that's been vamped out with crispy mushrooms cooked in the same pan. The mushrooms absorb all the heady chicken juices as they roast, turning golden and crunchy. It's sort of like they'd been fried in schmaltz, but a whole lot easier. You can use any mix of mushrooms here, but I especially love to include maitake (hen-of-the-woods). Their lacy edges turn potato-chip brittle, and it's very hard to stop eating them.

Roasted Tarragon Chicken with Crispy Mushrooms

SERVES 4 TO 6

—

1½ tablespoons finely chopped fresh tarragon leaves, plus 4 large sprigs

1¾ teaspoons fine sea salt, plus more as needed

1 teaspoon freshly ground black pepper

1 teaspoon finely grated lemon zest

1 whole (3½- to 4-pound) chicken, patted dry with paper towels

6 sprigs fresh thyme

8 ounces mixed mushrooms (any kinds you like), sliced ¼ inch thick

1½ tablespoons extra-virgin olive oil, plus more as needed

1 tablespoon unsalted butter

1 tablespoon chopped fresh parsley leaves

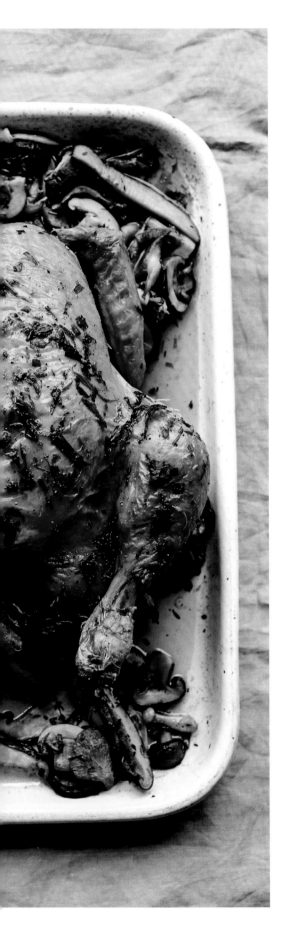

1. In a small bowl, mix together the chopped tarragon, salt, pepper, and lemon zest. Use this salt mixture to season the chicken inside and out. Refrigerate the chicken, uncovered, for 1 hour.

2. Heat the oven to 450°F.

3. Place the chicken, breast-side up, in a roasting pan or on a rimmed baking sheet. Stuff the cavity of the chicken with the tarragon and thyme sprigs. Roast for 30 minutes.

4. Meanwhile, in a medium bowl, toss together the mushrooms, oil, and a large pinch of salt.

5. After 30 minutes, baste the chicken with the pan juices, or drizzle it with a little olive oil if the pan is dry, and scatter the mushrooms around the chicken in the pan. Continue roasting until the chicken's juices run clear when the skin is pierced with a knife, 20 to 30 minutes more, tossing the mushrooms after 10 minutes.

6. When the chicken is done, transfer it to a cutting board and tent it with foil to keep it warm, leaving the mushrooms in the pan. Let the chicken stand for 10 minutes before carving.

7. Add the butter and parsley to the mushrooms in the roasting pan and toss to melt the butter. Serve the chicken with the buttery mushrooms on top.

Thinking Ahead

Chicken: You can marinate the chicken, uncovered, in the fridge for up to 24 hours.

Mushrooms: You can slice the mushrooms up to 24 hours ahead and store them in a sealed plastic bag in the fridge.

Ratatouille Sheet-Pan Chicken

SERVES 4

One of my favorite ratatouille hacks comes from a fashionable Parisian who taught me that the most convenient way to cook the vegetables is on sheet pans in the oven. Being already committed to the sheet-pan cause, it wasn't a huge leap for me to give up Julia Child's saucepan, which requires the cook to stand over the stove, sautéing each type of vegetable separately before combining them all. Sheet pans in the oven are more of a hands-off affair, and the method allows vegetables with similar cooking times to share the same pan (eggplant and onion in one pan, zucchini, peppers, and tomatoes in another).

In this recipe I've taken that basic ratatouille-in-the-oven technique and added a halved chicken to the pan. As the chicken cooks, the glorious chicken fat coats and crisps the vegetables, imbuing them with flavor. And the chicken absorbs the heady character of onion, peppers, and herbs. It's not as laissez-faire as other sheet-pan recipes—there's some rotating of pans so everything cooks evenly—but the combination of crisp chicken skin, fragrant herbs, and soft summer vegetables is well worth the work.

If you buy tomato paste in a tube, you won't worry about what to do with the leftover stuff in the can. Or you can freeze the excess.

4 tablespoons (½ stick) unsalted butter, room temperature

1½ teaspoons fine sea salt, plus more as needed

1 teaspoon chopped fresh rosemary leaves

1 teaspoon chopped fresh thyme leaves

½ teaspoon tomato paste

1 garlic clove, finely grated or minced

1 whole (3½- to 4-pound) chicken, patted dry with paper towels

2 medium eggplants (1½ pounds), cut into 1¼-inch chunks

1 large yellow onion, thinly sliced

5 tablespoons extra-virgin olive oil, plus more as needed

6 sprigs fresh thyme

3 sprigs fresh rosemary

2 bay leaves, torn into pieces

3 medium zucchini (1¼ pounds), cut into ¼-inch-thick slices

1 medium red bell pepper, sliced into ½-inch-wide strips

1 tomato, cut into 1-inch chunks

2 tablespoons chopped fresh basil leaves, for serving

Flaky sea salt and freshly ground black pepper, to taste

Lemon wedges, for serving

1. In a small bowl, mash together the butter, salt, rosemary, thyme, tomato paste, and garlic.

2. Using kitchen shears, cut down the sides of the chicken's backbone to remove it. Keep it for roasting later. Flip the chicken over and cut the chicken in half between the breasts.

3. Rub the butter mixture all over the chicken halves, getting it underneath the skin. Place the chicken halves on a rimmed baking sheet and let them marinate for at least 2 hours, and up to overnight, in the fridge (leave it uncovered, which will help the skin dry out and then crisp up when it roasts).

4. Arrange the racks in the top third, middle, and bottom third of the oven. Heat the oven to 450°F.

5. On a rimmed baking sheet, toss together the eggplants, onion, 5 tablespoons olive oil, and a big pinch of fine sea salt. Top the mixture with 2 thyme sprigs, 1 rosemary sprig, and a third of the bay leaf pieces. Place the reserved chicken backbone in the middle of the baking sheet next to the vegetables, and roast on the middle oven rack for 20 minutes, tossing the vegetables after 10 minutes. (The pan will be very full, and that's okay; the onion will reduce as it cooks.)

6. Meanwhile, in a large bowl, toss the zucchini, bell pepper, and tomato with just enough oil to coat, and add a big pinch of fine sea salt. Divide the vegetables between two rimmed baking sheets and spread them out into one layer. Top each pan of vegetables with half of the remaining thyme, rosemary, and bay leaf. Nestle half a chicken in among the vegetables on each pan. Make sure the chicken is resting on the pan, not the vegetables. Drizzle the chicken with olive oil.

7. Place these baking sheets on the top and bottom oven racks (the eggplant is on the middle rack). Roast for 15 minutes. Toss all the vegetables (including the eggplant and onion), and drizzle the chicken with a little more oil. Switch the top and bottom baking sheets (to help evenly brown the chicken) and roast for another 15 to 25 minutes, until the chicken registers 155°F when a thermometer is inserted into the thickest part of the thigh. Keep an eye on the vegetables, and transfer any that start to burn to a serving bowl.

8. If the chicken is done but the skin isn't brown enough for you, broil it for 1 to 2 minutes; then transfer the chicken to a serving platter and let it rest for 5 minutes. Transfer all the vegetables to a serving bowl, discarding the herb sprigs and bay leaf pieces, and toss them well with the pan drippings, any juice from the rested chicken, and the basil. Sprinkle the vegetables with flaky salt and plenty of black pepper, and then serve them alongside the chicken, with lemon wedges on the side.

Chicken Tagine with Blood Orange

SERVES 4

I ate my first tagine at a Moroccan restaurant in Paris. I was with my friend Stephanie, and we had left Barnard for a semester at Reid Hall. Finding restaurants that fit our student budget was challenging. Luckily, I discovered Patricia Wells's *Food Lover's Guide to Paris*, and I used it for tracking down the best bakeries, cafés, and smaller restaurants. (Wait, was I supposed to be taking classes, too?)

I don't recall the name of the Moroccan place, but I do remember the freezing December day when Stephanie and I set out to find it. We turned corners, walking one way then another, our noses stinging with cold and our breath fogging up around our hatless heads. Finally, we saw lights blazing in a damp window and knew couscous was at hand. It came topped with chicken tagine thick with prunes, olives, and plenty of turnips, and flavored with preserved lemons, which I had not tasted before. Their haunting, musky, citrus flavor has stayed with me.

This tagine, without any dried fruit, is a more savory take. Salted oranges replace the preserved lemons for a slightly fresher and more vivid taste. And it's just as warming on a damp, chilly day, whether you've been lost in Paris or are just longing to be.

FOR THE TAGINE

2 garlic cloves, minced

1½ teaspoons fine sea salt

¾ teaspoon ground coriander

¾ teaspoon ground turmeric

¾ teaspoon freshly ground black pepper

½ teaspoon ground ginger

Large pinch of saffron threads, pulverized with a mortar and pestle

Pinch of freshly grated nutmeg

1 (3½- to 4-pound) chicken, cut into 8 pieces

2 tablespoons extra-virgin olive oil

1 large white onion, diced

1 cup diced fresh or canned plum tomatoes

1 cinnamon stick

½ cup mixed pitted olives (use your favorite kinds)

½ cup chicken stock, preferably homemade

1½ tablespoons fresh lemon juice

½ cup chopped fresh cilantro leaves

Fresh orange wedges, for serving

Couscous, for serving

FOR THE QUICK-PRESERVED ORANGE

1 blood orange or small juice orange

¼ cup fresh lemon juice

3 tablespoons sugar

1½ tablespoons fine sea salt

1. **First, marinate the chicken:** In a large bowl, stir together the garlic, salt, coriander, turmeric, pepper, ginger, saffron, and nutmeg. Add the chicken pieces, rubbing the mixture all over to coat them, then cover the bowl

recipe continues

and let the chicken marinate at room temperature for at least 1 hour or overnight in the fridge.

2. **Meanwhile, make the preserved orange:** Trim the top and bottom from the orange (but do not peel it), and then quarter it lengthwise and remove the seeds. Slice the quarters crosswise into ⅛-inch-thick pieces.

3. Bring a small pot of water to a boil over high heat. Add the orange pieces, reduce the heat, and simmer for 5 minutes. Drain the orange pieces in a strainer, rinse them under cold running water to remove some of the bitterness, and then drain again.

4. In another small pot, combine ¼ cup water with the lemon juice, sugar, and salt. Bring to a simmer, stirring, until the sugar dissolves. Stir in the blanched orange pieces and simmer for 3 minutes. Then drain and pat them dry.

5. **Cook the tagine:** Heat the oil in a large ovenproof skillet or Dutch oven over medium heat. Add the chicken pieces, in batches if necessary, and brown them well on all sides, about 5 minutes per side. As they brown, transfer the pieces to a plate.

6. Reduce the heat under the skillet to medium-low and stir in the onion; cook until it is golden at the edges, 12 to 18 minutes. Stir in the tomatoes and cinnamon stick, and then add the browned chicken pieces, skin-side up, on top of the vegetable mixture. Pour in any chicken juices from the plate. Sprinkle the olives and preserved orange pieces over the chicken. Pour in the chicken stock and lemon juice.

7. Cover the skillet, bring the mixture to a simmer, and then reduce the heat to low. Cook until the chicken is done, 25 to 35 minutes. Top the chicken with the cilantro and fresh orange wedges, and serve it over couscous.

Thinking Ahead

Chicken: You can marinate the chicken, covered, up to 24 hours in the refrigerator.

Tagine: You can cook the tagine until the chicken is done in step 7. Let it cool, then cover and refrigerate it for up to 2 days. Reheat the tagine gently on the stove, adding more stock or water if the sauce is too thick. Top it with the cilantro and fresh orange wedges right before serving it over couscous.

Spatchcocked Chicken with Herbes de Provence Butter

SERVES 4 TO 6

4 tablespoons (½ stick) unsalted butter, room temperature

4 garlic cloves, finely grated or minced

2 teaspoons minced fresh parsley leaves

2 teaspoons minced mixed fresh herbs—any mix of mint, oregano, marjoram, and lavender buds (using no more than ¼ teaspoon lavender if you use it at all)

1½ teaspoons minced fresh thyme leaves

½ teaspoon minced fresh rosemary leaves

1¾ teaspoons fine sea salt

1 teaspoon herbes de Provence

½ teaspoon finely grated lemon zest

½ teaspoon freshly ground white pepper

½ teaspoon freshly ground black pepper

1 whole (3½- to 4-pound) chicken, spatchcocked and dried with paper towels (see note)

Lemon wedges, for garnish

Spatchcocking (also called butterflying) a chicken helps it to roast more evenly and much more quickly, giving you perfectly tender, juicy meat with golden skin. This one is slathered with herb butter, making it extra fragrant. If you like the idea of herb butter but you're more comfortable roasting a whole bird rather than spatchcocking, use the recipe for Roasted Tarragon Chicken on page 174, with or without the mushrooms, as a guide. And if you have some herb butter left over, freeze it, then use it on steaks or fish or roasted potatoes. Pulling out a well-flavored compound butter is one of those cheffy moves that makes almost everything taste better.

NOTE: To spatchcock a chicken, place the bird breast-side down on a work surface. Using a sharp knife or kitchen shears, start at the tail end and cut along one side of the backbone. Open the chicken up like a book, flip the chicken over, and press down on it to flatten it. Press firmly on the breastbone. You'll feel it pop.

1. In a medium bowl, mash together the butter, garlic, parsley, mixed herbs, thyme, rosemary, salt, herbes de Provence, lemon zest, white pepper, and black pepper. Rub three-quarters of the mixture all over the chicken, including under the skin (reserve the remaining herb butter for serving). Place the chicken, breast-up, on a rimmed baking sheet and refrigerate it, uncovered, for at least 2 hours and up to overnight.

2. Heat the oven to 450°F.

3. Roast the chicken until it is just cooked through (the meat will no longer be pink and the juices will run clear), 40 to 55 minutes. Let the chicken rest on a cutting board for 10 minutes before carving. Serve it topped with the reserved herb butter and lemon wedges.

Wine-Braised Chicken with Orange and Olives

SERVES 4

————

You'll find slowly stewed chickens simmered with wine and a bevy of aromatics all across France. *Coq au vin,* with red wine, onions, and mushrooms, is just one example, but there are countless other iterations, each a product of its region and the person who makes it. This one has white wine along with tomatoes and a little orange juice, which makes the sauce bright and very slightly sweet, along with spices (allspice, musky mace, and coriander) for depth. Green olives, added right at the end, add a briny note. Like all stews, this one begs for crusty bread, mashed potatoes, or generously buttered noodles or polenta to be served alongside to catch the sauce. It's rich, fragrant, and savory, and you won't want to lose one single drop.

1 small juice orange

1¾ teaspoons fine sea salt, plus more as needed

2 garlic cloves, finely grated or minced

¼ teaspoon ground allspice

¼ teaspoon ground mace (or nutmeg if you don't have mace)

¼ teaspoon ground coriander

¼ teaspoon freshly ground black pepper, plus more as needed

6 sprigs fresh thyme

1 bay leaf

3 pounds bone-in, skin-on chicken thighs and drumsticks

2 tablespoons extra-virgin olive oil, plus more as needed

1 large leek or 2 small leeks (white and light green parts only), halved lengthwise, cleaned, and thinly sliced

1 cup chopped fresh tomatoes

⅓ cup dry white wine

⅓ cup sliced pitted green olives, such as Picholines

Fresh lemon juice, if needed

Chopped fresh chives, for serving

1. Grate ¾ teaspoon zest from the orange, then juice the fruit into a measuring cup. Add enough water (if needed) to measure ⅓ cup. Refrigerate the juice until it's needed for cooking.

2. In a large bowl, combine the orange zest, salt, garlic, allspice, mace, coriander, pepper, thyme sprigs, and bay leaf. Add the chicken pieces and rub the marinade all over them; cover and refrigerate for at least 4 hours or up to 24 hours.

3. Heat the oven to 325°F.

Chicken: You can marinate the chicken for up to 24 hours in the fridge. You can also braise the chicken (through step 6) up to 1 day in advance. Let it cool and then store it in the refrigerator. Before serving, spoon off and discard any fat that has accumulated on the surface, then gently reheat the chicken over low heat for 20 to 30 minutes, stirring it often. (Alternatively, you can reheat it in the oven at 350°F for 30 minutes.) Garnish the chicken with the fresh chives right before serving.

4. Heat the oil in a Dutch oven over medium-high heat. Pat the chicken pieces dry and reserve any leftover marinade, including the thyme sprigs and bay leaf. Arrange the chicken pieces in a single layer in the pot (if they won't all fit, cook them in batches) and cook until they are well browned on all sides, turning them often, 10 to 15 minutes total, reducing the heat if they start to burn. Transfer the chicken pieces to a plate as they finish browning.

5. Stir the leeks into the chicken drippings in the pot, adding a little more oil if the pot looks dry, and cook over medium heat until they have softened, about 6 minutes. Then stir in the tomatoes, wine, reserved orange juice, and any reserved marinade. Nestle the chicken pieces, along with any accumulated juices, into the pot, cover, and bake in the oven for 35 minutes.

6. Raise the oven temperature to 450°F. Stir the chicken, making sure it is coated with the pan juices, then scatter the olives over the top. Bake, uncovered, for 10 to 15 minutes, until the chicken is cooked through and falling off the bones. Transfer the chicken pieces to a serving platter. If the juices in the pot look thin, place the pot on the stove and simmer the sauce until it has thickened slightly. Remove the thyme sprigs and bay leaf, taste, and season the sauce with more salt and some pepper. Add a squeeze of lemon if the sauce seems flat.

7. Serve the sauce over the chicken, topped with fresh chopped chives.

Poule au Pot Pie

SERVES 8

Poule au pot, a classic and very cozy French supper, describes a dish in which a whole chicken is cooked in a covered Dutch oven, steaming in its own succulent juices. In some recipes the chicken is stuffed with sausage meat and vegetables; in others the bird shares the pot with hunks of brisket and pork sausages. Julia Child's recipe calls for so much beef and pork that, she writes in *Mastering the Art of French Cooking*, when she finally pulls the chicken out at the very end, her guests are always surprised to find it hiding at the bottom of the pot.

This is a comparatively simple chicken-only take on *poule au pot*. Instead of adding any meat, I cover the top with puff pastry as an edible lid. It's a bit like a tricked-out chicken pot pie, but with a whole bird nestled with mushrooms, leeks, peas, and wine beneath its golden, buttery crust.

A vibrant sauce is traditionally offered with *poule au pot* to perk up the juicy, soft chicken. Here a creamy, herbal aioli does the job, adding both body and depth.

See photograph on **page 168**.

FOR THE CHICKEN

3¼ teaspoons fine sea salt, plus more as needed

1 tablespoon minced fresh thyme leaves, preferably lemon thyme

1 garlic clove, finely grated or minced

½ teaspoon freshly ground black pepper

1 whole (3½- to 4-pound) chicken, rinsed and patted dry

1 large egg

1 sheet or square all-butter puff pastry, thawed if frozen (about 9 to 14 ounces, brands vary)

2 tablespoons extra-virgin olive oil

2 large leeks (white and light green parts only), halved lengthwise, cleaned, and thinly sliced (about 8 cups)

2 large carrots, thinly sliced (about 1⅓ cups)

4 ounces cremini mushrooms, halved or quartered if large (about 2 cups)

2 tablespoons unsalted butter

3 tablespoons all-purpose flour

4 cups chicken stock, preferably homemade

1 cup dry white wine

½ cup fresh or frozen peas

¼ cup chopped mixed fresh herbs (such as parsley, basil, tarragon, chervil, dill, and/or chives)

Flaky sea salt, for serving

FOR THE AIOLI

1 teaspoon fresh lemon juice, plus more as needed

1 large garlic clove, grated

¼ teaspoon fine sea salt, plus more as needed

Freshly ground black pepper, as needed

2 tablespoons chopped fresh parsley leaves

1 tablespoon chopped fresh tarragon leaves

1 large egg, plus 1 large egg yolk

½ cup neutral oil, such as grapeseed

⅓ cup extra-virgin olive oil

recipe continues

Chicken: You can refrigerate the marinated chicken, uncovered, for up to 24 hours.

Pastry: You can roll out and freeze the pastry, well covered, up to 2 weeks in advance.

Aioli: You can make the aioli up to 1 week in advance. Store it, covered, in the refrigerator.

1. **Cook the chicken:** In a small bowl, combine 2 teaspoons of the salt with the thyme, garlic, and pepper. Smear the mixture all over the chicken, and let it rest, uncovered, in the fridge for at least 2 hours or overnight.

2. In a small bowl, lightly whisk the egg with 1 teaspoon water to make an egg wash. On a lightly floured surface, roll out the pastry so it will fit over the top of a large Dutch oven; don't make it too thin. Transfer the pastry to a large plate or cookie sheet. Brush it with the egg wash, cut a few slits in the center, then refrigerate it until you are ready to bake the chicken.

3. In a large Dutch oven, heat the oil over medium-high heat. Stir in the leeks, carrots, mushrooms, and ¼ teaspoon of the salt; cook until the vegetables have softened and are just starting to brown, about 10 minutes. Push the vegetables to one side of the pot and melt the butter in the other side (to make the roux). Stir the flour into the butter and cook until it is lightly browned, about 2 minutes. Stir the roux into the vegetables. Nestle the chicken in the pot and add the chicken stock, wine, and remaining 1 teaspoon salt. Bring to a low simmer, cover, and continue to barely simmer for 30 minutes.

4. Meanwhile, place a rimmed sheet pan in the oven and heat the oven to 425°F.

5. Remove the Dutch oven from the heat and uncover it. Stir in the peas and mixed herbs, and then carefully drape the prepared puff pastry over the pot. Transfer the Dutch oven to the sheet pan in the oven and bake until the pastry is puffed and golden, 20 to 25 minutes.

6. **Make the aioli:** Combine the lemon juice, garlic, salt, and pepper in a blender; let the ingredients stand for 1 minute. Add the parsley, tarragon, egg, and egg yolk. Cover and blend briefly on medium speed. With the motor running, drizzle in both oils in a slow steady stream until just combined. Taste and add more lemon juice and/or salt if needed.

7. Transfer the chicken to a cutting board to carve. Serve the chicken in soup plates with some of the broth and with pieces of the golden crust. Serve the aioli on the side for drizzling, with flaky sea salt for sprinkling.

Crispy Duck Legs with Satsumas

SERVES 8

Whenever I run out of duck fat—which I always keep in the fridge for potato-roasting—I just throw some duck legs into the oven to make some more. True, I can buy duck fat separately. But it seems like a waste, because I can get it for free when I cook the legs, which, after their stint in the oven, become practically confited for a tasty dinner.

Here, that same faux confit of duck legs makes a base for my take on *canard à l'orange*. The legs stand in for the roasted whole duck. And instead of an elaborate demi-glace and orange juice–based butter sauce, I serve the duck with a sweet-tart mix of fresh satsuma sections tossed with vinegar, soft herbs, crunchy olive oil–fried almonds, and diced dried apricots for sweetness and texture.

If you don't want to make a fake duck leg confit for this recipe, you can buy real duck confit and use it instead (heat the oven to 425°F and go straight to step 8). In either case, you'll end up with a company-worthy dish that's fresh and modern, but still rich, crisp-skinned, and thoroughly elegant.

FOR THE DUCK

- 8 duck legs (3½ to 4 pounds total)
- 2½ teaspoons fine sea salt
- 1 teaspoon freshly ground black pepper
- 1 teaspoon dried juniper berries, crushed with the side of a knife
- 3 garlic cloves, finely grated or minced
- 8 sprigs fresh thyme, torn into several pieces
- 3 sprigs fresh rosemary, torn into several pieces
- 2 medium satsuma mandarins or large clementines (or other seedless tangerines), peeled and pulled into sections
- ½ cup fresh chervil leaves and tender stems (or use parsley or cilantro)

FOR THE SAUCE

- 2 medium satsuma mandarins or large clementines (or other seedless tangerines), peeled and pulled into sections
- ⅓ cup chopped dried apricots
- 2 tablespoons white wine vinegar, plus more to taste
- Fine sea salt
- 3 tablespoons extra-virgin olive oil
- ⅓ cup coarsely chopped whole (unpeeled) almonds
- ½ cup thinly sliced red onion
- Large pinch of crushed red pepper flakes

1. **Prepare the duck:** Pat the duck legs dry with a paper towel. Then use the tip of a sharp paring knife to make tiny slits through the duck skin without piercing the flesh. The easiest way to do this is to hold the knife parallel to the duck, rather than perpendicular (which would be the intuitive way to do it).

2. In a small bowl, combine the salt, pepper, and juniper berries. Rub this mixture all over the duck, paying more

recipe continues

attention to the exposed flesh on the bottom rather than the skin (though get that, too). Then rub the garlic all over the duck in the same way. Scatter the herb sprigs in a rimmed baking sheet or other large dish and put the duck legs, flesh-side down, on top of them. Refrigerate, uncovered, for 24 to 72 hours (the longer the better).

3. **Cook the duck:** Heat the oven to 325°F. Place 3 or 4 of the duck legs, fat-side down, in a large ovenproof skillet and heat them over medium-high heat until the fat starts to render. When the duck is very browned on one side and has rendered most of its fat, after about 10 minutes, transfer the duck, browned-side up, to a large roasting pan. Repeat with the remaining duck. When all the duck is browned, cover the pan with foil and place it in the oven. Roast the legs for 1½ hours.

4. Remove the foil, raise the oven temperature to 375°F, and continue roasting the duck until it is golden brown, 30 minutes to 1 hour. Let the duck cool slightly in the pan, 15 to 30 minutes (the fat should stay liquid).

5. While the duck is cooling, heat the oven to 425°F.

6. Remove the duck legs from the pan and pour the fat into a container. Reserve the fat for future potato-roasting.

7. Return the duck to the roasting pan and scatter the satsuma sections around the legs but not on top of them. Roast until the duck is hot and crisp and the satsumas are wilted, 15 to 30 minutes.

8. **Make the sauce:** While the duck is crisping, coarsely chop the satsuma sections and place them in a medium bowl. Add the apricots, vinegar, and a pinch of salt.

9. In a small skillet, heat the oil. Add the almonds and cook until they are golden brown, about 5 minutes. Pour the almonds into the bowl containing the apricots and let them cool. Then stir in the onion, red pepper flakes, and salt to taste and let the mixture sit for at least 10 minutes for the flavors to meld. Taste and add more salt and/or vinegar just before serving.

10. To serve, arrange the duck and satsumas on a platter, top with the chervil, and spoon the apricot-almond sauce over all.

Thinking Ahead

Duck legs: You can roast the duck legs up to 1 week in advance. Store them, covered, in the refrigerator.

Sauce: You can make the sauce and let it sit at room temperature for up to 6 hours in advance of serving.

Duck fat: Rendered fat will keep for months in a sealed container in the fridge.

Chicken Liver Mousse with Bourbon

MAKES 2⅓ CUPS

The key to a great chicken liver mousse is to use almost as much butter as liver, so the whole thing becomes silky smooth and perfectly spreadable. I like to spike mine with a little bourbon to give it a heady, boozy character, along with some dry mustard powder for a tangy bite. If you've never made your own chicken liver mousse, you might be surprised to see how easy it is—thanks to the food processor—not to mention exceedingly impressive. Serve it with thinly sliced bread or with crackers, and spread it on thick. Then offer puckery cornichons on the side to balance the lovely creamy richness.

Thinking Ahead

Mousse: Chill the mousse, covered in plastic wrap, for at least 4 hours and up to 1 day in advance. Let it come to room temperature 30 minutes before serving. Leftover mousse can be frozen for up to 1 month.

1 cup (2 sticks) unsalted butter, room temperature

1 small onion, diced

2 bay leaves

1 pound chicken livers, membranes removed

2 garlic cloves, thinly sliced

¼ cup bourbon (or you can use brandy)

1 teaspoon fine sea salt, plus more to taste

1 teaspoon dry mustard powder

½ teaspoon freshly ground black pepper

½ teaspoon ground allspice

⅛ teaspoon freshly grated nutmeg

Pinch of ground cloves

Crackers or toasted baguette slices, for serving

Cornichons, for serving

1. Melt ½ cup of the butter in a large skillet over medium heat. Stir in the onion and bay leaves; cook, stirring often, until the onions start to brown at the edges, about 10 minutes.

2. Stir in the chicken livers and garlic, and cook until the livers are golden on the outside but still rosy on the inside, 6 to 10 minutes. Discard the bay leaves and transfer the contents of the skillet to a food processor. Add the remaining ½ cup butter and the bourbon, salt, mustard powder, pepper, allspice, nutmeg, and cloves. Process until very smooth, scraping down the sides of the processor bowl. Taste and add more salt if needed.

3. Pour the mixture into a 1-quart crock or serving dish, or into four 6-ounce ramekins. Cover with plastic wrap and refrigerate for at least 4 hours.

4. Remove the mousse from the refrigerator at least 30 minutes before serving. Serve it at room temperature with crackers or baguette slices and cornichons alongside.

Back before you could find them here in the States, the top item on my mother's supermarket shopping list when we were in France was *magrets de canard*, boneless duck breasts as thick and meaty as steak, covered in a glorious layer of fat and skin on one side. No matter how short our stay or how small our kitchen, it wasn't vacation without at least one meal of Mom's homemade *magrets*.

To cook the duck, she'd score the skin in a crosshatch, then sear it until the fat melted into the pan. (She always stuck a container of the rendered fat in the freezer, completely sure the people we exchanged homes with would appreciate her unctuous gift when they returned.) As for the duck breast, she kept the meat rare and the skin burnished, and we'd eat slices with a quickly made pan sauce spiked with wine or vinegar or fruit juice, depending on what was within arm's reach.

I like to keep the giddy spirit of my mom's *magrets*, but I add a few layers of flavor. First I rub a salted spice mix on the meat the night before cooking. It seasons the duck, and it also allows the skin to dry out a bit, which helps it crisp up in the hot pan. Second, I like to caramelize some figs in the pan juices to serve on the side. Add a green salad and some good bread and you can practically pretend you're on vacation in France. I know I always do.

Seared Duck Breasts with Figs, Rosemary, and Lemon

SERVES 2 TO 3

Finely grated zest of ½ lemon

1 fat garlic clove, finely grated or minced

1 teaspoon plus 1 tablespoon rosemary leaves, finely chopped, divided

¾ teaspoon fine sea salt

⅛ teaspoon freshly ground black pepper

2 (10- to 12-ounce) duck breasts, patted dry

6 fresh figs, halved

Juice of ½ lemon (or use balsamic vinegar), for serving

Extra-virgin olive oil, for serving

Flaky sea salt, for serving

1. In a medium bowl, combine the lemon zest, garlic, 1 teaspoon rosemary, the salt, and pepper.

2. Using a sharp knife, cut shallow slits in a crosshatch pattern into the duck skin and fat, making sure not to pierce the flesh underneath. Rub the garlic mixture all over both breasts, then transfer them to a small rimmed baking sheet. Refrigerate, uncovered, for at least 6 hours or overnight.

3. Remove the duck from the fridge at least 30 minutes prior to cooking to allow it to come to room temperature, and heat the oven to 350°F.

4. Place the duck, fat-side down, in a large (unheated) ovenproof skillet. Place the skillet over medium heat and cook until the fat has rendered and the skin is crispy and golden, 8 to 12 minutes. Pour or spoon most of the fat from the skillet into a container and save it for future potato-roasting (it will keep for at least 3 months in the fridge).

5. Flip the duck pieces over, remove the skillet from the heat, and scatter the figs and remaining 1 tablespoon rosemary in the skillet but not on top of the duck. Place the skillet in the oven and cook the duck for 3 to 5 minutes for medium (135°F on a meat thermometer). Remove the skillet from the oven and turn on the broiler. Transfer the duck to a cutting board, cover it with foil, and let it rest for 5 minutes.

6. Return the skillet, still containing the figs, to the oven and broil until the figs are lightly charred, 1 to 2 minutes.

7. Slice the duck and serve it with the figs on the side, with a squeeze of lemon juice or a drizzle of balsamic vinegar, a drizzle of olive oil, and a sprinkle of flaky sea salt.

Thinking Ahead

Duck: You can marinate the duck breasts up to 24 hours in advance. Store them, uncovered, in the refrigerator. Let them come to room temperature before cooking.

Marrowbones with Horseradish Parsley Sauce

SERVES 6 TO 8

Marrow is the butter of roasted bones, waiting to be swabbed up with chunks of crunchy toast and savored in all its glorious beefy richness. You can buy halved marrowbones from most butchers (though you may have to order them ahead), and roasting them couldn't be easier. Just pop them in a very hot oven and leave them there until the firm white marrow softens, turning liquid at the edges and threatening to leak but not quite doing so. Then immediately serve the bones with coarse salt for seasoning and bread for dunking. I also like to serve some kind of sharp and tangy counterpoint to cut the marrow's richness. Here, a rustic mix of herbs and horseradish offers the needed pizzazz. The marrowbones work well as a hearty appetizer or as a light main course with a salad on the side.

3 to 4 pounds marrowbones, preferably canoe cut (lengthwise)

¾ cup fresh parsley leaves and tender stems, coarsely chopped

3 scallions, thinly sliced

1 teaspoon prepared white horseradish, plus more to taste

Squeeze of fresh lime juice

Flaky sea salt, to taste

1 to 2 tablespoons extra-virgin olive oil

Crusty toasted bread, for serving

1. Heat the oven to 425°F.

2. Place the bones, cut-side up, on a rimmed baking sheet. Roast for 12 to 20 minutes, until the marrow softens and starts to separate from the bones. Some of it will render and melt away, but the majority should just soften up. Don't overcook it or it will all melt and you'll lose it.

3. Meanwhile, in a small bowl, toss together the parsley, scallions, horseradish, lime juice, and salt. Taste, and add more lime juice, salt, and/or horseradish to taste. Drizzle in the oil.

4. To serve, put the bones on a platter and sprinkle the parsley sauce over them. Have guests spoon the marrow and parsley onto toast, then sprinkle it with flaky sea salt before eating.

Seared Steaks
with Basil Béarnaise

SERVES 4

It can be easy to brush béarnaise aside as one of those old-fashioned French sauces that are too finicky to be worth the effort. At least, that's how I once felt about it, relegating béarnaise to the same stodgy category as espagnole (brown sauce) and velouté (flour-thickened cream sauce). But then béarnaise and I got reacquainted at a Parisian bistro, and I remembered just how lively and sparkling a dinner companion it could be, especially when paired with a nice rare steak. Based on a hollandaise, the classic béarnaise recipe calls for egg yolks to be emulsified with white wine vinegar and butter, and flavored with licorice-flavored tarragon. Here I replace tarragon with basil for a slightly spicier green flavor.

Hanger steaks are the classic cut for bistro *steak frites*, but feel free to use any good steak here. Just keep the meat as rare as you can, so its juices can mingle with the béarnaise. It's a fantastic combination—and even better served with potato gratin (page 245).

FOR THE BÉARNAISE

- 3 tablespoons white wine vinegar, plus more if needed
- ¼ cup dry white wine or dry white vermouth
- 1 tablespoon minced shallots
- 3 tablespoons minced fresh basil leaves
- ⅛ teaspoon freshly ground black pepper
- Pinch of salt
- 3 egg yolks
- 2 tablespoons cold unsalted butter, divided
- ½ cup (1 stick) unsalted butter, melted

FOR THE STEAKS

- 4 (6- to 8-ounce) hanger steaks (or use your favorite boneless steak), about 1 inch thick
- Kosher salt, to taste
- Freshly ground black pepper, to taste
- 2 tablespoons unsalted butter
- 1 tablespoon extra-virgin olive oil
- Chopped fresh chives, for serving

1. **Make the béarnaise sauce:** In a heavy nonreactive (i.e., stainless-steel, not cast-iron) 9- or 10-inch skillet or medium-size pot, bring the vinegar, wine, shallots, basil, pepper, and salt to a simmer over medium heat. Cook until the liquid has reduced to 2 tablespoons, about 5 minutes. Let the mixture cool slightly.

2. In a small bowl, whisk the egg yolks until they become thick and sticky, about 1 minute. Slowly pour the vinegar mixture into the egg yolks, whisking constantly. Add 1 tablespoon of the cold butter, but do not beat it in.

recipe continues

Thinking Ahead

Béarnaise: The sauce will keep
for up to 5 days in the fridge. Press
plastic wrap directly on the surface so
that a skin doesn't form. Bring it to
room temperature before serving
it on the hot steaks.

3. Scrape the egg mixture back into the skillet, and place it
    over very low heat. Whisk the yolks until they thicken,
    1 to 2 minutes. Whisk in the remaining 1 tablespoon
    cold butter, and then whisk in the melted butter in a
    slow steady stream, whisking constantly until the sauce
    thickens like mayonnaise. Taste, and add salt and/or
    vinegar if necessary. Keep the sauce warm, not hot, for
    serving.

4. **Cook the steaks:** Season the steaks with salt and pepper.
    Heat a cast-iron or other heavy skillet over medium-
    high heat. Stir in the butter and oil, then add the steaks
    and sear them until browned on both sides, about
    3 minutes per side for medium-rare, 4 minutes per side
    for medium. (If your steaks are thinner than 1 inch,
    cook them a bit less; thicker steaks might need another
    minute or two per side.) Transfer the steaks to a cutting
    board and let them rest for 5 minutes before slicing and
    serving with the béarnaise and chives.

Beef Daube with Carrots and Honey Vinegar

SERVES 6 TO 8

A *daube* is a slowly braised Provençal beef stew with myriad interpretations. Usually cooked in either red or white local wine, the hallmark of the dish is a rather inexpensive cut of meat simmered until it's coated in a thick onion-rich sauce and is tender enough to eat with a spoon.

Some cooks add olives; others throw orange peel or lavender into the pot. I like to replace the onions with shallots, added toward the end of cooking so they maintain a little of their integrity, and to finish with a dash of honeyed wine vinegar, which brings both acid and sweetness. Also, while the beef is braising in the oven, I throw a pan of carrots in there, too, so they can become tender and caramelized while the stew bubbles away above them. Their vivid color breaks up all the brown tones of the meat and shallots, and adds a soft texture to the mix.

Fine sea salt, as needed

1 teaspoon freshly ground black pepper

4 garlic cloves, finely grated or minced

3 teaspoons fresh thyme leaves, chopped, divided

2 teaspoons rosemary leaves, chopped

4 pounds boneless beef stew meat, cut into 2-inch chunks (or use boneless short ribs)

¼ cup white wine vinegar, plus more to taste

1½ tablespoons honey

5 tablespoons extra-virgin olive oil, plus more as needed

1 (750-ml) bottle dry red wine

2 bay leaves

½ teaspoon freshly grated nutmeg

1½ pounds carrots (about 7 large), cut into ½-inch-thick rounds

1 pound shallots (about 8), sliced ⅛-inch thick

Finely grated zest of 1 small orange

½ cup fresh parsley leaves, chopped

Flaky sea salt

1. In a large bowl, stir 1 tablespoon fine sea salt with the pepper, garlic, 2 teaspoons of the chopped thyme, and the chopped rosemary; add the beef and toss to coat. Cover and let sit in the refrigerator for at least 2 hours or preferably overnight.

2. Meanwhile, in a small bowl, whisk together the vinegar, honey, and remaining 1 teaspoon chopped thyme. Cover and let it sit at room temperature.

3. Position one rack in the center of the oven and another one underneath it. Heat the oven to 325°F.

recipe continues

Beef: You can marinate the beef in the refrigerator up to 24 hours ahead.

Carrots: You can roast the carrots up to 1 day in advance. Store them, loosely covered, in the refrigerator, then bring to room temperature before adding them to the beef at the end.

Daube: You can make the daube (through step 7) up to 3 days in advance. Let it cool, then cover and refrigerate. Before reheating it, scoop up and discard any fat that has accumulated on the surface. Gently rewarm the daube on the stove, and then stir in the roasted carrots and honey-vinegar mixture just before serving.

4. Heat the olive oil in a large Dutch oven over medium-high heat. Add the beef, in batches, and sear until it is well browned on all sides, about 3 minutes per side, adding more oil if the pan dries out. Take your time with this—the more color you get on the meat, the richer the sauce will be. As the beef chunks are browned, transfer them to a plate.

5. Whisk the wine into the pot, scraping up the browned bits from the bottom. Add the bay leaves, nutmeg, and browned beef and any juices. Bring to a simmer, then cover and bake in the oven for 2 hours. At this point the meat will be about halfway done. (Total beef cooking time is 3 to 3½ hours.)

6. Put the carrot slices on a rimmed baking sheet and toss them with oil and ½ teaspoon fine sea salt. Place the baking sheet on the rack below the beef and roast for 30 minutes.

7. At this point, the beef will have been cooking for 2½ hours, and the carrots for 30 minutes. Give the carrots a stir. Add the shallots and orange zest to the pot with the beef, stirring them in. Cover the pot and continue to cook for 30 to 60 minutes longer, removing the carrots from the oven when they are caramelized and the beef when it is very tender.

8. When the carrots are roasted, drizzle them with half of the honey-vinegar mixture, give them a stir, then cover the pan with foil or another overturned sheet pan to keep warm.

9. When the beef is tender, stir the carrot mixture into the pot. Then drizzle some or all of the remaining honey-vinegar mixture into the pot, tasting as you go. If the dish seems flat, stir in a little more white wine vinegar and salt. Ladle the daube into individual soup bowls and top with the parsley and flaky sea salt.

Braised Brandied Short Ribs

SERVES 6 TO 8

4 garlic cloves, finely grated or minced

2½ teaspoons fine sea salt, plus more as needed

1 teaspoon freshly ground black pepper

3 sprigs fresh rosemary

1 bay leaf, torn

1 star anise pod

1 tablespoon coriander seeds

¼ cup brandy

4 pounds bone-in beef short ribs

2 tablespoons extra-virgin olive oil

2 tablespoons unsalted butter

1 medium onion, diced

1 large fennel bulb, trimmed and diced (reserve the fronds for garnish)

4 cups beef or chicken stock, preferably homemade

½ cup dry white wine

Chopped fresh parsley leaves or chives, for garnish (optional)

The chef Daniel Boulud taught me how to cook short ribs when we were working on his cookbook *Braise*. The trick, he said, is the browning of the meat. The more patience you have to stand there, turning each piece until it is mahogany on all sides, the deeper and richer your sauce will be. And as any French chef will tell you, when it comes to *haute cuisine*, the sauce is everything.

In this recipe, bone-in beef short ribs are marinated in garlic, herbs, and freshly toasted star anise and coriander seeds before they get their deep, dark sear; then they're braised in both wine and brandy, with onion and fennel. The beef bones add marrow to the sauce, making it extremely silky and fla-vorful. Make sure to find a fennel bulb with lots of luxuriant green fronds still attached—you'll need them for garnish. Lacking those, some chopped fresh chives or parsley will work to add color and freshness to the heady brown stew.

Try to make this a day or two before you plan to serve it. The flavors get even better after sitting in the fridge.

1. In a large bowl, combine the garlic, salt, pepper, rosemary sprigs, and bay leaf.

2. Heat a small dry skillet over medium heat. Add the star anise and coriander seeds, and toast until they are fragrant, about 1 minute. Transfer the spices to a cutting board and lightly smash them with the flat of a knife (or do this with a mortar and pestle).

3. Scrape the coriander and star anise into the bowl containing the garlic mixture, and stir to combine. Stir in the brandy, then add the short ribs and toss to combine. Cover and refrigerate for at least 2 hours or up to 24 hours.

Short ribs: You can marinate the ribs, covered, in the refrigerator up to 24 hours in advance.

Stew: It's best to cook the stew a day ahead. Let the short ribs cool in the liquid, then chill them in the pot overnight. It will be easy to remove the fat from the cold stew—simply spoon it off. Then remove the meat and simmer the sauce to reduce it as directed in step 7. Return the meat to the pot and reheat it in the sauce just before adding the garnish.

4. Heat the oil and butter in a large Dutch oven over medium-high heat. Arrange the short ribs in a single layer in the pot with ample space around each one— you'll have to brown these in batches. (Reserve any of the marinade that's still left in the bowl.) Cook until browned on all sides, 3 to 5 minutes per side, reducing the heat if necessary to prevent burning. Take your time with the browning; the more color you get on the meat, the richer the sauce will be. As they are browned, transfer the short ribs to a plate, leaving the fat in the pot.

5. Heat the oven to 325°F.

6. Reduce the heat under the Dutch oven to medium, and stir in the onion, fennel, and a pinch of salt. Cook until the vegetables are softened and translucent, about 10 minutes. Stir in any reserved marinade and cook for another minute. Then nestle the short ribs into the pot and top with the stock and wine. Bring to a simmer, cover, and transfer the pot to the oven; cook until the beef is tender and falling off the bone, about 3 hours.

7. Using tongs, transfer the short ribs to a bowl. Return the Dutch oven to the stove and bring the liquid to a simmer. Cook until the sauce has thickened slightly, 10 to 20 minutes. Spoon off the fat on the surface if desired, then taste and add more salt if needed. Return the short ribs to the sauce and reheat them if necessary. Serve garnished with the fennel fronds or chopped herbs, if you like.

Roasted Pork Loin with Rosemary

SERVES 6 TO 8

A juicy roasted loin of pork with crackling skin and an herby, winey pan sauce is one of the simplest yet most alluring things you can serve at a dinner party, at least when there are carnivores in attendance. This one, scented with fennel seeds and rosemary, goes beautifully with a pan of duck fat–roasted potatoes (see page 246). But then again, there are few meats that don't.

NOTE: To lightly crush the spices, you can use a mortar and pestle or a spice grinder, or press down on the spices with the flat side of a knife.

Thinking Ahead

Pork: You can marinate the pork as long as overnight, covered and stored in the refrigerator.

5 garlic cloves, finely grated or very finely minced

3 tablespoons chopped fresh rosemary leaves

3 tablespoons chopped fresh thyme leaves

2 teaspoons whole-grain mustard, plus more for serving

1¾ teaspoons fine sea salt, plus more as needed

1½ teaspoons fennel seeds, lightly crushed (see note)

1 teaspoon freshly ground black pepper

1 (2½- to 3-pound) boneless pork loin (not tenderloin)

1 tablespoon extra-virgin olive oil

½ cup dry white wine

4 tablespoons (½ stick) unsalted butter, cubed

Chopped fresh fennel fronds or parsley, for serving

1. In a large bowl, stir together the garlic, rosemary, thyme, mustard, salt, fennel seeds, and pepper. Rub the mixture all over the pork, cover, and refrigerate to marinate for at least 2 hours or up to overnight.

2. Heat the oven to 400°F. Pat the pork dry and place it, fat-side down, in a large ovenproof skillet. Drizzle the roast with the oil. Roast for 25 minutes, then turn it over and roast until it reaches 135°F on a meat thermometer, 15 to 25 minutes longer. Transfer the pork to a plate and tent it with foil.

3. Place the skillet over medium-high heat and whisk in the wine, scraping up the browned bits. Simmer until the liquid is reduced by half, about 1 minute, then add any juices from the plate holding the roast. Whisk in the butter, a little at a time, until the sauce emulsifies; then simmer until it has thickened, 1 minute. Taste and add more salt if needed.

4. To serve, thinly slice the pork. Drizzle the slices with the sauce and top them with the fennel fronds or parsley. Serve with whole-grain mustard on the side.

Oxtail Bourguignon with Caramelized Mushrooms and Garlic

SERVES 4 TO 6

In my version of *boeuf bourguignon*, oxtails replace the usual chunks of stewing beef. Rich with marrow that leaks out of their bones as they cook, the oxtails—along with the requisite bacon and mushrooms—make the sauce particularly intense while the meat itself turns succulent. The usual garnish for *boeuf bourguignon* is a crown of golden pearl onions and mushrooms that are fried separately in butter. Here I add whole garlic cloves to that pan, which turn very sweet and soft and give the stew a little extra verve.

If you're tempted to use frozen pearl onions to save time, let me try to dissuade you. With all their liquid, they won't caramelize as nicely as fresh peeled onions. But if you want to substitute bone-in short ribs for the oxtail, that's perfectly fine; they work just as well in this hearty stew.

FOR THE STEW

- 5 ounces thick-cut bacon, diced
- 2½ pounds oxtail, cut into 1½-inch chunks
- 1½ teaspoons fine sea salt, divided
- ½ teaspoon freshly ground black pepper
- 2 large leeks (white and light green parts only), halved lengthwise, cleaned, and thinly sliced
- 1 large carrot, sliced into ¼-inch-thick rounds
- 3 fat garlic cloves, minced
- ½ teaspoon tomato paste
- 1½ tablespoons all-purpose flour
- 1 (750-ml) bottle dry red wine, preferably a pinot noir from Burgundy
- 1 bay leaf
- 1 large sprig fresh thyme

FOR THE MUSHROOM GARNISH

- ½ cup chicken stock, preferably homemade
- 8 ounces pearl onions, peeled (about 3 cups)
- 6 ounces cremini mushrooms, halved if large (about 3 cups)
- 12 medium garlic cloves, peeled but left whole
- 1 tablespoon extra-virgin olive oil
- Salt and freshly ground black pepper, to taste
- Pinch of sugar
- Chopped fresh parsley leaves, for serving

1. **Make the stew:** In a heavy pot or Dutch oven, cook the bacon over medium-low heat until the fat is rendered. Raise the heat to medium and cook until the bacon is crisp, 10 to 15 minutes. Transfer the bacon to a paper towel–lined plate. Reserve the fat in the pot.

Bourguignon: You can make the stew through step 5, let it cool, and store it, covered, in the refrigerator overnight. The next day, spoon off and discard any fat that has accumulated on the surface. Gently reheat the stew on the stove. If the sauce looks thin, reduce it as directed in step 7. Don't cook the mushroom garnish in step 6 until right before serving the mushrooms and onions; they don't reheat as perfectly as the stew does.

2. Season the oxtail with 1 teaspoon of the salt and the pepper. Raise the heat under the pot to medium-high and heat the bacon fat until it is hot but not smoking. Lay about half of the oxtail chunks in a single layer in the pot, leaving some space between the pieces. Cook, turning the meat as it sears, until it is well browned on all sides, about 10 minutes; transfer the meat to a plate as it browns. Take your time with this, browning the meat in batches; the more color you get on the meat, the richer the sauce will be.

3. Stir in the leeks, carrot, and remaining ½ teaspoon salt and cook, stirring occasionally, until the vegetables are soft, about 10 minutes. Reduce the heat if necessary to prevent burning.

4. Meanwhile, heat the oven to 350°F.

5. Stir the garlic and tomato paste into the vegetables and cook for 1 minute, until fragrant. Stir in the flour, cook for 1 minute, and then add the wine, 1 cup of water, and the bay leaf and thyme sprig, scraping up the browned bits on the bottom of the pot. Add the browned oxtail pieces and half of the cooked bacon to the pot, cover it with a tight-fitting lid, and transfer it to the oven. Bake until the oxtails are very tender, 2½ to 3 hours, turning the pieces halfway through.

6. **Meanwhile, make the mushroom garnish:** In a large skillet set over high heat, combine the stock, pearl onions, mushrooms, garlic, olive oil, and a pinch each of salt, pepper, and sugar. Bring the mixture to a simmer, then cover the skillet and reduce the heat to medium. Cook for 15 minutes. Then uncover the skillet, raise the heat to medium-high, and cook, tossing the vegetables frequently, until they are well browned and caramelized, 3 to 5 minutes.

7. Transfer the oxtails to a serving bowl, and then spoon off the fat on the surface of the sauce in the pot. If the sauce looks thin, simmer it over high heat until it reduces and thickens. Add sauce to the serving bowl with the oxtails. To serve, scatter the mushroom garnish and remaining cooked bacon over the stew, then top it with the parsley.

Lentil Stew with Garlic Sausage and Goat Cheese

SERVES 4 TO 6

This cozy lentil stew, simmered with leeks and herbs and studded with springy pink sausages, would be completely traditional if it weren't for the bits of goat cheese crumbled over the top at the end. I love the way the creamy, funky cheese gives the whole thing a quiet, salty complexity. It may be out of the ordinary, but it's a hearty combination that's deeply and wonderfully satisfying. French green lentils hold their shape better in stews like this, but regular brown lentils will work if that's what you've got.

1 tablespoon extra-virgin olive oil, plus more for serving

6 ounces garlic sausage or kielbasa, cut into bite-size rounds or chunks

2 small leeks (white and light green parts only), halved lengthwise, cleaned, and thinly sliced

½ teaspoon sweet smoked paprika (or use a pinch of hot smoked paprika), plus more to taste

2 carrots, diced

1¾ cups French green lentils (lentilles du Puy) or brown lentils

4 cups chicken or vegetable stock, preferably homemade

2 teaspoons fine sea salt, plus more to taste

5 sprigs fresh parsley, plus chopped fresh parsley leaves for serving

4 sprigs fresh thyme

2 sprigs fresh rosemary

1 large bay leaf

2 garlic cloves, finely grated or minced

Fresh lemon juice, for serving

4 ounces (1 cup) goat cheese, diced, room temperature

Freshly ground black pepper

1. Heat the oil in a large heavy pot over medium-high heat. Stir in the sausage pieces and cook until they are browned and crisp, about 8 minutes, reducing the heat if necessary to prevent burning. Transfer the sausage to a paper towel–lined plate.

2. Reduce the heat to medium and stir the leeks into the pot. Cook until they are golden and soft, stirring occasionally and scraping up the browned bits from the bottom of the pot, about 10 minutes. Stir in the paprika and cook for 30 seconds to 1 minute to bloom it (you should be able to smell it).

Thinking Ahead

Stew: You can make the stew up
to 3 days in advance. Let it cool
and then keep it, covered, in the
refrigerator. Gently reheat it on the
stove and serve it with the toppings.

3. Stir in the carrots, lentils, stock, 3 cups of water, and
   the salt. Using kitchen twine, tie the sprigs of parsley,
   thyme, and rosemary and the bay leaf into a bundle,
   and throw that in, too (or, if you don't have twine, just
   throw the herbs in the pot, but be prepared to fish them
   out later). Partially cover the pot and bring the mixture
   to a simmer. Continue to simmer, stirring occasionally,
   until the lentils are tender, about 35 minutes. If the pot
   starts to dry out before the lentils are done, add a bit
   more water. Remove and discard the herb bundle.

4. Use an immersion blender to partially blend the stew.
   Don't overdo it—it should stay fairly chunky. (You can
   also do this in a regular blender; just purée about a third
   of the lentil mixture, then return it to the pot.)

5. Stir the sausage back into the stew, add the garlic, and
   return it to a simmer; let it simmer for 2 minutes to meld
   the flavors, stirring frequently. Taste, and add lemon
   juice to taste and more paprika and salt if needed. Serve
   the stew topped with the goat cheese, a drizzle of oil, the
   chopped parsley, and a generous grinding of pepper.

Chive-Stuffed Rack of Lamb with Crispy Potatoes

SERVES 6 TO 8

In this very elegant dish, racks of lamb are coated in a garlicky, gingery herb paste, then roasted over a bed of potatoes that catch the rendering fat and juices. Then, while the lamb rests, the potatoes are blasted with high heat so they turn crunchy and golden. There's a little bit of Asian fish sauce in the lamb marinade. You won't really taste it, but it adds an umami depth, like a couple of anchovies would, but with a subtler flavor.

½ cup chopped fresh chives, any blossoms reserved for garnish

½ cup chopped fresh parsley or basil leaves or a combination

¼ cup extra-virgin olive oil, plus more as needed

6 garlic cloves, finely grated or minced

2 tablespoons grated fresh ginger

1½ teaspoons fine sea salt, plus more as needed

1 teaspoon Asian fish sauce

1 teaspoon freshly ground black pepper, plus more as needed

Pinch of crushed red pepper flakes

2 racks of lamb (1½ to 2 pounds each), frenched

3 pounds fingerling or small round potatoes

Mustard, for serving

1. In a blender or a mini food processor, combine the chives, parsley, oil, garlic, ginger, salt, fish sauce, black pepper, and red pepper flakes. Process until everything is finely chopped and well mixed. If you are using a blender, you may need to add a little more oil to make everything blend smoothly.

2. Season the lamb all over with salt and pepper. Then, using the tip of a paring knife, make vertical slits between the bones of the racks of lamb (the slits should be just large enough for a finger to fit in, so you can push in the marinade). Rub the herb mixture all over the lamb, including pushing it down into the slits. Let the lamb marinate at room temperature while you prepare the potatoes.

3. Heat the oven to 475°F.

recipe continues

4. Put the potatoes in a pot, add water to cover, and season the water with salt until it tastes salty. Bring the water to a boil. Cook until the potatoes are tender when poked with the tip of a knife, 10 to 15 minutes, depending on their size. Drain them well, pat them dry, and place them in a large roasting pan or a rimmed baking sheet.

Thinking Ahead

Lamb: You can marinate the lamb for up to 2 hours at room temperature, or covered and refrigerated overnight.

Potatoes: You can boil and store the potatoes, loosely covered, in the refrigerator for up to 5 days in advance. Crush the potatoes right before roasting them.

4. Put the potatoes in a pot, add water to cover, and season the water with salt until it tastes salty. Bring the water to a boil. Cook until the potatoes are tender when poked with the tip of a knife, 10 to 15 minutes, depending on their size. Drain them well, pat them dry, and place them in a large roasting pan or a rimmed baking sheet.

5. Using your hands or the back of a spoon, flatten the potatoes until they crack open. Drizzle them with olive oil and sprinkle with salt.

6. Place the racks of lamb on top of the potatoes, fat-side facing up (the bones should curve downward). Place the pan in the oven and roast for 5 minutes. Then reduce the oven temperature to 425°F and continue to roast until the lamb is done to taste, another 18 to 23 minutes for rare meat (115°F to 120°F on a meat thermometer). Or roast the meat for a bit longer if you like it medium-rare or medium.

7. Transfer the lamb to a cutting board and tent it with foil to keep warm (the internal temperature will also rise by a few degrees as it sits). Meanwhile, raise the oven temperature to 500°F, flip the potatoes over, drizzle a little more oil over them if they look dry, and continue to roast until they are golden, 8 to 12 minutes.

8. Cut the lamb into chops, slicing between the bones, and serve them sprinkled with chive blossoms, if you've got them, pulled apart into individual florets, along with the potatoes and with mustard on the side.

When I'm grilling for a large group of guests, all of whom have different meat-doneness preferences, I reach for a butterflied leg of lamb. With the bone extracted and the lamb leg sliced into a slab (which your butcher can do for you), it's a cut of meat that's by its nature uneven—in a very good way. When you grill it, the thicker parts stay redder than the thinner bits, and both rare-meat-lovers and their medium-to-well-loving counterparts end up happy, without your having to fuss with various cooking times or putting slices of meat back on the grill after you've carved it.

Marinating the lamb with fennel seeds and anchovies gives it so much flavor, it doesn't even need a sauce. I usually just put out a little pot of mustard for guests to use—or not—as they see fit. Meat this juicy and flavorful doesn't lack for a thing.

Note that you can also broil the leg of lamb if grilling isn't on the agenda.

Grilled Butterflied Leg of Lamb with Fennel and Anchovy

SERVES 12

1½ tablespoons fennel seeds

1 tablespoon cumin seeds

1 tablespoon coriander seeds

2 tablespoons minced fresh fennel fronds or basil leaves (or a combination)

5 garlic cloves, finely grated or minced

4 oil-packed anchovy fillets, minced

1 tablespoon finely grated lemon zest (from 1 to 2 lemons)

1 tablespoon fine sea salt

½ tablespoon freshly ground black pepper

1 to 2 tablespoons extra-virgin olive oil, plus more as needed

1 (5½- to 6-pound) boneless leg of lamb, butterflied, well trimmed of fat

Mustard, for serving (optional)

1. Heat a medium-size dry skillet over medium heat. Stir in the fennel, cumin, and coriander seeds and cook until they are toasted and fragrant, 1 to 3 minutes. Using a mortar and pestle, pound until the seeds start to break down but are not pulverized (or use the flat of a knife to crush the seeds).

2. In a large bowl, combine the crushed toasted seeds with the fennel fronds, garlic, anchovies, lemon zest, salt, and pepper. Drizzle in as much oil as needed to make a paste, then rub the paste all over the lamb. Cover the lamb (or stuff it into a resealable plastic bag), and let it marinate in the refrigerator for at least 2 hours or as long as overnight.

3. When you are ready to cook, heat an outdoor grill to high (or heat a broiler with the rack set 3 inches below the heat source).

4. Grill or broil the lamb for 7 to 12 minutes per side. For medium-rare lamb, you're looking for an internal temperature of 125°F on a meat thermometer, which will climb to 130°F or 135°F before you slice it. I like it rare, so I usually pull it off at about 115°F. Let the lamb rest (it will continue to cook), loosely covered with foil, for at least 10 minutes before slicing it. Serve the mustard alongside if you like.

Thinking Ahead

Lamb: You can marinate the lamb up to 24 hours in advance.

Lamb Shank Cassoulet

SERVES 8

Cassoulet, a sumptuous dish of soft, aromatic beans and meats baked under a crisp bread-crumb crust, may not be the kind of thing you'll find in fancy French restaurants, but what it lacks in refinement it makes up for in rustic, brawny charm. Named for the earthenware pot in which it is traditionally cooked (the *cassole*), cassoulet has its roots in the rural cooking of the Languedoc region, where the usual meats stirred in are duck and pork. In my version, I substitute lamb, both shanks and sausages, which gives the dish a slightly more sophisticated character.

Like all cassoulets, this one does take time. You have to braise the lamb shanks, soak and simmer the dried beans, brown the sausages, then combine everything and cook it all again beneath the savory bread-crumb topping. Just give yourself up to the rhythm of roasting, sautéing, and long, slow simmering. The final stew, a glorious pot of velvety beans and chunks of tender meat covered by a burnished crust, is completely worth the effort. Then serve it with a rich red wine and a crisp green salad. You won't need anything else to round out this hearty, meaty meal.

FOR THE LAMB

1½ teaspoons fine sea salt, plus more as needed

¾ teaspoon sweet paprika

½ teaspoon freshly ground black pepper

2 teaspoons minced fresh thyme leaves

1 teaspoon minced fresh rosemary leaves

6 garlic cloves, finely grated or minced, divided

4 lamb shanks (about 1 pound each)

2 tablespoons extra-virgin olive oil, plus more as needed

1 large yellow onion, diced

2 carrots, diced

2 celery stalks, diced

1 teaspoon tomato paste

1 teaspoon harissa (see note, page 218)

2 cups robust wine (red, white, or a combination)

2½ cups lamb or chicken stock, preferably homemade, plus more as needed

FOR THE BEANS

1 pound dried white beans, such as flageolet, navy, Great Northern, or cannellini (do not substitute canned beans)

3 teaspoons fine sea salt, plus more as needed

3 sprigs fresh thyme

3 sprigs fresh parsley, plus ¼ cup minced fresh parsley leaves

2 sprigs fresh rosemary

1 bay leaf

1 pound lamb sausage (or pork or turkey sausage)

1½ tablespoons extra-virgin olive oil, plus more as needed

1 yellow onion, diced

4 garlic cloves, finely grated or minced, divided

½ teaspoon freshly ground black pepper

1 cup tomato purée or crushed tomatoes

1 cup chicken stock, preferably homemade

1 teaspoon grated lemon zest

recipe continues

3 tablespoons unsalted butter, melted (or substitute olive oil)

1 teaspoon chopped fresh rosemary leaves

1 garlic clove, finely grated or minced

1 teaspoon grated lemon zest

¼ teaspoon fine sea salt

1 cup panko bread crumbs

NOTE: If you don't have harissa, substitute an extra 1 teaspoon tomato paste along with ¼ teaspoon cayenne pepper and ½ teaspoon ground cumin.

1. **Marinate the lamb:** In a small bowl, combine the salt, paprika, pepper, thyme, rosemary, and half of the garlic (save the remaining garlic for sautéing). Rub the mixture all over the lamb shanks. Place the lamb in a bowl or dish, cover it, and refrigerate for at least 4 hours or overnight.

2. **Soak the beans:** Place the beans in a bowl and add enough cold water to cover them by 2 inches. Stir in 1 teaspoon of the salt and let them soak at room temperature for at least 4 hours or overnight.

3. Heat the oven to 325°F.

4. **Cook the lamb:** Heat the oil in a large Dutch oven over medium-high heat. Add the lamb shanks, in batches if necessary, and brown the meat all over, 3 to 5 minutes per side. Take your time with this (it will likely take 15 to 20 minutes all told); the more color you get on the meat, the richer the sauce will be. Transfer the meat to a plate as it browns.

5. If the Dutch oven looks dry, drizzle in a little more oil. Add the onion, carrots, celery, remaining garlic, and a pinch of salt and sauté until the vegetables are tender and golden at the edges, 5 to 7 minutes. Add the tomato paste and harissa and cook until the pastes darken, 30 seconds to 1 minute. Add the wine to the pot and cook until it has reduced by half, 3 to 5 minutes. Add the stock and bring the liquid to a simmer.

6. Return the lamb and any juices to the pot, cover, and place it in the oven. Let the lamb braise, turning it every 30 minutes, until the meat is very tender, 1½ to 2 hours.

7. **While the lamb braises, cook the beans:** Drain the beans and place them in a pot with enough water to cover them by 2 inches; add the remaining 2 teaspoons salt.

Using kitchen twine, tie the thyme sprigs, parsley sprigs, rosemary sprigs, and bay leaf into a bundle and add it to the pot (or just throw the herbs into the pot if you don't have twine). Bring to a simmer and cook for 30 minutes.

8. Add the sausage to the beans and let it poach in the bean liquid for 15 minutes (the sausage will not be fully cooked at this phase). Using tongs, transfer the sausage to a cutting board to cool slightly. Continue to cook the beans until they are tender, which can take anywhere from another 15 minutes to 2 hours, depending upon what kind you used and how fresh they were. (If the water level gets too low, add some boiling water to the pot.) Drain the beans in a colander set over a bowl to catch the liquid, and discard herbs. Reserve the bean cooking liquid.

9. When the lamb shanks are cool enough to handle, tear the meat off the bones and put it in a bowl. Discard the bones or save them for stock. Use a slotted spoon to scoop out all the vegetables from the pot and add them to the lamb. Taste the cooking liquid left in the pot. If it tastes bland and seems thin and watery, simmer it on the stove until it thickens slightly, then season it to taste with salt and pepper. Transfer the liquid to a measuring cup and spoon the fat off the top. You should have between 1 and 1½ cups liquid (if it's more than that, put it back in a small pot on the stove and reduce it a little longer; if it's less than that, add a little more stock); reserve the liquid. Reserve the Dutch oven for baking the cassoulet (you don't need to wash it).

10. To finish the beans, heat the oil in a large skillet over medium-high heat. When the oil shimmers, add the onion, half the garlic, the pepper, and a pinch of salt. Sauté until the onion is translucent, about 4 minutes.

11. Dice the reserved lamb sausage into ¾-inch pieces and add them to the skillet. Sauté until the sausage and onions are golden at the edges, 5 to 10 minutes. Add the tomato purée and simmer until the oil separates out and the sauce reduces a bit, about 10 minutes.

Thinking Ahead

Lamb: You can marinate the lamb as long as overnight, covered and refrigerated. You can braise the shanks 1 day in advance. Shred the meat, separate the sauce, and store both separately in the refrigerator. Scoop off and discard any fat that accumulates on the surface of the liquid before reheating.

Beans: You can let the beans soak, covered and refrigerated, as long as overnight. You can cook them (before adding them to the sausage mixture) up to 5 days in advance. Store the cooled and drained beans and the bean liquid in separate airtight containers in the refrigerator.

Cassoulet: You can make the cassoulet, through step 14, up to 3 days in advance. Store it, covered, in the refrigerator. Bring it to room temperature before topping it with the crust for the final baking.

recipe continues

12. Add the drained beans and the chicken stock, and simmer until the beans are moist and very soupy, 12 to 15 minutes, stirring occasionally. Add some of the reserved bean cooking liquid if the mixture dries out at any point. Stir in the remaining grated garlic, the lemon zest, and the minced parsley. Taste, and add more salt if needed.

13. Turn the oven temperature up to 350°F.

14. Spoon half the beans into the Dutch oven, top them with the lamb and vegetables, and then cover with the remaining beans. Pour the reserved lamb cooking liquid around the edges of the pot until it reaches the top layer of beans but does not cover them. If there's not enough lamb liquid, add some of the reserved bean cooking liquid.

15. **Make the topping:** Mix the melted butter, rosemary, garlic, lemon zest, and salt in a small bowl. Add the panko and use your fingers to mix in the bread crumbs well, making sure the butter is well distributed. Sprinkle the mixture evenly on top of the beans in the pot.

16. Bake until the crust is very lightly browned, about 30 minutes. Use the back of a large spoon to lightly crack the crust; the liquid will bubble up. Use the spoon to drizzle this liquid all over the top of the crust. If there is not enough liquid in the pot to drizzle all over the crust, drizzle it lightly with some of the reserved bean cooking liquid. Return the pot to the oven and bake for 30 minutes to 1 hour more, cracking the crust and drizzling with the bean liquid every 20 minutes or so, until the crust is well browned and the liquid is bubbling. (The total baking time should be 1¼ to 1½ hours.) Remove the pot from the oven and let the cassoulet cool slightly, then serve.

Artichokes with Feta-Dill Dressing, **page 228**

Vegetables

Asparagus Almondine

SERVES 6

2 bunches asparagus, woody ends trimmed

7 tablespoons unsalted butter

½ cup sliced almonds

¼ teaspoon fine sea salt

Juice of ½ lemon

2 tablespoons chopped fresh parsley leaves

1 tablespoon chopped fresh tarragon leaves

1 tablespoon chopped fresh chives, plus any chive blossoms for serving (optional)

Freshly ground black pepper, for serving

Flaky sea salt, for serving

Asparagus season is too short for all the things I long to do with the verdant spears. Usually by the time I eat my way through my roster of roasting, pan-frying, and sautéing, summer has arrived with its wave of tomatoes and cucumbers, the asparagus gone until next spring. This does not, however, stop me from constantly expanding my repertory, and this buttery dish is a recent addition. In it, steamed asparagus is treated like delicate trout fillets, covered with a toasted-almond brown butter and seasoned with lemon juice and herbs. It's simple but devastatingly good. I like to serve it as a first course, where it can command all the attention, rather than as an easily overlooked side dish. Lavender-hued chive blossoms, pulled apart with the fluffy bits sprinkled on top, make this even prettier than it already is.

1. In a large pot fitted with a steamer rack, bring an inch of water to a boil. Add the asparagus to the rack and steam until the spears are slightly less tender than you like them (you'll finish cooking them later), 3 to 10 minutes depending upon the thickness of the spears. Transfer the asparagus to a clean dish towel and blot them dry.

2. Melt the butter in a large skillet over medium heat. Stir in the almonds and cook until the butter is deeply golden and smells nutty and the almonds are a very pale gold, 2 to 5 minutes.

3. Add the asparagus to the skillet, season it with the fine sea salt, cover the skillet, and shake it well over medium-high heat so the sauce coats the spears. Cook, shaking the skillet, until the asparagus is cooked a bit more and the almonds and butter deepen in color by a shade, going from dark gold to light brown. Take care not to overcook the asparagus.

4. Sprinkle the lemon juice, parsley, tarragon, chives, and pepper over the asparagus and shake the pan a few more times to distribute everything. Serve the spears topped with flaky sea salt and chive blossoms, if possible, making sure to spoon all the almonds and melted butter over the spears.

Radishes Anchoïade

SERVES 4 TO 6

Anchoïade is France's answer to Italy's *bagna cauda*—a wonderfully fishy, pungently garlicky sauce that loves nothing more than crisp, juicy vegetables for dunking. The biggest difference between the two sauces is that *bagna cauda*, from northern Italy, is always served warm (the name translates to "warm bath"). *Anchoïade*, from sunny Provence, is served at room temperature, which makes life easier for the cook. Although practically any vegetable will work here for dipping, I particularly love the combination of crisp, spicy radishes with the anchovies. Or for the most stunning impact, put out an array of veggies, including radishes of all colors, fennel, cucumber, multi-hued carrots, and/or lightly steamed cauliflower, broccoli, and asparagus. Chunks of baguette, with their soft crumb soaking up maximum sauce, would also be a welcome addition.

1 fat garlic clove, finely grated or minced
1½ teaspoons white wine vinegar
12 to 16 oil-packed anchovy fillets
2 to 4 tablespoons extra-virgin olive oil
2 bunches radishes, scrubbed, trimmed, and halved if large
Unsalted butter, room temperature, for serving

1. Put the garlic and vinegar in the bowl of a mini food processor or blender, and let them sit for 1 minute to mellow the garlic. Then add the anchovies and pulse to blend. Pour in 2 tablespoons of the oil and pulse until the sauce is just combined, adding more oil if needed. You should have a thick, chunky, rough paste.

2. Arrange the radishes on a platter. Heap some of the anchoïade next to the radishes, and some butter in a mound next to that. Guests can spread either anchoïade or butter—or both—onto the radishes before eating.

Thinking Ahead

You can make the anchoïade up to 1 week in advance. Store it in a sealed container in the refrigerator.

When I eat artichokes, I do so with gusto. In artichoke season, I'll happily devour one or two of the thorny thistles as my dinner, messily using the petals to scoop up an herb-flecked creamy sauce like this one, then tearing into the tender heart with my fingers. It's the kind of meal I prefer to have at home, where I can take full advantage of its sensuous nature. Naturally, the French are far more refined about the whole thing. They may still use their hands for petal-dunking (traditionally in bowls of melted butter or mayonnaise), but it's a daintier maneuver followed by a bath in a finger bowl, and the hearts are dispatched with knife and fork.

No matter how you choose to eat them, artichokes are not hard to prepare at home. If you have an electric pressure cooker, they'll be done fairly quickly (in under 15 minutes), which makes them weeknight-friendly. But even when using a regular pot on the stove, their earthy, nutty flavor and velvety flesh make them worth the 45 minutes or so they take to steam.

See photograph on **page 222**.

Artichokes with Feta-Dill Dressing

SERVES 4

FOR THE ARTICHOKES

Fine sea salt

4 medium to large artichokes

½ lemon

FOR THE FETA-DILL DRESSING

½ cup (2 ounces) crumbled feta cheese

3 tablespoons chopped fresh dill fronds

1½ tablespoons fresh lemon juice

Fine sea salt

Freshly ground black pepper

¼ cup extra-virgin olive oil

¼ cup whole-milk fromage blanc or Greek yogurt

1. **Prepare the artichokes:** Fill a large pot or an electric pressure cooker insert with 1 inch of water. Add a large pinch of salt, and place a steamer basket inside.

2. Remove any browned outer leaves from the artichokes. Cut off the top quarter of each artichoke, and use kitchen shears to trim away any pointy ends on remaining outer leaves. Use a vegetable peeler to remove the tough outer layers of the stems; then immediately rub all cut edges with the lemon half to prevent browning.

3. Place the artichokes in the steamer basket, stem-side up, and squeeze any remaining juice from the lemon half into the water. If you are using a regular pot, cover and steam until tender, 30 to 50 minutes, making sure to add more water as the pot starts to dry out. To check for doneness, gently poke an artichoke base with a knife tip; if it slides in easily, the artichokes are done.

    If using an electric pressure cooker, cook at high pressure for 10 minutes, then release the pressure manually. If the artichokes are not done, reseal the pot and cook for 2 to 4 minutes longer, depending on how firm they still feel.

4. **While the artichokes are cooking, make the dressing:** In a small bowl, whisk together the feta, dill, lemon juice, a large pinch of salt, and black pepper to taste. Whisk in the oil and fromage blanc, taste, and adjust the seasoning if necessary. Serve with the artichokes.

Thinking Ahead

Artichokes: You can steam them up to 4 hours ahead and keep them at room temperature.

Dressing: You can make the feta dressing up to 2 days ahead. Store it in a sealed container in the fridge, but bring it back to room temperature before serving.

Roasted Tomatoes with Lemony Anchovy Crumbs

MAKES 8 SIDE DISH SERVINGS OR 4 MAIN COURSE SERVINGS

If you make this dish in tomato season, when colorful heirlooms are in markets everywhere just waiting to become dinner, you won't really be surprised by its juicy profundity of flavors—a gorgeous mix of sweet, salty, pungent, and umami, all baked until golden and bubbling on top. But what's so especially appealing about this dish is that it's also amazing when made with, meh, out-of-season tomatoes, those hydroponic specimens that you buy because, well, waiting until July seems impossible. In both cases, the garlicky, lemony bread crumbs, anchovy oil, and Parmesan will work their magic, seasoning the vegetables while they roast. Serve this as a side dish, or make it the star of a light meal, with some crusty bread to mop up all those luscious, tangy juices.

4 large tomatoes, preferably heirlooms, cut into fat wedges

1 cup cherry or grape tomatoes, preferably a mix of colors

12 oil-packed anchovy fillets, minced, divided

½ cup (1½ ounces) grated Parmesan cheese

½ cup panko bread crumbs

2 fat garlic cloves, finely grated or minced, divided

2 teaspoons fresh thyme leaves, finely chopped

1 teaspoon finely grated lemon zest

Pinch of crushed red pepper flakes

6 tablespoons extra-virgin olive oil, divided, plus more as needed

Large pinch of fine sea salt

Fresh basil or mint leaves, torn, for serving

1. Heat the oven to 375°F.

2. Arrange the tomato wedges in a gratin dish or a 9 × 13-inch baking dish, or use individual gratin dishes. Scatter the cherry tomatoes around and in between the tomato wedges.

3. In a medium bowl, mix about a quarter of the minced anchovies with the Parmesan, panko, half the garlic, the thyme, lemon zest, and red pepper flakes. Mix in 1 tablespoon of the oil and toss to combine. Sprinkle the crumbs over the tomatoes.

4. In a small saucepan, combine the remaining 5 tablespoons olive oil, remaining anchovies, remaining garlic, and the salt, and bring to a simmer. Cook, stirring, until the anchovies start to break down and the garlic is fragrant, 1 to 2 minutes. Drizzle the mixture over the tomatoes, adding more olive oil if it looks dry.

5. Bake until the top is golden and crispy, 40 to 45 minutes. Serve hot or warm, garnished with the basil or mint.

Tomato, Eggplant, and Zucchini Tian

SERVES 4

A tian is really just a humble casserole that prefers to go by its French designation, lending it an air of chic mystery. As with any casserole, you can add almost any combination of vegetables to the pan and they will bake up gloriously golden on top and soft in the center. Here, zucchini, tomatoes, and eggplants are first roasted on sheet pans until very tender, then layered in a gratin dish with confited garlic, herbs, and Parmesan before being baked again. The initial roasting allows maximum caramelization of the vegetables before their flavors are allowed to mingle in the close proximity of the gratin dish.

You can do most of the work a few days in advance, then pop this in the oven just before serving. It's an exuberantly summery dish that's equally good served next to roasted or grilled meats or fish, or as the main course, especially if you dollop it with some salted yogurt first.

2 small zucchini, sliced ¼ inch thick

2 medium eggplants, sliced ¼ inch thick

3 medium tomatoes, sliced ½ inch thick

3 tablespoons extra-virgin olive oil, divided, plus more for drizzling

Fine sea salt, as needed

5 garlic cloves: 3 smashed, 2 finely grated

6 sprigs fresh thyme, plus 1 teaspoon chopped fresh thyme leaves

4 sprigs fresh rosemary

2 bay leaves, torn in half

¾ cup (3 ounces) coarsely grated Parmesan cheese

Chopped fresh basil leaves, for serving (optional)

Plain whole-milk Greek yogurt, for serving (optional)

1. Heat the oven to 375°F.

2. Arrange the zucchini in a single layer on one rimmed baking sheet, the eggplant on a second baking sheet, and the tomatoes on a third. Drizzle the vegetables liberally with oil, and sprinkle each trayful generously with salt. Divide the smashed garlic, thyme sprigs (not the chopped thyme), rosemary sprigs, and bay leaves evenly across the baking sheets. Roast the vegetables until they are very tender and very browned: 25 to 30 minutes for the tomatoes, 35 to 40 minutes for the eggplant, and 50 to 60 minutes for the zucchini. Flip the eggplant and zucchini over halfway through (no need to flip the tomatoes). Reserve the roasted smashed garlic cloves; discard the thyme and rosemary sprigs and the bay leaf pieces.

3. Raise the oven temperature to 450°F.

recipe continues

4. On a cutting board, sprinkle salt over the reserved roasted garlic cloves and then finely chop them into a paste. Spread this paste all over the bottom of a gratin dish, baking dish, or pie plate. Over the garlic, layer the vegetable slices, alternating among tomato, zucchini, and eggplant. Drizzle with the 3 tablespoons oil to coat and sprinkle with salt.

5. In a medium bowl, combine the Parmesan, grated garlic, and chopped thyme, rubbing them together with your fingertips. Spread the mixture evenly on top of the vegetables, and bake until the top is golden brown, 18 to 23 minutes. Serve hot, warm, or at room temperature, topped with the chopped basil and yogurt, if you like, and seasoned to taste with salt.

Roasted vegetables: You can roast the vegetables 2 days before layering them into the gratin dish. Store them in containers in the fridge.

Tian: The tian can be assembled up to 3 hours before baking. You can bake it up to 8 hours before serving; keep it at room temperature until you're ready to eat, then heat it up in a 300°F oven if you'd like to serve it warm.

Roasted Eggplant with Herbs and Hot Honey

SERVES 4

The best way to get crisp-skinned, velvet-fleshed eggplant is to fry it. But roasting it in a very hot oven with plenty of oil comes close (and is much less messy), and it's the method I use all the time, varying the seasonings to suit my mood. This combination is inspired in part by southern France, with its herbes de Provence, garlic, and lemon juice, and in part by Brooklyn, with its drizzle of trendy hot honey. The dish is both sweet and savory, with a pronounced herbal kick. If you don't have hot honey on hand, you can substitute regular honey spiked with a pinch of cayenne or a dash of hot sauce. You're looking for a touch of sweetness and a bit of heat to round out the lemon and garlic.

1 tablespoon fresh lemon juice

1 teaspoon herbes de Provence

1 garlic clove, finely grated or minced

½ teaspoon fine sea salt, plus more as needed

¼ cup extra-virgin olive oil

2 pounds eggplant, cut into ¾-inch cubes

Hot honey, for serving

Chopped fresh herbs, such as basil, cilantro, mint, parsley, chives, or chervil, or a mixture, for serving

Lemon wedges, for serving

1. Heat the oven to 450°F.

2. In a large bowl, whisk together the lemon juice, herbes de Provence, garlic, and salt. Slowly whisk in the oil, a little at a time, until the dressing is creamy and emulsified.

3. Toss the eggplant with the dressing, then scrape it onto a rimmed baking sheet (make sure to get all the dressing, too). Spread it out in an even layer and roast, tossing the eggplant every 15 minutes, until the cubes are golden and caramelized, 35 to 45 minutes.

4. Drizzle the eggplant with the hot honey and fresh herbs, and serve it with lemon wedges.

Roasted Cauliflower with Brown Butter, Raisins, and Capers

This combination of ingredients—nutty brown butter, salty capers, sweet raisins, and cauliflower—was inspired by Jean-Georges Vongerichten, who has been serving it as a sauce for scallops at his restaurant Jean-Georges since it opened in 1997. He simply isn't allowed to take it off the menu—the mix of flavors is just too magical. Here I've nixed the scallops and focused on the cauliflower, roasting it until it is well caramelized, then topping it with the brown butter mixture. Or if you'd like to reclaim those lost scallops, add some to the brown butter along with the raisins and sauté them for a couple of minutes, until just cooked through. It's a slightly different end result from Jean-Georges's crisp and brown seared scallops, but easier to do at home and still compelling to eat.

1 medium head cauliflower (about 1¾ pounds), florets and stem cut into bite-size pieces

2 tablespoons extra-virgin olive oil

½ teaspoon fine sea salt, plus more as needed

⅓ cup pine nuts

4 tablespoons (½ stick) unsalted butter

3 tablespoons golden raisins

¼ teaspoon freshly grated nutmeg

2 tablespoons capers, coarsely chopped

2 tablespoons fresh parsley leaves, chopped

Lemon wedges, for serving

1. Heat the oven to 425°F.

2. On a rimmed baking sheet, toss together the cauliflower, oil, and salt. Roast until the cauliflower is caramelized, 30 to 35 minutes, tossing it once more halfway through.

3. Meanwhile, heat a small skillet over medium heat. Stir in the pine nuts and cook, tossing them frequently, until toasted, about 5 minutes. Transfer the pine nuts to a plate.

4. Return the skillet to medium heat and melt the butter in it. Continue cooking, swirling the skillet occasionally, until the butter is brown and nutty, 5 to 7 minutes. Remove the skillet from the heat and continue to swirl it occasionally as it cools; the butter will continue to cook as it sits; swirling helps prevent overbrowning.

5. Bring 1 cup of water to a boil in a small pot or kettle. Put the raisins in a mesh strainer and then pour the boiling water over them. Let the drained raisins cool for 5 minutes, then pat them dry and stir them into the browned butter. Add the nutmeg to the brown butter as well.

6. When the cauliflower comes out of the oven, pour the brown butter, toasted pine nuts, and capers over it on the baking sheet. Toss to combine, then scrape the mixture onto a serving platter. Top with the parsley and more salt, and serve with lemon wedges.

Thinking Ahead

You can refresh the raisins with boiling water up to 1 day ahead. Store them in a container at room temperature.

Moroccan Eggplant Salad

SERVES 4

2 large green bell peppers

4 large ripe tomatoes (1½ pounds)

½ cup extra-virgin olive oil, divided, plus more as needed

¼ cup chopped fresh parsley leaves

2 garlic cloves, finely grated or minced

1 teaspoon sweet paprika

1 teaspoon fine sea salt, plus more as needed

¾ teaspoon ground cumin

Pinch of cayenne pepper

1 tablespoon minced preserved lemon, or more to taste (optional)

1 large eggplant, cut into ¼-inch-thick slices

Fresh lemon juice, for drizzling

½ cup fresh cilantro leaves, torn

½ cup fresh mint leaves, torn

Plain yogurt, for serving (optional)

Most of the time, when it comes to frying eggplant, I simply don't. It's just such a messy, splattering process that even when I start out with frying intentions, I usually end up throwing the whole thing in the oven to roast at high heat.

But when I do want to go that extra mile for some eggplant euphoria, I'll make this deeply nuanced dish. Yes, it requires two skillets—one for the spiced tomato and bell pepper sauce, and one for the eggplant itself. And yes, both the eggplant and the tomato mixture will spray hot juices and oil all over your stovetop, floor, and apron (definitely remember to put one on before frying). But it's worth the mess for this salad's hauntingly rich flavor and crisp-edged texture. Every eggplant-lover should fry it at least once.

That said, if eggplant-frying is not on your agenda today (or ever), go ahead and roast the eggplant here. Just coat the slices liberally with olive oil and salt, and roast them in a 450°F oven until they are nicely browned all over, 25 to 35 minutes. Topped with a tomato sauce seasoned with cumin and preserved lemon, this fragrant salad will still be delightful, albeit a bit less silky and rich.

1. Over the open flame of a burner, on a grill, or on a rimmed baking sheet under the broiler (in which case, halve the peppers), roast the peppers until they are evenly charred, about 10 minutes, turning them often. Transfer the peppers to a heatproof bowl, cover it with a plate to trap the steam, and let the peppers sit until they are cool enough to handle, about 15 minutes. Then peel off the skins (using paper towels helps), seed the peppers, and chop the flesh into ¾-inch pieces.

2. Halve the tomatoes crosswise and squeeze out the seeds. Dice the flesh into 1-inch pieces.

3. Heat ¼ cup of the oil in a large skillet over medium-low heat. Stir in the tomatoes, parsley, garlic, paprika, salt, cumin, and cayenne. Cover and cook, stirring occasionally, until the tomatoes are soft, about 10 minutes. Stir in the green peppers and continue to cook, uncovered, until the liquid has evaporated, another 20 to 25 minutes. Stir in the preserved lemon

recipe continues

if using, adding more to taste if you like. Season the vegetables with more salt if needed. Remove from the heat and reserve.

4. Heat the remaining ¼ cup oil in a separate large skillet over medium-high heat. Season the eggplant slices with salt. When the oil is hot but not smoking, add as many slices as will fit in the skillet in one layer, and fry until they are golden brown, 3 to 5 minutes per side. Transfer the eggplant to a paper towel–lined plate or two and sprinkle with more salt while it is still warm. Repeat, frying in batches until all the eggplant is cooked, adding more oil if the pan dries out.

5. To serve, arrange the eggplant on a serving platter, and top it with the tomato mixture. Drizzle with olive oil and a squeeze of lemon. Sprinkle with the torn cilantro and mint leaves. If you like, whisk the yogurt with a pinch of salt and serve it on the side.

Thinking Ahead

Tomato-pepper mixture: You can make the tomato mixture up to 8 hours before serving. Keep it at room temperature, covered.

Eggplant: You can fry the eggplant up to 2 hours in advance. It loses some of its crispness, but the flavor will still be good. Store it uncovered at room temperature.

Chickpea and Vegetable Tagine with Couscous

SERVES 4 TO 6

Imbued with a freshly ground spice mix of coriander, cumin, and caraway, this is a highly fragrant vegetarian stew, loaded with chickpeas and myriad colorful vegetables. You can change up the vegetables to suit whatever you have on hand—just make sure to use a variety for the most interesting texture and flavor. I like to cook my own dried chickpeas for this; their flavor is better and the texture not quite as mushy as those from a can. Canned chickpeas work well, too, but look for the kind that is seasoned with salt. Sodium-free chickpeas are bland. In any case, do try to get the preserved lemons for this. With their salty-funky flavor, they add depth to the vegetables and spices.

Thinking Ahead

Spice mix: You can make the spice mix up to 1 week in advance and store it, covered, at room temperature.

Tagine: You can prepare the tagine up to 4 days ahead. Store it in the fridge, and reheat it gently on the stove before serving.

FOR THE TAGINE

- 1 teaspoon coriander seeds
- 1 teaspoon cumin seeds
- ½ teaspoon caraway seeds
- ½ teaspoon crushed red pepper flakes
- ½ teaspoon ground ginger
- ½ teaspoon sweet paprika
- ¼ teaspoon ground turmeric
- 2 tablespoons extra-virgin olive oil
- 1 large onion, diced
- 1 red bell pepper, seeded and diced
- 2 teaspoons fine sea salt, divided, plus more as needed
- 4 garlic cloves, finely grated or minced
- 1½ tablespoons tomato paste
- 2 cups vegetable stock, preferably homemade
- 2 cups chickpea cooking liquid (or use more vegetable stock)
- 1¾ cups cooked chickpeas, either homemade (see sidebar, page 242) or from a 14-ounce can, drained
- ½ preserved lemon, quartered lengthwise, seeded, and thinly sliced, plus more to taste
- 2 medium carrots, cut into ½-inch pieces
- 2 medium turnips, cut into 1-inch pieces
- 1 pound butternut squash, cut into 1-inch pieces (3½ cups)
- 1 large zucchini, cut into 1-inch pieces
- ¼ cup chopped fresh mint or parsley leaves
- ¼ cup chopped fresh cilantro leaves
- 2 scallions, white and green parts, thinly sliced

FOR THE COUSCOUS

- 3 cups couscous
- 3 tablespoons unsalted butter, room temperature
- ½ teaspoon fine sea salt, plus more to taste
- 5½ cups boiling water

recipe continues

How to Cook Chickpeas

To cook chickpeas from scratch, soak 8 ounces dried chickpeas in 2 quarts of cold water containing 1 teaspoon fine sea salt for at least 6 hours or as long as overnight. Drain, and put the chickpeas in a pot. Add another teaspoon of salt and enough fresh cold water to cover the peas by 2 inches. If you like you can also add any or all of the following for extra flavor: a bay leaf, a couple of rosemary sprigs, a celery stalk, a halved onion, 4 garlic cloves, a drizzle of olive oil. (I like to use all of it—it makes the chickpea liquid taste a bit like chicken broth.) Bring to a simmer and cook until the chickpeas are just tender, 1 to 2 hours, adding more water if the level descends below the chickpeas. (To use an Instant Pot, cook at high pressure for 20 to 25 minutes, depending on how long you soaked them. Let pressure release naturally.) Drain. You'll have 3½ cups cooked chickpeas. Store in a container in the fridge for up to 5 days.

1. **Cook the tagine:** Heat a small dry skillet over medium heat, and then stir in the coriander, cumin, and caraway seeds. Toast until fragrant, about 1 minute.

2. Transfer the spices to a spice grinder or a mortar and pestle, and grind to a powder. Stir in the red pepper flakes, ginger, paprika, and turmeric.

3. Heat the oil in a Dutch oven or heavy pot over medium heat. Stir in the onion, bell pepper, and ½ teaspoon salt, and cook until the vegetables are soft, about 5 minutes. Stir in the garlic, tomato paste, and spice mixture and cook for 1 minute more.

4. Stir in the vegetable stock and chickpea liquid, chickpeas, preserved lemon, and the remaining 1½ teaspoons salt. Bring to a simmer, then stir in the carrots, turnips, and butternut squash. Partially cover the pot and cook for 15 minutes. Then stir in the zucchini, partially cover the pot, and continue to cook until all the vegetables are tender, stirring occasionally, another 15 to 20 minutes.

5. **Meanwhile, make the couscous:** In a large heatproof bowl, combine the couscous, butter, and salt. Stir in the boiling water, then cover the bowl (a plate works well here) and let it stand for 10 minutes. Fluff with a fork.

6. Remove the tagine from the heat and stir in more preserved lemon and/or salt if you like. Top it with the mint, cilantro, and scallions, and serve it with the couscous. Or pile the tagine on top of the couscous before garnishing it with the herbs and scallions.

Scalloped Potato Gratin

SERVES 8 TO 10

4 tablespoons (½ stick) unsalted butter, plus more for the foil, room temperature

3 cups heavy cream

¼ cup chopped fresh sage leaves

4 fat garlic cloves, finely grated or minced

¼ teaspoon freshly grated nutmeg

1½ teaspoons fine sea salt, plus more as needed

5 large eggs

4 pounds (about 6 large or 8 medium) russet potatoes

Freshly ground black pepper, to taste

2¼ cups (8½ ounces) grated Gruyère cheese

Is there anything better than a molten, golden-topped potato gratin? I don't think so, either. This one stays fairly classic—scented with sage, garlic, and nutmeg, then showered with lots of nutty Gruyère cheese. My tweak is in form rather than flavor. Instead of piling the potatoes an inch or two deep in a gratin dish, I shingle the slices in a shallow sheet pan. It gives the whole thing a more elegant look, and you get maximum browning and crunch on top. There's less of the gooey center, but what it loses in ooze it makes up for in increased surface area for the crisp-edged baked cheese.

Thinking Ahead

Assembling: You can assemble the gratin up to 4 hours ahead of baking. Store it, loosely covered, in the fridge.

Baking: The gratin can be baked 4 hours ahead, kept uncovered at room temperature, and then reheated in a very hot oven (450°F) until the top is shiny. It's not quite as gooey as when freshly baked, but it's still quite good.

1. Heat the oven to 350°F and brush the 4 tablespoons butter on a rimmed 17 × 13-inch baking sheet. Brush one or two pieces of foil (enough to cover the top of the pan) with more butter. Set the foil aside.

2. In a medium pot, bring the cream, sage, garlic, nutmeg, and a pinch of salt to a simmer. Simmer until reduced by one fourth, about 15 minutes.

3. In a large heatproof bowl, lightly beat the eggs. Beating constantly, gradually add a little of the hot cream to the eggs, then slowly pour in the rest of the hot cream, whisking to prevent the eggs from curdling. Reserve.

4. Using a mandoline or a sharp knife, slice the potatoes into ⅛-inch-thick rounds.

5. Arrange one layer of potatoes on the buttered baking sheet, slightly overlapping the slices. Sprinkle with ¾ teaspoon of the salt, add pepper to taste, then pour half the egg mixture over the potatoes. Top with ½ cup of the cheese. Repeat the layers of potato, seasoning, and egg mixture. Top with the remaining 1¾ cups cheese. Cover the baking sheet with the foil (buttered-side down) and bake for 20 minutes. Remove the foil and bake until the potatoes and cheese are browned and bubbling, 25 to 30 minutes. Let cool slightly, then serve.

Once I started dunking my French fries in the combination of mustard and mayo when I was a kid traveling in France, I never went back to plain old ketchup. These duck fat potatoes are the grown-up oven-roasted version of those creamy, salty fries. The duck fat plus high heat turns the fingerlings very crisp and golden. The salsa verde, tangy with anchovies, garlic, vinegar, and lemon, gives them a mustard-like jolt. And the mayonnaise adds the luscious creamy note. This dish is just as good with store-bought mayonnaise as it is with homemade—it's a slightly different taste, sweeter rather than more pungent—but I like them equally. So feel free to use either one here. Or if you want to go full blast on the garlic, use aioli (see page 19). And if you don't have duck fat on hand, you can substitute olive oil.

Duck Fat–Roasted Potatoes with Anchovy Salsa Verde and Mayonnaise

SERVES 4

1½ pounds fingerling potatoes, scrubbed

1 teaspoon fine sea salt, plus more as needed

3 tablespoons duck fat, melted

1 cup fresh parsley leaves and tender stems, chopped

1 cup fresh cilantro leaves and tender stems, chopped

½ cup fresh mint leaves, chopped

10 oil-packed anchovy fillets, chopped

1 shallot, finely chopped

1 garlic clove, finely grated or minced

Finely grated zest of ½ lemon

1½ tablespoons fresh lemon juice

½ teaspoon white wine vinegar

¼ teaspoon crushed red pepper flakes

¼ cup extra-virgin olive oil

Turkish red pepper (*urfa biber*), or more crushed red pepper flakes, for serving

Mayonnaise (purchased or homemade; see page 21)

1. Put the potatoes in a large pot and add enough water to cover them by at least 1 inch. Add several large pinches of salt, until the water tastes like the sea. Bring the water to a boil, then simmer until the potatoes are tender, 10 to 15 minutes. Drain the potatoes and let them cool until you can handle them.

2. Heat the oven to 450°F.

3. Cut the potatoes in half lengthwise. On a rimmed baking sheet, toss the potatoes with the salt and the duck fat. Arrange them in a single layer, cut-side down, and roast until they are a deep golden brown on the bottom, 25 minutes. Then flip the potatoes over and roast until they are crispy on the outside and fork-tender on the inside, another 10 to 15 minutes.

4. **Meanwhile, make the anchovy salsa verde:** In a medium bowl, combine the parsley, cilantro, mint, anchovies, shallot, garlic, lemon zest, lemon juice, vinegar, and red pepper flakes. Stir in the oil. Taste and add a pinch of salt if needed.

5. Serve the crispy potatoes topped with the anchovy salsa verde, sprinkled with Turkish pepper or more red pepper flakes, and drizzled with mayonnaise.

Thinking Ahead

Anchovy salsa verde: You can prepare the salsa verde up to 1 day in advance. Store it in a covered container in the refrigerator and bring it to room temperature before serving.

Potatoes: You can boil and halve the potatoes up to 8 hours ahead of roasting them. Keep them covered at room temperature.

Roasted Carrots and Fennel with Pomegranate Vinaigrette

SERVES 4 TO 6

This is a glorious side dish to make in winter, when the unrelenting palette of browns, beiges, and golds—no matter how delicious they taste—becomes oppressive to look at. Here, the pops of orange from the carrots, green from the herbs, and scarlet from juicy pomegranate seeds serve as needed refreshment. It's complexly flavored, too, with a combination of reduced pomegranate juice and sour pomegranate molasses adding zing to the sweetness of the carrots and fennel. Serve it with roasted or stewed meats to brighten your winter table and, if necessary, your winter doldrums, too.

Thinking Ahead

Pomegranate juice: You can reduce the pomegranate juice up to 2 weeks ahead and store it in the fridge. Extra reduced juice can be frozen for up to 6 months. Or use any extra juice to spike seltzer or sparkling wine.

1 pound carrots, halved or quartered lengthwise into long skinny wedges

2 fennel bulbs, trimmed and cut into ¾-inch-thick wedges (reserve the fronds)

¾ teaspoon fine sea salt, plus more as needed

Freshly ground black pepper, to taste

4 tablespoons extra-virgin olive oil, divided

1 teaspoon cumin seeds

½ cup pomegranate juice

1½ teaspoons pomegranate molasses

⅓ cup pomegranate seeds

2 tablespoons coarsely chopped chervil leaves (or dill fronds)

Fennel fronds (or dill fronds), for serving

1. Heat the oven to 375°F.

2. On a rimmed baking sheet, toss together the carrots, fennel, salt, pepper, and 3 tablespoons of the oil. Roast for 20 minutes. Then flip the vegetables over, sprinkle them with the cumin seeds, and roast for another 20 to 25 minutes, until the vegetables are golden and soft.

3. Meanwhile, bring the pomegranate juice to a simmer in a small pot and continue to simmer until it has reduced by half, about 10 minutes.

4. In a small bowl, whisk together 1 tablespoon of the reduced pomegranate juice, the pomegranate molasses, a large pinch of salt, and pepper to taste. Slowly whisk in the remaining 1 tablespoon oil until emulsified.

5. Toss the warm carrots and fennel with dressing to taste (you might not need all of it), then transfer them to a serving platter. Top with the pomegranate seeds, chervil, and fennel fronds and serve.

Mushroom and Goat Cheese Toasts

These elegant toasts, with their topping of creamy goat cheese and earthy sautéed mushrooms, work equally well served as an hors d'oeuvre or as a first course—or even as a light main course. Make sure the goat cheese is one that's soft enough to spread easily, and then spread it on the warm toasts as soon as you have rubbed them down with garlic. You want the cheese to melt, creating what becomes almost a sauce for the browned mushrooms. Use as many different kinds of mushrooms as you can here; the greater the variety in textures and flavors, the better.

———

4 tablespoons (½ stick)
unsalted butter

1 pound mixed mushrooms
(a combination of shiitakes,
oyster mushrooms, hen-
of-the-woods if you can
find them, and cremini is
especially good), sliced

3 shallots, diced

1 tablespoon chopped fresh
thyme leaves

Fine sea salt, as needed

2 tablespoons Fino sherry or
dry white vermouth

3 tablespoons chopped fresh
chives, plus more for garnish

1 (10-inch) demi-baguette
(or use a piece of a longer
baguette)

Extra-virgin olive oil, as
needed

1 garlic clove, cut in half

5 ounces (1¼ cups) goat
cheese, room temperature

Freshly ground black pepper,
as needed

1. Melt the butter in a large skillet over medium heat. Stir in the mushrooms and shallots and cook, stirring only occasionally so the vegetables can brown, until golden, about 10 minutes. Then stir in the thyme and cook until well browned, another 5 to 10 minutes. Season with salt to taste.

2. While the mushrooms are cooking, heat the oven to 400°F.

3. Stir the sherry into the mushrooms and cook, stirring, until it evaporates, about 1 minute. Then stir in the chives and remove the skillet from the heat.

4. Halve the baguette lengthwise as if you were making a sandwich, then cut it crosswise into sixths to make 12 equal pieces. Arrange them, cut-side up, in one layer on a rimmed baking sheet, drizzle them with olive oil, sprinkle with salt, and bake until they are golden on the edges, 6 to 10 minutes.

5. Remove the toasts from the oven and immediately rub the cut sides with the garlic halves, pressing hard so the garlic oils are released onto the toasted bread. Then smear each baguette piece with about 1 scant tablespoon of the goat cheese.

6. Put the skillet of mushrooms back over medium-high heat for a minute or two to warm them up. Spoon the mushroom mixture on top of the goat cheese toasts, and sprinkle with chopped chives and freshly ground black pepper. Serve hot or warm.

Thinking Ahead

You can cook the mushrooms up to 4 hours in advance. Keep them in a covered container at room temperature and reheat before serving.

Sautéed Chanterelles with Garlic and Parsley

SERVES 2 TO 4

¼ cup extra-virgin olive oil

10 ounces chanterelle mushrooms, sliced

2 garlic cloves, minced

¼ cup chopped fresh Italian parsley leaves

Freshly ground black pepper

Fine sea salt, as needed

Fresh lemon juice, for serving

It used to be nearly impossible to find fresh chanterelle mushrooms in New York. I remember how excited my father would get whenever he spotted some at Balducci's in Greenwich Village. That's where he'd go once or twice a month to stock up on hard-to-find "gourmet" ingredients, the kinds of things I take for granted at my local supermarket these days, like olive oil imported from Italy and good Parmigiano-Reggiano cheese. When chanterelles appeared, no matter how pricy, he'd bring them home and sauté them in Italian olive oil, with loads of garlic and parsley. We ate them in France in the summer, too, sautéed in salty French butter. But maybe because they were such a rarity in Brooklyn, I usually picture them quickly cooked in my parents' copper-bottomed skillet, the smells of sizzling garlic and woodsy mushrooms mingling while we all waited. Then we ate them straight from the pan.

This is pretty much my dad's recipe. It's basic, but perfect in its simplicity—delicate, oily, garlicky, and bright with herbs. I like them as a first course on their own, but they also work beautifully topped with some fresh ricotta cheese, or a fried egg, to round them out.

1. In a very large (preferably 12-inch) skillet, heat the oil over medium-high heat. Stir in the mushrooms and cook, stirring infrequently to allow them to brown, for 5 to 10 minutes or until they are golden all over. Then stir in the garlic, parsley, and several grinds of black pepper, and cook for another minute, until the garlic is fragrant.

2. Remove the skillet from the heat and season the mushrooms with salt to taste. Transfer them to a serving dish and serve immediately, with a squeeze of fresh lemon juice.

Sautéed Cabbage with Gruyère and Jalapeños

SERVES 4 TO 6

This is what I cook when I'm alone in the house but want to feed myself something hearty, comforting, and slightly rich. Since neither my husband nor my daughter likes sautéed cabbage as much as I do (which for them is not at all and for me is a lot), I wait until I get one of those precious solitary evenings to make this. Usually, my night begins with a plate of this caramelized cabbage and ends in the bathtub with a bourbon and a book. Dreamy.

In this recipe, I've increased the quantities to feed a larger group in the hopes that just maybe you're lucky enough to come from a family of cabbage-lovers. If so, this soft and tender vegetable with its puddles of melted Gruyère and spicy green chiles will feed them well.

4 tablespoons (½ stick) unsalted butter

1 to 2 jalapeños, halved, seeded, and thinly sliced

3 garlic cloves, thinly sliced

10 cups sliced cabbage (from 1 small or ½ large head)

1 teaspoon fine sea salt, plus more as needed

¼ cup chicken or vegetable stock, preferably homemade

1¼ cups (5 ounces) shredded Gruyère cheese

¼ cup (1 ounce) grated Parmesan cheese

1. Heat the broiler.

2. Melt the butter in a large cast-iron or other broiler-proof skillet over medium heat. Stir in the jalapeños and garlic, and cook until they are fragrant and starting to brown, about 2 minutes.

3. Stir in the cabbage, salt, and stock. Raise the heat to medium-high and continue to cook, stirring often, until the cabbage is soft, the liquid has cooked off, and the edges of the cabbage are starting to brown, about 10 minutes. Taste, and add more salt if needed.

4. Sprinkle the Gruyère and Parmesan evenly over the cabbage. Transfer the skillet to the oven and broil until the cheese is bubbly and golden, 2 to 3 minutes. Serve warm.

Roasted Butternut Squash with Lime and Hazelnuts

SERVES 4 TO 6

Plush slices of roasted butternut squash are one of the joys of autumn. I like to roast them at a high heat so their undersides caramelize and turn a deep golden brown, then top the squash with some sort of vibrant dressing. Here, lime and red pepper flakes bring out the sweetness of the squash with their contrasting pungency while hazelnuts add crunch. I always peel my butternut squash with a vegetable peeler. The skins just slip right off. Or, if you've got a nice-looking squash without a lot of blemishes on the skin, you can leave it unpeeled. The skin is perfectly edible and turns crisp when you roast it.

Thinking Ahead

You can prepare the vinaigrette up to 1 day in advance. Store it in the fridge and bring it to room temperature before serving it on the squash.

3 tablespoons extra-virgin olive oil, plus more as needed

1 (2-pound) butternut squash, peeled, halved, seeds removed, sliced ½ inch thick

¼ teaspoon fine sea salt, plus more as needed

Freshly ground black pepper, as needed

2 tablespoons fresh lime juice

½ teaspoon finely grated lime zest

1 garlic clove, finely grated or minced

Pinch of crushed red pepper flakes

3 oil-packed anchovy fillets, minced

¼ cup chopped toasted hazelnuts (or use walnuts or pecans)

2 scallions (white and green parts), thinly sliced

1. Heat the oven to 425°F.

2. Oil a rimmed baking sheet and arrange the squash slices on it in a single layer. (If it doesn't all fit, oil another sheet and use that as well.) Brush the top of the squash slices with more oil and sprinkle them with the salt and black pepper to taste. Roast until the squash is golden brown on the bottom, 15 to 20 minutes. Then flip the slices over and roast until they are very tender, about 10 minutes longer.

3. Meanwhile, make the vinaigrette: In a small bowl, combine the lime juice, zest, garlic, red pepper flakes, and a pinch of salt. Let the ingredients sit for a minute, then whisk in the anchovies and 3 tablespoons oil until emulsified. Taste and add more salt and/or lime juice as needed.

4. Serve the squash covered with the vinaigrette and sprinkled with the hazelnuts and scallions.

Apricot Tarte Tatin, **page 290**

After Dinner

Rustic Buckwheat Apple Ginger Cake

SERVES 10

A simple, luscious cake with chunks of raw apple baked into the batter, this is based on a recipe in Dorie Greenspan's wonderful cookbook *Around My French Table*. She sort of got it from a fashionable Parisian friend, Marie-Hélène Brunet-Lhoste, who, like many French cooks, can throw together a cake without a recipe, just eyeballing the ingredients and mixing by feel. Dorie did the measuring and weighing for us. Then I tweaked the basic formula, replacing some of the white flour with buckwheat flour for an earthy richness, and stirring some candied ginger into the batter, bits of which pop up in chewy, sweet-spicy mouthfuls. Dorie says to use a mix of apples (Rome, Gala, Braeburn, Mutsu, Granny Smith, MacIntosh) for their different nuances and textures, and I absolutely agree. Or substitute pears for another take on these lovely autumnal flavors.

Thinking Ahead

This is best served on the same day that it is baked.

8 tablespoons (1 stick / 113 grams) unsalted butter, melted and cooled, plus more for the pan

¾ cup (97 grams) all-purpose flour, plus more for the pan

3 tablespoons (23 grams) buckwheat flour

¾ teaspoon baking powder

¼ teaspoon fine sea salt

2 large eggs, room temperature

¾ cup (150 grams) sugar

3 tablespoons brandy

1 teaspoon vanilla extract

4 medium apples (about 1½ pounds), peeled, cored, and diced into 1-inch cubes

⅓ cup finely chopped candied ginger

Whipped crème fraîche or sour cream, for serving

1. Position a rack in the center of the oven and heat the oven to 350°F. Butter and flour an 8-inch springform pan, and line the bottom with parchment paper. Place the pan on a rimmed baking sheet.

2. In a medium bowl, whisk together the all-purpose flour, buckwheat flour, baking powder, and salt.

3. In a large bowl, whisk the eggs until frothy, then whisk in the sugar, brandy, and vanilla. Whisk in half of the melted butter until it is just incorporated, then whisk in half the flour mixture. Repeat with the remaining butter and flour. Fold in the apples and candied ginger, making sure to coat them with the batter.

4. Scrape the batter into the prepared pan, smooth the top, and bake until a toothpick inserted in the center comes out clean, 60 to 70 minutes. Let the cake cool in the pan for 5 minutes, then run a small spatula around the inside rim and release the sides. Serve the cake warm or at room temperature, with dollops of crème fraîche.

French Yogurt Cake with Cherries and Cardamom

SERVES 8 TO 10

I love the one-bowl-and-a-whisk ease of a French yogurt cake—and the incredibly moist, soft texture of the crumb after it bakes. I throw these together all the time, stirring whatever fruit I have into the batter: apricots or berries in summer, diced blood orange or tangerine pieces in winter, fresh figs or plums in the fall. This one is perfect to make in July, when fresh cherries are at their juiciest and most abundant. But frozen cherries work nearly as well. Don't thaw them first; just bake the frozen cherries right into the cake. If you're serving this for dessert, you might want to add a scoop of ice cream or sorbet to dress it up. I like it for an afternoon snack or a sweet breakfast, served with a little plain Greek yogurt spooned on top.

Thinking Ahead

This cake is best served on the same day that it's baked, but it's still quite good when made the day before. Wrap the cooled cake in a clean kitchen towel or plastic wrap and store it at room temperature.

Unsalted butter, room temperature, for the pan
1⅔ cups (215 grams) all-purpose flour
1 teaspoon baking powder
1 teaspoon ground cardamom
½ teaspoon baking soda
½ teaspoon fine sea salt
1⅓ cups (266 grams) sugar
1 cup (240 grams) plain whole-milk yogurt (not Greek)
½ cup (120 milliliters) grapeseed, sunflower, or canola oil
2 large eggs
1 cup (8 ounces) pitted sweet cherries or blueberries, fresh or frozen

1. Heat the oven to 350°F and butter a 9 × 5-inch loaf pan.

2. In a large bowl, whisk together the flour, baking powder, cardamom, baking soda, salt, and sugar. In a separate large bowl, whisk together the yogurt, oil, and eggs, beating the mixture until it's well combined. Scrape the egg mixture into the flour mixture and whisk until smooth. Fold in the cherries.

3. Pour the batter into the prepared loaf pan and bake until the top is golden and a cake tester inserted in the center comes out clean, 50 to 60 minutes. Transfer the cake to a wire rack and let it cool completely in the pan.

4. Unmold the cake by running a thin spatula around the edges and inverting the pan over a serving plate. Serve it in thick slices.

Campari Olive Oil Cake

SERVES 8

When I posted a photo of this very modest-looking cake on Instagram, I was blown away by the response. Honestly, it didn't look like much—a generic yellow cake with a golden top. I think just the very notion of putting Campari and olive oil in a cake is what made people stop and "like" it. And it *is* a pretty terrific flavor combination—the citrusy bittersweet character of the Campari goes really well with the fragrant olive oil, to which I also add melted butter for richness as well as lots of fresh citrus juice and zest. The flavors are both fresh and intense, with a fluffy, moist crumb.

On its own it's a pretty plain-looking thing, but you can dress it up for a party, adding orange segments, berries, and dollops of whipped cream or crème fraîche to the top. Or if you want to go one step further, simmer some Campari and a bit of sugar down to a syrup, and drizzle that all over the cake. It makes it pretty, pinker, and accentuates the boozy flavor of the cake.

Thinking Ahead

This cake is best served on the same day that it's baked.

4 tablespoons (½ stick / 56 grams) unsalted butter, melted, plus more for greasing the pan

2 cups (260 grams) all-purpose flour

1⅔ cups (335 grams) sugar

1 teaspoon fine sea salt

1 teaspoon baking powder

½ teaspoon baking soda

⅔ cup (150 milliliters) whole milk

⅔ cup (150 milliliters) mild olive oil

3 large eggs

⅓ cup (80 milliliters) Campari

1 tablespoon grated grapefruit zest

1 tablespoon grated orange zest

1 teaspoon grated lemon zest

¼ cup (60 milliliters) fresh grapefruit juice

2 tablespoons (30 milliliters) fresh orange juice

1 tablespoon (15 milliliters) fresh lemon juice

Whipped crème fraîche or whipped cream, sweetened or not as you like, for serving

1. Heat the oven to 350°F. Grease a 9-inch springform pan, and line the bottom with parchment paper. (You can use a regular 9-inch cake pan that is at least 2 inches deep, but the cake will be harder to unmold.)

2. In a medium bowl, whisk together the flour, sugar, salt, baking powder, and baking soda. In a large bowl, whisk together the milk, oil, butter, eggs, Campari, citrus zests, and citrus juices. Fold in the dry ingredients, then scrape the batter into the prepared pan.

3. Bake until the top is golden and springs back when lightly pressed in the center, 45 minutes to 1 hour. (A cake tester might emerge with a few crumbs, which is okay.)

4. Let the cake cool completely in the pan. Then run a butter knife around the edges and release the sides. Serve with dollops of whipped crème fraîche.

Pain d'Epices

SERVES 8 TO 12

French gingerbread, called *pain d'épices*, is stickier, denser, and more compact than what we are used to here in the States, thanks in part to the large amount of honey whisked into the batter. That honey is integral to both flavor and texture, adding a haunting, syrupy character to the crumb, especially if you use a forthright variety like wildflower or chestnut. I first fell in love with the cake when I was a student in Paris. A small bakery near my walk-up sold slices of it, and ordering that cake was what taught me the word *tranche*, meaning "slice," because I bought so many of them. Rich with spices and candied fruit, it's a recipe that dates back to the Middle Ages but is still beloved today. I like to serve the cake in thin slices, either buttered or plain, with tea as an afternoon snack. Or you can use it for the base of the gingery mousse on page 311.

Thinking Ahead

The cake can be baked up to 3 days before serving. Store it, wrapped in plastic wrap, at room temperature.

6 tablespoons (¾ stick / 85 grams) unsalted butter, cubed, room temperature, plus more for the pan

½ cup (120 milliliters) water (or use brewed tea or coffee)

1 teaspoon grated fresh ginger

½ teaspoon ground cinnamon

½ teaspoon ground ginger

¼ teaspoon ground allspice

¼ teaspoon ground cloves

¼ teaspoon freshly grated nutmeg

⅛ teaspoon ground coriander

⅛ teaspoon freshly ground black pepper

⅓ cup (120 grams) good rich honey, such as wildflower

¼ cup (55 grams) finely chopped candied citron or orange zest (or use candied ginger and 1 tablespoon grated orange zest)

1¼ cups (162 grams) rye flour

¾ cup (98 grams) bread flour

½ cup (100 grams) sugar

1½ teaspoons baking powder

¼ teaspoon fine sea salt

1. Heat the oven to 350°F. Butter an 8 × 4-inch loaf pan.

2. In a small pot over medium heat, whisk the water, ginger, cinnamon, ground ginger, allspice, cloves, nutmeg, coriander, and pepper; bring to a boil. Remove the pot from the heat, stir in the butter, and let it sit for 10 minutes. Whisk in the honey and candied citron.

3. In the bowl of an electric mixer, use the paddle to mix the rye flour, bread flour, sugar, baking powder, and salt. Add the spice mixture, and mix until combined.

4. Scrape the batter into the prepared pan and smooth the top. Bake until the top is browned and a cake tester inserted in the center comes out clean, 55 to 65 minutes. Transfer to a rack and cool for 30 minutes. Run a knife around the edges and invert the cake; let it finish cooling on the rack. Serve in slices.

French Rye-Chocolate Cake with Spiced Crème Anglaise

MAKES 12 SMALL RICH SERVINGS

With a texture that falls somewhere between a chocolate truffle and a fudgy brownie, French chocolate cakes are about as dark, dense, and decadent as desserts get. This one has a small amount of rye flour mixed into the batter, which gives the cake an appealing earthiness. I like to pair very small slices with a crème anglaise infused with ginger, pepper, cloves, and nutmeg. But if you'd rather not make the crème anglaise, the cake is also excellent served with whipped cream that has been lightly sweetened with a little maple syrup or maple sugar.

Thinking Ahead

Cake: The cake can be made up to 5 days in advance and stored, well wrapped in plastic wrap, in the refrigerator. You can serve it cold and fudgy, or let it come to room temperature, when it will be a bit softer.

Creme anglaise: After it cools, you can cover the crème anglaise with plastic wrap pressed directly onto its surface, and chill it for up to 1 week. Note that it thickens after chilling, so if you want a thicker custard, plan ahead.

FOR THE CAKE

12 tablespoons (1½ sticks / 170 grams) unsalted butter, cubed, plus more for the pan

Unsweetened cocoa powder, as needed, for the pan

12 ounces (340 grams) bittersweet chocolate, chopped

1 cup (200 grams) sugar

⅛ teaspoon fine sea salt

5 large eggs, whites and yolks separated

⅓ cup (43 grams) rye flour

FOR THE CRÈME ANGLAISE

5 large egg yolks

½ cup (100 grams) sugar

1 cup (240 milliliters) heavy cream

1 cup (240 milliliters) whole milk

½ teaspoon ground ginger

¼ teaspoon freshly ground white pepper

¼ teaspoon ground cloves

¼ teaspoon freshly grated nutmeg

Pinch of fine sea salt

1. **Bake the cake:** Heat the oven to 350°F. Butter a 9-inch springform pan, and dust the bottom and sides with cocoa powder, tapping out the excess. Wrap the outside of the pan tightly in two layers of foil, to make sure the water doesn't seep into the pan.

2. In a large microwave-safe bowl, melt the chocolate and the butter together in 30-second bursts in the microwave, stirring in between, until just melted (or do this in a pot on the stove over low heat). Stir in the sugar

recipe continues

and salt, whisking until the mixture is no longer hot. Stir in the egg yolks until smooth, then stir in the flour.

3. In the bowl of an electric mixer fitted with the whisk attachment, beat the egg whites to form stiff peaks. Carefully and gently fold one-third of the whites into the chocolate mixture to lighten it, then fold in the remaining egg whites. Take your time with this so you don't deflate the whites; a few white streaks in the batter are okay. Scrape the batter into the prepared springform pan, then set the pan into a large roasting pan.

4. Fill the roasting pan with enough hot tap water to reach halfway up the springform's sides. Bake until the cake is just set, with firm sides and a slight jiggle in the center, about 60 minutes. Transfer the pan to a wire rack to cool.

5. **Make the crème anglaise:** In a medium bowl, whisk together the egg yolks and sugar. In a medium pot, bring the cream, milk, ginger, white pepper, cloves, nutmeg, and salt to a simmer over medium heat. Remove the pan from the heat.

6. Pour a little of the hot cream mixture in a thin steady stream into the yolks, whisking continuously, then scrape the yolk-cream mixture back into the pot. Return the pot to medium heat and cook, stirring constantly, until the custard has thickened enough to coat the back of a spoon, about 5 minutes. Strain the mixture to remove any cooked bits of yolk, and let the crème anglaise cool.

7. To serve, run a butter knife around the inner edge of the pan to loosen the cake, then release the sides. Slice the cake and serve it with the crème anglaise.

Chestnut Icebox Cake Stacks

SERVES 8

My madeleine is the mass-produced chestnut mousse called Maron Sui's that's sold in plastic tubs next to the yogurts in supermarkets all over France. I'd make a beeline for it every summer when our family did the first big shopping at the *hypermarché* near whatever house we were staying in that August. While my sister scouted the aisles for Nutella (then available only in France), I'd do dairy-case duty, piling packages of Maron Sui's and La Vache Qui Rit (Laughing Cow) cheese into our cart.

I've been making a homemade version of Maron Sui's ever since I figured out that all I needed was heavy cream and sweetened chestnut paste, either purchased or homemade (see page 268). Just whip them together with a little rum and vanilla and voilà—a nearly instant mousse with a buoyant texture and earthy flavor. Here I layer the mousse with homemade chocolate wafer cookies for a French twist on American icebox cake. While the cookies and mousse sit in the fridge, the cookies soften, turning into something velvety and cakelike as they absorb all the cream.

If you'd rather use Nabisco Famous Chocolate Wafers—the traditional cookie of the icebox cake—you can substitute them for the homemade wafers.

FOR THE WAFERS

- 1½ cups (195 grams) all-purpose flour
- ¾ cup (88 grams) Dutch-process cocoa powder
- ¾ teaspoon baking powder
- ¾ teaspoon fine sea salt
- 12 tablespoons (1½ sticks / 170 grams) unsalted butter, room temperature
- 1 cup (200 grams) sugar
- 1 large egg yolk
- 2 tablespoons (30 milliliters) heavy cream
- 1 teaspoon vanilla extract

FOR THE CHESTNUT CREAM

- 1½ cups (420 grams) chestnut crème or jam (see page 268)
- 1½ cups (360 milliliters) very cold heavy cream
- 1 tablespoon (15 milliliters) dark rum
- 1 teaspoon vanilla extract

Shaved chocolate, for serving (see note, page 277)

1. **Make the wafers:** In a medium bowl, whisk together the flour, cocoa powder, baking powder, and salt.

2. In the bowl of an electric mixer fitted with the paddle attachment, cream the butter and sugar together until pale and fluffy, about 3 minutes. Beat in the egg yolk, cream, and vanilla, scraping the sides of the bowl with a rubber spatula. Add the flour mixture and mix until just combined. Scrape the dough onto a clean work surface and form it into a 10-inch-long log. Wrap it in plastic wrap and refrigerate for at least 1 hour.

3. Heat the oven to 350°F and line two baking sheets with parchment paper.

recipe continues

Chestnut Crème

Sweetened chestnut crème (*crème de marrons*), also called chestnut spread, paste, or jam, is made from chestnuts that have been cooked in sugar syrup with a vanilla bean until very soft, then puréed. You can buy it at specialty markets and online. I like the Faugier brand. You can also make it yourself using either freshly roasted and peeled chestnuts or purchased vacuum-packed or jarred roasted chestnuts.

To make chestnut crème: In a medium pot, combine 2 cups (21 ounces / 600 grams) chopped peeled roasted chestnuts with 1½ cups sugar, a halved vanilla bean if you like, and 2½ cups water. Simmer, partially covered, over low heat until the chestnuts are very soft, 25 to 40 minutes. If the pan dries out, add a little more water. Discard the vanilla bean and purée the chestnuts and their liquid in a food processor or blender until very smooth (this will take 3 to 5 minutes). If the mixture has little lumps of chestnut in it, and if this bothers you, press the paste through a fine-mesh sieve. You'll end up with about 1½ cups of chestnut crème.

4. Slice the log into ⅛-inch-thick slices and place them on the prepared baking sheets, spacing them about 1 inch apart (you should have 48 cookies). Bake for 12 minutes, until the cookies are firm and the edges have darkened slightly, rotating the baking sheets halfway through. Transfer the pans to wire racks and let the cookies cool completely.

5. **Make the chestnut cream:** In the bowl of an electric mixer fitted with the whisk attachment, beat the chestnut crème until smooth. Pour in the heavy cream, rum, and vanilla; whisk until medium peaks form.

6. **To assemble the stacks:** Place 8 cookies on a serving platter, 2 to 3 inches apart. Spoon 1 tablespoon chestnut crème on top of each cookie and gently spread it out to the sides. Top with another cookie, and repeat the layers until the crème and cookies are used up and you've made 8 cute little individual stacks. Drape the platter very loosely with plastic wrap and refrigerate it for at least 8 hours or overnight. To serve, sprinkle the stacks with chocolate shavings.

Thinking Ahead

Dough: The dough log can be made up to 5 days ahead and stored, well wrapped, in the refrigerator, or frozen for up to 2 months. Thaw frozen dough overnight in the fridge.

Cookies: The cookies can be baked up to 1 week before you assemble the stacks. Store them in an airtight container at room temperature.

Stacks: These are best eaten within 48 hours of assembling.

Cocoa Hazelnut Financiers

MAKES 2 DOZEN FINANCIERS

At first glance, these diminutive treats might look like brownie bites, with their cocoa color and small disk shape. But that's as far as the resemblance goes. While brownies are fudgy and chewy, these are tender and delicate, infused with the Nutella flavors of chocolate and hazelnut, and with a melt-in-the-mouth texture that's soft and tender rather than moist and dense. If you can't find the hazelnut flour, almond flour works just as well. Serve these refined little cakes as part of a *petits fours* plate, or on their own, with a mid-afternoon shot of espresso or a cup of strong milky tea.

Thinking Ahead

Batter: You can mix the batter up to 4 days before baking. Store it, covered, in the fridge.

Financiers: These are best served within 2 days of baking. Store them in a sealed container at room temperature.

8 tablespoons (1 stick / 113 grams) unsalted butter, plus more for the pans

1¼ cups (155 grams) confectioners' sugar

½ cup (56 grams) hazelnut flour

⅓ cup (43 grams) all-purpose flour, plus more for the pans

⅓ cup (33 grams) Dutch-process cocoa powder

¼ teaspoon fine sea salt

4 large (120 grams) egg whites

24 whole hazelnuts, for garnish (optional)

1. Heat the oven to 400°F.

2. In a small saucepan, melt the butter, letting it cook until it turns a dark golden brown and smells toasted, about 3 minutes. Do not let it get too brown; you're looking for a deep golden color but not dark brown—it's a blond butter rather than a brown butter. Pour it into a heatproof bowl or a coffee mug and let it cool.

3. In the bowl of an electric mixer, combine the confectioners' sugar, hazelnut flour, all-purpose flour, cocoa powder, and salt. Using the mixer's whisk attachment on low speed (or a hand whisk and a strong arm), beat in the egg whites until the flour mixture is damp. Add the reserved butter and beat on medium-high speed (or vigorously by hand) until the batter is very smooth, about 2 minutes.

4. Butter and flour 24 mini muffin cups (or coat with nonstick spray). Divide the batter among the cups and top each one with a hazelnut, if using.

5. Bake until the financiers are firm and the tops spring back when lightly pressed with a finger, 11 to 17 minutes. Let them cool on a wire rack before unmolding.

Thinking Ahead

Sugar mix: The sesame sugar mix can be ground up to a week in advance of baking. Store it, covered, at room temperature.

Cookies: These are best served within 4 days of baking. Store them in an airtight container at room temperature.

Black Sesame Palmiers

MAKES ABOUT 2 DOZEN COOKIES

1 cup (200 grams) sugar
¼ cup (35 grams) black sesame seeds
¼ teaspoon fine sea salt
1 pound all-butter puff pastry, thawed if frozen

Black sesame is having a moment in Paris, where you'll find the smoky, earthy seeds baked into cookies and croissants, stirred into sauces, and infused into all manner of custards, syrups, and ice creams. I like to use them to flavor *palmiers,* where they add a haunting, nutlike richness that's heady and intense next to the buttery puff pastry.

To make the *palmiers,* I grind black sesame seeds with sugar to form a speckled gray powder, then roll up the sugar in puff pastry coils, which are sliced and baked until darkly caramelized and very crunchy. Because you don't have to make your own puff pastry, it's a fairly easy dessert to put together. The key here is not to underbake them. You need to make sure that the sugar melts so that when the *palmiers* cool, they are crackling and crisp and shatter into sugary crumbs in your hands when you break one in half.

You can also make these cookies with white sesame seeds, but they will have a subtler flavor. And, without the kaleidoscope of browns, blacks, and grays, they are not nearly as arresting on the plate.

1. Heat the oven to 425°F and line two rimmed baking sheets with parchment paper.

2. In a food processor, electric spice grinder, or blender, grind together the sugar, sesame seeds, and salt until the mixture looks like gray volcanic ash with speckles of black. Be careful not to overdo it and process it into a paste.

3. On a clean work surface, sprinkle about ½ cup of the sugar mixture in a roughly 14 × 14-inch square. Place the puff pastry in the middle, and sprinkle the remaining sugar mixture evenly across the top.

4. Roll the puff pastry out to form a 14 × 14-inch square to cover the sugar. (It doesn't have to be exact, since brands of puff pastry vary in size; the aim here is to roll the pastry out on the sugar so the sugar adheres.) Using your hands, roll the bottom and top edges in toward each other in the middle, bringing them together to touch. They will look like two cylinders lined up next to each other. If your dough has warmed up, transfer it to the fridge until chilled. Leave any sugar left on the work surface (you'll need it later), or transfer the sugar to a plate and reserve it.

5. Slice the logs of dough crosswise into ⅜-inch-thick pieces, and dip each flat side into the leftover sugar. Transfer the cookies to the prepared baking sheets, spacing them 1 inch apart.

6. Bake for 10 minutes, then flip the cookies over. Bake for another 5 to 7 minutes, until browned on the tops and the bottoms. Do not underbake. Transfer to racks to cool completely.

A peanut butter pie with a chocolate cookie crust is one of those quintessentially American desserts of my childhood—salty-sweet, and as luscious and dense as the cream-filled centers in a box of chocolate bonbons. This is my Frenchified version of it. I substitute hazelnut butter for the peanut butter and add an elegant garnish of raspberries and chocolate shavings. The hazelnut-chocolate combination gives the pie a Nutella-like appeal, though in a less sweet and far more sophisticated guise. If you served this at a fancy dinner party, I doubt anyone would recognize its humble inspiration. Or, you can take the pie in the opposite direction and use peanut butter here instead. One bite might even evoke your childhood, but only the good parts.

Make sure your cream cheese is soft before you start beating it. A brief stint in the microwave can help if your kitchen is cold or if you forgot to take the cheese out ahead of time.

Hazelnut Butter Raspberry Pie

SERVES 8

FOR THE CRUST

Unsalted butter, room temperature, for the pan

8 ounces (227 grams) chocolate wafer cookies, such as Nabisco Famous (about 30 cookies) or homemade (page 267)

6 tablespoons (¾ stick / 85 grams) unsalted butter, melted

2 tablespoons (25 grams) granulated sugar

FOR THE FILLING

8 ounces (1 cup / 227 grams) smooth unsweetened hazelnut butter (or use peanut or almond butter)

8 ounces (227 grams) cream cheese, room temperature

½ cup (60 grams) confectioners' sugar

2 teaspoons vanilla extract

Pinch of fine sea salt

1 cup (240 milliliters) cold heavy cream

1 cup (4 ounces) fresh raspberries

Chocolate shavings, for garnish (optional, see note)

1. Heat the oven to 350°F and generously butter a 9-inch pie pan.

2. **Make the crust:** Crush the cookies into fine crumbs in a food processor, or place them in a plastic bag and smack it with a rolling pin until they are crumbled. In a bowl, mix the cookie crumbs with the melted butter and sugar until thoroughly combined. Press the mixture into the prepared pie pan, pushing it up the sides as far as possible. Bake until the crust is firm, 8 to 10 minutes. Let it cool completely on a wire rack.

3. **Make the filling:** In the bowl of an electric mixer fitted with the whisk attachment, cream together the hazelnut butter, cream cheese, confectioners' sugar, vanilla, and salt (use a pretty big pinch if your hazelnut butter is unsalted). Beat for 2 to 3 minutes, until the mixture is smooth. Then beat in the cream, which will lighten the mixture and make it a bit more airy. (You can also whirl this together in a food processor, but it won't be as airy.) Scrape the filling into the cooled crust and smooth the top with a spatula.

4. Refrigerate the filling until it is set, 2 to 3 hours.

5. Just before serving, top the pie with the raspberries and a sprinkle of chocolate shavings.

NOTE: To make chocolate shavings, grate a bar of your favorite bittersweet or milk chocolate on a hand grater. The larger grater holes make chunky, big pieces of chocolate that are like oversized sprinkles. Smaller holes make more powdery, fluffy gratings. Both are delicious and pretty, so use either one or try a combination. Another option is to make chocolate curls with a vegetable peeler.

Thinking Ahead

Crust: You can bake the crust up to 1 day ahead. Store it, well wrapped, at room temperature.

Pie: You can make the pie up to 24 hours ahead; top it with the raspberries and chocolate shavings just before serving.

Gâteau Breton with Plums and Cardamom

Based on a classic *gâteau Breton*, this buttery, crumbly cake is filled with sliced fresh plums instead of the usual purée of prunes or dried apricots. The fresh fruit makes the cake moister in the center than the traditional recipe, and a bit less sweet, too, since there's a lot less sugar in the filling. The egg yolk–rich dough, which bakes up into something akin to a soft and tender shortbread, is especially easy to make in a food processor.

If you don't have a food processor, substitute superfine sugar for the granulated, and make the dough by hand according to the directions on page 117, adding the egg yolks in place of the other liquid. If it doesn't come together at first, just add a tablespoon or two of water.

1 cup (200 grams) sugar, plus more for the plums

2⅓ cups (303 grams) all-purpose flour

1¼ teaspoons ground cardamom, divided

¾ teaspoon finely grated lemon zest

½ teaspoon fine sea salt

1 cup (2 sticks / 226 grams) cold unsalted butter, diced, plus more for the pan

7 large egg yolks, divided

2 to 3 medium plums (about 6 ounces), halved, pitted, and sliced ¼-inch thick

1. In a food processor, process the sugar until it is powdery and fine, about 1 minute. Add the flour, 1 teaspoon of the cardamom, the lemon zest, and the salt; pulse to combine. Add the butter and pulse until the mixture resembles coarse bread crumbs. Then add 6 egg yolks and pulse until the mixture comes together. Divide it in half, form the halves into disks, and wrap them in plastic wrap. Chill for at least 2 hours or until firm.

2. Heat the oven to 350°F. Butter an 8-inch springform pan.

3. Between two sheets of parchment paper or plastic wrap, roll one of the dough disks out to form an 8-inch round. Transfer the dough to the prepared springform pan, pressing it into the edges. Arrange the plum slices, overlapping, in concentric circles on the dough, leaving a ¾-inch border around the outside edge. Sprinkle 2 to 4 tablespoons sugar over the plums, depending on how sweet they are. (Use more than you think you need! The plums can get tart during baking.) Then sprinkle with the remaining ¼ teaspoon cardamom.

4. Roll the second piece of dough into an 8-inch round, transfer it to the pan, and press around the outside edge to stick the dough pieces together and seal in the fruit.

5. In a small bowl, combine the remaining egg yolk with 1 teaspoon water and beat together lightly. Brush this egg wash over the top of the cake, and then use a fork to score a crisscross pattern into the dough. Bake until the top is golden brown, about 55 minutes (cover it with foil if the cake is browning too quickly). Let the cake cool in the pan for 15 minutes; then run a butter knife around the inside edge of the pan and release the sides. Let the cake cool completely before serving.

Thinking Ahead

Dough: The dough can be made up to 5 days in advance and refrigerated, well wrapped. Or it can be frozen for up to 3 months. Just make sure it's well wrapped in plastic if you're freezing it.

Cake: This gâteau is best served on the same day that it's made; after about 24 hours the juices released from the fruit start to turn the pastry to mush.

Tarte au Fromage with Goat Cheese, Crème Fraîche, and Honey-Drizzled Figs

SERVES 12

Tarte au fromage is how the French do cheesecake—or, at least how they traditionally did, before they fell in love with the New York–style cream cheese–based version, which has currently invaded their dessert status quo.

This ethereal, moist cake harkens back to the more classic incarnations, with its not-too-sweet filling that's tender and relatively fluffy, lightened with beaten egg whites. The usual cheese for a *tarte au fromage* is *fromage blanc*, a supremely mild, yogurt-like white cheese that's hard to find in the United States. In my version, I substitute a mix of savory goat cheese and crème fraîche, which gives the filling a pronounced tang that I balance with a sweet cookie crust.

The topping couldn't be simpler if you can get fresh figs: Just pile them on top of the cake and drizzle them with the darkest, most intense honey you've got. I like chestnut honey, but buckwheat honey is good, too. And if you can't get good fresh figs, use whatever fresh juicy fruit you can find—berries, apricots, or peaches in summer, or tangerine segments or pineapple in winter. Or serve slices of this naked on the plate, which is exactly how it's done in France.

1¼ cups (125 grams) crushed sablé cookies, butter cookies, or shortbread cookies (I like La Mère Poulard brand sablés; digestive biscuits will also work but are not quite as rich-tasting; ditto graham crackers; see page 277 for crushing instructions)

4 tablespoons (½ stick / 56 grams) unsalted butter, melted

1 cup (8 ounces / 227 grams) crème fraîche

4 ounces (1 cup) goat cheese, softened

2 large eggs, yolks and whites separated

⅓ cup plus 1 tablespoon (80 grams) sugar

1 pint (12 ounces) fresh figs, quartered

1 to 2 tablespoons chestnut honey (or other good dark honey)

Fennel fronds or torn fresh mint leaves, for garnish (optional)

1. Position a rack in the center of the oven and heat the oven to 375°F.

2. In a medium bowl, combine the ground cookies with the melted butter. Then press the mixture evenly into a 10-inch tart pan. Place the pan on a rimmed baking sheet and bake until the crust is golden all over, 10 to 13 minutes. Transfer the tart pan to a wire rack, but leave the baking sheet in the oven. Let the crust cool while you prepare the filling; the crust can be warm or completely cool when you fill it.

3. While the crust is baking, prepare the filling: In the bowl of an electric mixer fitted with the paddle attachment, beat together the crème fraîche, goat cheese, egg yolks, and the ⅓ cup sugar until smooth (or use a bowl, a whisk, and some elbow grease).

4. In the clean bowl of an electric mixer fitted with the whisk, beat the egg whites until they are lightly frothy, about 1 minute. Add the remaining 1 tablespoon sugar and continue to beat until medium-stiff peaks form.

5. Using a spatula, gently but firmly fold the beaten whites into the cheese mixture, taking care not to deflate the whites. Scrape the batter into the tart shell, and carefully place the tart on the hot baking sheet. Bake until the center of the tart barely jiggles, 35 to 40 minutes. Transfer the tart to a rack to cool completely. Then cover and refrigerate it for at least 2 hours before serving.

6. When you are ready to serve it, arrange the figs on top of the tart, drizzle them with the honey, and sprinkle with fennel fronds or mint if you like.

Thinking Ahead

The baked tart can be kept, covered, in the refrigerator for up to 3 days before serving. Add the figs, honey, and garnish just before serving.

Meyer Lemon Tart with Olive Oil and Fleur de Sel

SERVES 8

The combination of lemon, olive oil, and salt is my go-to for seasoning pretty much anything savory, from salad to fish to pizza. But it's also fantastic turned into dessert—in this case, a lemony curd and piled into an almond-rich tart crust and baked until golden and crisp. The flavors and textures here are a bit like lemon squares but more refined.

You will likely have a bit of dough left over after making the tart crust, and I like to turn it into butter cookies: Form the dough scraps into a log, then chill it, wrapped in plastic wrap, until it is very firm, 2 to 3 hours. Slice the log into ¼-inch-thick rounds, sprinkle them with Demerara sugar, and bake at 350°F until golden, about 10 minutes. You can save the dough log in the fridge until the tart is finished (up to 5 days). Then, before you have a chance to become sad at the lack of dessert around the house, you can bake the cookies and prolong the sugary joy.

NOTE: If you can't get Meyer lemons, use the zest of regular lemons and substitute ¾ cup fresh lemon juice mixed with ¼ cup fresh orange juice.

FOR THE DOUGH

- 1½ cups (195 grams) all-purpose flour, plus more for rolling
- ½ cup (50 grams) almond flour or blanched sliced almonds
- 2 tablespoons (25 grams) sugar
- ¼ teaspoon fine sea salt
- 8 tablespoons (1 stick / 113 grams) very cold unsalted butter, cubed
- 1 large egg, lightly beaten with 1 tablespoon water

FOR THE FILLING

- 5 to 6 Meyer lemons (see note)
- 8 large eggs
- 1 cup (200 grams) sugar
- 8 tablespoons (1 stick / 113 grams) unsalted butter, cubed
- ¼ cup (60 milliliters) extra-virgin olive oil
- ⅛ teaspoon fine sea salt

Fleur de sel, for serving (optional)
Whipped crème fraîche, for serving (optional)

1. **Make the dough:** In a food processor, combine the flour, almond flour or sliced almonds, sugar, and salt; pulse to mix if using almond flour, or process until the nuts are finely ground if using sliced almonds. Add the butter and pulse just a few times to break the pieces into chickpea-size chunks. Drizzle in the beaten egg, then pulse until the dough comes together. If the dough seems very crumbly, add a little water, 1 tablespoon at a time, until it just holds together. Pat it into a 1-inch-thick disk and wrap it in plastic wrap. Chill in the refrigerator for at least 1 hour.

recipe continues

Curd: The curd will keep for up to a
week when stored in the fridge; cover
it with plastic wrap pressed directly
on the surface.

Crust: The dough can be made up
to 5 days ahead and stored, well
wrapped, in the fridge, or up to
1 month ahead and frozen. Thaw
frozen dough overnight in the
refrigerator.

Tart: For the crunchiest crust, serve
the tart within 12 hours of baking.

2. **Make the filling:** Grate the zest of 5 of the lemons and
   reserve it. Juice the zested lemons to make 1 cup juice;
   if you're a bit short, use the 6th lemon. (You'll need the
   zest of 5 lemons and 1 cup lemon juice.)

3. In a large heatproof bowl with a dish towel placed
   beneath it to hold it steady, whisk the eggs well. In a
   medium pot over medium heat, stir together the lemon
   zest, lemon juice, sugar, butter, oil, and fine sea salt.
   Once the mixture is simmering and the butter has
   melted, slowly pour or ladle about a third of the mixture
   into the eggs, whisking constantly, to temper them.
   Then return the egg-lemon mixture to the pot. Reduce
   the heat to medium-low and cook, stirring constantly
   with a heatproof spatula or a wooden spoon, until the
   curd thickens enough to coat the back of a spoon, about
   5 minutes. Strain it into a medium bowl and set it aside
   to cool.

4. When you are ready to bake the tart, roll the dough out
   on a lightly floured surface to form a 13-inch round,
   about ¼ inch thick. Line a 10-inch tart pan with the
   dough, trim the edges, and prick it all over with a fork.
   Chill the shell, uncovered, for 30 minutes.

5. Meanwhile, heat the oven to 350°F.

6. Line the tart shell with foil and baking weights (or dried
   beans or raw rice), and bake it for 15 minutes. Then
   remove the foil and weights and bake until the crust is
   golden brown, another 5 to 10 minutes. Transfer the tart
   pan to a wire rack and let the crust cool slightly, about
   5 minutes. Reduce the oven temperature to 325°F.

7. Scrape the curd into the tart shell, smoothing the top.
   Bake until the filling is set around the edges and jiggles
   only slightly in the center when the pan is shaken, 45
   to 55 minutes. The curd may brown slightly and that is
   okay, but cover the edges of the tart with foil if the crust
   starts to get *too* brown.

8. Transfer the tart to a wire rack and let it cool completely.
   Before serving, sprinkle the top with fleur de sel if you
   like. Serve the tart with crème fraîche if desired.

Blackberry Frangipane Tart

SERVES 8

You can use any berries in this summery tart, though I particularly love blackberries because they tend to be larger than raspberries and blueberries and look especially striking, like purple gems set into the soft almond filling that puffs up all around them.

If you'd rather use almond flour instead of whole almonds, you can; you'll need 150 grams, which is about 1½ cups. I've seen almond flour sold both blanched and unblanched, and if you have a choice, I'd go for the unblanched. Those bits of skin add a subtle rustic texture and complexity to the frangipane.

This tart doesn't need an accompaniment—it can hold its own on the plate—but if you can't resist adding a little something, a scoop of berry or lemon sorbet would adorn it well.

FOR THE CRUST

8 tablespoons (1 stick / 113 grams) unsalted butter, room temperature

¼ cup (50 grams) sugar

Large pinch of fine sea salt

1 large egg yolk

1¼ cups (162 grams) all-purpose flour

FOR THE FILLING

1 cup (140 grams) whole raw (unblanched) almonds

¾ cup (150 grams) sugar

2 tablespoons (32 grams) all-purpose flour

Large pinch of fine sea salt

12 tablespoons (1½ sticks / 170 grams) unsalted butter, room temperature

3 large eggs

1 tablespoon brandy

¼ teaspoon almond extract

1½ cups (6 ounces) fresh blackberries

Sliced almonds, for garnish

1. **Make the crust:** In the bowl of an electric mixer fitted with the paddle attachment, cream the butter, sugar, and salt together until fluffy, about 3 minutes. Beat in the egg yolk, scraping the sides of the bowl as necessary. Add the flour and mix until just combined. Pat the dough into a 1-inch-thick disk, wrap it in plastic wrap, and chill it for at least 1 hour.

2. Between two pieces of parchment or waxed paper, roll the dough out to form a 12-inch round, ¼ inch thick. Remove the paper and transfer the dough to a 10-inch tart pan, pressing the dough into the edges and up the sides. Trim

recipe continues

Thinking Ahead

Crust: The dough can be made up to 5 days ahead, wrapped in plastic wrap, and stored in the fridge, or up to 1 month ahead and frozen. Thaw frozen dough overnight in the refrigerator.

Filling: The frangipane filling can be made up to 3 days ahead and refrigerated, covered. Let it come to room temperature before using.

Tart: For the crunchiest crust, serve the tart within 12 hours of baking.

the top, prick the dough all over with a fork, and then chill the shell, uncovered, for at least 30 minutes.

3. Heat the oven to 375°F.

4. Line the tart shell with foil and fill it with pie weights (or dried beans or raw rice). Bake for 17 minutes. Then remove the pie weights and foil and continue to bake until the crust is pale golden, another 5 to 10 minutes.

5. **Meanwhile, make the filling:** In a food processor, process the almonds, sugar, flour, and salt until finely ground. Pulse in the butter, scrape the sides of the bowl with a spatula, and then pulse in the eggs, brandy, and almond extract. Process until smooth.

6. Scrape the filling into the tart shell, smoothing the top (it's okay if the crust is still warm when you do this). Arrange the blackberries over the top, then sprinkle sliced almonds around the edges. Return the tart to the 375°F oven and bake until the filling is puffed and golden, 40 to 50 minutes. Transfer the tart to a wire rack to cool completely before serving.

Peach Cobbler Tatin

SERVES 8

This whimsical confection takes the syrupy fruit and biscuit crust of a peach cobbler and quite literally turns it on its head, *tarte Tatin*–style. To make it, the peaches are caramelized with sugar in a skillet, just the way apples are in a classic *tarte Tatin*. But then, instead of covering the fruit with pie dough or puff pastry, I top it with fluffy biscuit dough. While it's baking, the dough rises and browns and creates a golden, tender pillow on which the jammy fruit lands when it's all unmolded. The whole thing is a bit more cakelike in texture than the usual crisp-crusted *Tatin*, and it has the juicy allure of ripe fresh peaches. Both sophisticated and homey, it's a hybrid confection unlike any other.

FOR THE BISCUITS

2½ cups (325 grams) all-purpose flour, plus more for rolling

6 tablespoons (75 grams) granulated sugar

1 tablespoon plus 1 teaspoon (16 grams) baking powder

1 teaspoon baking soda

¼ teaspoon fine sea salt

8 tablespoons (1 stick / 113 grams) cold unsalted butter, cubed

1 cup (240 milliliters) plus 1 tablespoon (15 milliliters) heavy cream, divided

2 tablespoons (25 grams) Demerara or raw sugar

FOR THE FILLING

¾ cup (150 grams) granulated sugar

Pinch of fine sea salt

1 teaspoon honey

4 tablespoons (½ stick / 56 grams) unsalted butter, cut into pieces, room temperature

6 to 7 small ripe peaches (2 pounds), halved and pitted

Crème fraîche, for serving

1. **Make the biscuit dough:** Place a piece of parchment or wax paper on a small rimmed baking sheet or a large plate.

2. In a food processor, pulse together the flour, sugar, baking powder, baking soda, and salt. Pulse in the butter just until the mixture looks like lima beans. Drizzle in 1 cup cream and pulse just to combine. (Alternatively, you can do this in a bowl, cutting the butter into the flour mixture with a pastry cutter or two knives, then mixing in the cream.)

3. Transfer the dough to a lightly floured surface and pat it together, incorporating any stray or dry pieces. Divide the dough into 8 equal pieces and roll them into balls. Transfer the dough balls to the parchment-lined baking

sheet or plate, and flatten the balls into ¾-inch-thick
disks; cover the baking sheet loosely with plastic wrap
or another overturned baking sheet, and chill it for at
least 20 minutes.

Thinking Ahead

Caramel: You can make the caramel up to 6 hours ahead; just leave it in the skillet. It will harden, but that's okay—just heat it up on the stove until it melts.

Biscuit dough: You can prepare the disks of biscuit dough up to 6 hours ahead; store them on the baking sheet in the fridge until you're ready to bake the *Tatin*.

4. Heat the oven to 350°F.

5. **Prepare the filling:** In a 9-inch nonstick ovenproof skillet, combine ¼ cup water with the sugar, sea salt, and honey. Bring the mixture to a boil, stirring. Then stop stirring and continue to simmer, swirling the pan occasionally, until the caramel is the deep amber-brown color of an Irish setter, 4 to 8 minutes.

6. Remove the skillet from the heat and whisk in the butter (stand back—the caramel may bubble up and splatter).

7. Arrange the peaches, cut-side up, in the skillet, placing them as close together as possible. Top with the biscuits. Brush the biscuits with the remaining 1 tablespoon cream, then sprinkle them with the Demerara sugar.

8. Place the skillet on a rimmed baking sheet (to catch any overflowing filling), and bake until the biscuits are golden brown, 45 to 55 minutes. Remove the skillet from the oven and let it cool slightly. Then carefully flip the tart onto a serving platter, replacing any peaches that stuck to the skillet. Note that the tart will come out most easily if it's still a bit hot when you flip it. Serve warm, within 2 hours of baking, with crème fraîche.

Using apricots instead of apples in a *tarte Tatin* transforms an inherently autumnal dessert into the very essence of summer. To keep things on the simpler side (relative to *Tatin*), I use purchased puff pastry here instead of making my own crust. I love the buttery, crunchy bits that shatter when you bite down, contrasting with the honeyed fruit. A few sprigs of fresh thyme add a lovely herbal perfume to the apricots, but if you don't have them, you can leave them out or substitute lemon zest. This tart really benefits from something creamy served alongside. A bit of whipped cream or crème fraîche, or ice cream, will melt and mingle with the caramel, creating a rich and lovely sauce.

See photograph on **page 256**.

Apricot Tarte Tatin

SERVES 8

¾ cup (150 grams) sugar

1 teaspoon honey

Pinch of fine sea salt

4 tablespoons (½ stick / 56 grams) unsalted butter, room temperature

4 sprigs fresh thyme, preferably lemon thyme (or use ½ teaspoon finely grated lemon zest)

All-purpose flour, for rolling

1 sheet or square all-butter puff pastry, thawed if frozen (about 9 to 14 ounces; brands vary)

7 to 8 apricots (18 ounces), halved and pitted

Crème fraîche or whipped cream, or ice cream, for serving (optional)

1. Heat the oven to 425°F.

2. In a 9-inch ovenproof skillet, combine ¼ cup water with the sugar, honey, and salt. Bring the mixture to a boil; then reduce the heat and simmer, swirling the pan occasionally, until the sugar is caramelized and is the deep amber-brown color of an Irish setter, 4 to 8 minutes.

3. Remove the skillet from the heat and whisk in the butter (the caramel may bubble up and splatter, so stand back). Then stir in the thyme sprigs. Let the mixture sit while you prepare the puff pastry.

4. On a lightly floured surface, roll the pastry to form an 11-inch round about ⅛ inch thick, trimming it if necessary (it may have started out as a rectangle). Arrange the apricots, cut-side up, in the skillet atop the caramel, placing them as close together as possible. Drape the pastry over the apricots and then tuck the edges of the pastry into the skillet. Prick the pastry all over with the tip of a knife.

5. Place the skillet on a rimmed baking sheet (to catch any overflowing filling), and bake until the pastry is browned and puffed, 30 to 35 minutes. Remove the skillet from the oven and let the tart cool slightly. Then run a butter knife or an offset spatula around the outer edge of the pastry to unstick it from the pan. Carefully flip the tart onto a serving platter, replacing any apricots that stuck to the pan. Note that the tart will come out most easily if it's still a bit hot when you flip it.

6. Serve the tart warm or at room temperature (within 6 hours of baking), drizzled with the caramel from the skillet, and topped with crème fraîche, whipped cream, or ice cream if you like.

Thinking Ahead

Caramel: You can make the caramel up to 6 hours ahead; just leave it in the skillet. It will harden, but that's okay— just heat it up on the stove until it melts.

Pastry: You can roll the pastry out up to 6 hours ahead; store it on a cookie sheet in the fridge until you're ready to use it.

Pumpkin Brûlée Tart with Crème Fraîche

SERVES 8

Pumpkin pie is not a traditional dessert in France, but if it were, I'd imagine an Escoffier-elegant confection like this one. It has a sweet shortbread crust, an ultra-creamy pumpkin custard gently spiced with nutmeg, cardamom, and vanilla, and, to cap it all off, a candy-like layer of burnt sugar that crunches when you take a bite before it instantly melts on your tongue. If you don't want to brûlée this tart, you can skip that step; the tart is still excellent, even without the glossy sugar topping. Serve it with whipped crème fraîche or vanilla ice cream.

FOR THE CRUST

12 tablespoons (1½ sticks / 170 grams) unsalted butter, room temperature, plus more for the foil

½ cup (60 grams) confectioners' sugar

1 large egg yolk

½ teaspoon vanilla extract

¼ teaspoon fine sea salt

1¾ cups (227 grams) all-purpose flour, plus more for rolling

FOR THE FILLING

1 cup (225 grams) pumpkin purée

⅔ cup (152 grams) crème fraîche

⅓ cup (79 milliliters) heavy cream

Scant ½ cup (90 grams) dark brown sugar

4 large egg yolks

1¼ teaspoons ground cardamom

1½ teaspoons vanilla extract

⅛ teaspoon fine sea salt

⅛ teaspoon freshly grated nutmeg

2 tablespoons (25 grams) granulated sugar, for the brûlée

1. **Make the crust:** In the bowl of an electric mixer fitted with the paddle attachment, cream the butter and confectioners' sugar until smooth. Beat in the egg yolk, vanilla, and salt, scraping the sides of the bowl as necessary. Mix in the flour until just combined. Form the dough into a 1-inch-thick disk, wrap it in plastic wrap, and refrigerate it for at least 1 hour.

2. On a lightly floured surface, roll the dough out to form a 12-inch, ¼-inch-thick round. Transfer it to a 10-inch tart pan, pressing it into the bottom and sides. Trim the excess dough away, then push the sides up ¼ inch above the rim of the tart pan. Prick the dough all over with a fork, and chill it, uncovered, for at least 30 minutes.

Crust: The dough can be made up to 5 days ahead, wrapped in plastic wrap, and stored in the fridge, or up to 1 month ahead and frozen. Thaw frozen dough overnight in the refrigerator.

Tart: The tart can be baked up to 12 hours ahead, but don't brûlée the top until just before serving.

3. Heat the oven to 375°F.

4. Butter a piece of foil and press it, buttered-side down, onto the tart crust. Top the foil with pie weights (or dried beans or raw rice). Transfer the tart pan to a rimmed baking sheet and bake for 15 minutes. Then remove the foil and pie weights and bake until the crust is lightly golden, about another 10 minutes. Transfer the tart pan to a wire rack and let it cool while you make the filling. Reduce the oven temperature to 325°F.

5. **Make the filling:** In a large bowl, whisk together the pumpkin purée, crème fraîche, cream, brown sugar, egg yolks, cardamom, vanilla, salt, and nutmeg.

6. Pour the filling into the crust (it can be cooled or warm), return it to the oven, and bake until the edges are set but the center is still wobbly, 30 to 35 minutes. Turn off the oven, prop the oven door open about 1 inch by sticking the handle of a wooden spoon between the door and the oven, and let the tart cool in the oven for 1 hour (this will gently finish its cooking). Then remove the tart from the oven and continue to let it cool to room temperature.

7. When you're ready to serve the tart, sprinkle the granulated sugar evenly over the top. Use a kitchen torch or the broiler to melt and evenly brown the sugar (some black spots are okay). Serve immediately.

Hazelnut Dacquoise with Coffee-Cardamom Buttercream

A hazelnut dacquoise from Julia Child's *Mastering the Art of French Cooking* was the first "fancy" cake I ever made, for my father's birthday. It was quite an undertaking. I had to toast whole hazelnuts, rub the skins off in a dish towel, grind them in a food processor in batches so they wouldn't turn to butter, and then press them through a sieve. And that was just to make the nut flour for the batter! I also had to beat egg whites to make a meringue, whip together a coffee buttercream, and, to decorate the top of the cake, dip blanched almonds and hazelnuts in chocolate. I think there were dried apricots involved, too, and I recall trying, and failing, to candy mint leaves from the garden. Nevertheless, it was a huge hit, and I remember being very pleased with my sixteen-year-old self.

This is a much simpler version, using purchased hazelnut flour, which is getting easier to find. And instead of dipping whole nuts in chocolate, I decorate the buttercream with chocolate coffee beans. It's still a stunning, elegant cake worthy of your father's birthday—or some other occasion just as celebratory.

FOR THE HAZELNUT DACQUOISE

- ¾ cup (150 grams) sugar
- 1 cup (100 grams) hazelnut flour (see note, page 297)
- 1 tablespoon plus 1 teaspoon (16 grams) cornstarch
- ¾ teaspoon ground cardamom
- Large pinch of fine sea salt
- 5 large egg whites
- ¼ teaspoon cream of tartar

FOR THE BUTTERCREAM

- 5 large egg whites
- 1½ cups (300 grams) sugar
- ¼ teaspoon fine sea salt
- 2 cups (4 sticks / 454 grams) unsalted butter, cubed, room temperature
- ¾ teaspoon ground cardamom
- 1½ tablespoons instant espresso powder dissolved in 1½ tablespoons hot water

FOR THE GANACHE

- 3 ounces (85 grams) milk chocolate
- 3 ounces (85 grams) bittersweet chocolate (74% cacao)
- Pinch of fine sea salt
- ¼ teaspoon ground cardamom
- ¾ cup (175 milliliters) heavy cream
- Chocolate coffee beans, for decoration (optional)

1. **First, make the dacquoise:** Heat the oven to 275°F and line an 11 × 17-inch rimmed baking sheet with parchment paper.

recipe continues

Dacquoise: The dacquoise can be baked 1 day ahead. Store it, wrapped airtight, at room temperature.

Buttercream: You can make the buttercream up to 5 days ahead. If you are storing it for 24 hours or less, leave it at a cool room temperature. For longer storage, or if your kitchen is very hot, cover and chill it. You will likely have to re-beat it before using. Bring the chilled buttercream to room temperature before re-beating. Cold buttercream won't beat up nicely.

Ganache: You can make the ganache up to 1 week ahead. Store it, covered, for up to 2 days at a cool room temperature. For longer storage, or if it's very hot in your kitchen, cover the ganache and chill it. Let it come to room temperature before using.

Assembled cake: Serve this cake within 12 hours of assembling it. After that, the dacquoise can start to get soggy, though it still tastes great.

2. In a medium bowl, whisk together the sugar, hazelnut flour, cornstarch, cardamom, and salt.

3. In the bowl of an electric mixer fitted with the whisk attachment, beat the egg whites with the cream of tartar on high speed until the mixture forms stiff peaks. Using a rubber spatula, fold a third of the hazelnut mixture into the whites, taking care not to deflate them. Gently fold in another third of the hazelnut mixture, and then fold in the remaining hazelnut mixture. Do not overmix—a few white streaks are okay.

4. Transfer the meringue to a large resealable plastic bag and snip off a ½-inch corner (or use a pastry bag). Leaving a 1-inch border around the edge of the prepared baking sheet, pipe the batter, forming the outline of a rectangle inside the baking sheet. Then pipe batter in the center of the rectangle. Use an offset spatula to lightly and gently smooth the top (don't press down or you'll deflate the meringue).

5. Bake until the meringue is firm, dry, and golden brown, 1½ to 2 hours. Transfer the pan to a wire rack and let the dacquoise cool completely.

6. To unmold, run an offset spatula between the meringue and the parchment paper and lift the meringue onto a cutting board. Use a serrated knife to cut the rectangle crosswise into thirds, so that each piece measures about 5¼ × 10 inches (you'll want to be able to stack them on top of one another later).

7. **Next, make the buttercream:** Fill a medium pot with 1 inch of water and bring it to a simmer. In the heatproof bowl of an electric mixer, combine the egg whites, sugar, and salt. Then balance the mixer bowl on the pot of simmering water, and using a pot holder to hold the bowl steady with one hand, whisk with the other hand until the mixture reaches 140°F and the sugar has completely melted. You can also use a hand mixer. (If you don't have a thermometer, rub some of the whites between your fingers; it shouldn't burn, and there shouldn't be any grit, indicating that the sugar is dissolved.) Transfer the bowl to the electric mixer, fit it with the whisk attachment, and beat the whites on high

speed until they are fluffy and reach room temperature, about 5 minutes. (You can also do this using a double boiler and a handheld mixer.)

8. One cube at a time, beat in the butter. Then beat in the cardamom and the dissolved instant espresso until combined.

9. **Finally, make the ganache:** Place both chocolates, the salt, and the cardamom in a heatproof bowl. In a medium pot or in a bowl in the microwave, bring the cream to a simmer. Pour the cream over the chocolate and let it sit for 1 minute. Then whisk until the mixture is melted and smooth. Let the ganache cool thoroughly at room temperature until you are ready to assemble the dacquoise.

10. To assemble, spread a scant ½ cup ganache over one of the dacquoise rectangles. Top it with a generous ½ cup buttercream, then repeat the dacquoise/ganache/ buttercream layers two more times, stacking them on top of one another. Spread the remaining buttercream all over the top and sides of the cake.

11. If you want to be fancy, you can decorate the top of the cake with more buttercream piped through a pastry bag (or you can keep it simple and store the remaining buttercream in the freezer and use it to top cupcakes at some later date). Garnish the cake all over with the chocolate coffee beans if you like. Use a serrated knife to cut and serve cake.

NOTE: If you can't find hazelnut flour, you can grind your own peeled hazelnuts in a food processor. To do so, it's best to weigh the nuts (you'll need 100 grams), then pulse them with 2 tablespoons of the sugar until finely ground. Make sure not to overdo it, though—you don't want to end up with hazelnut paste.

Jam-Filled Sablés

MAKES ABOUT 30 COOKIES

The word *sablé* means "sandy" in French, and that perfectly describes the texture of these crumbly butter cookies with their deeply browned edges. What sets *sablés* apart from other shortbread cookies is the European-style butter used for the dough. European butter is richer than American supermarket butter in two distinct ways. The first is a higher butterfat content mandated to be at least 82 percent, as compared to 80 percent in the United States. And the second is the flavor. European butter has been cultured, meaning that instead of being churned from mild, sweet cream, it's made from cultured cream (like crème fraîche), which has a nuttier, tangier character. While you can make *sablés* with regular supermarket butter (they will still be delicious), using the good stuff gives them a more complex flavor.

Thinking Ahead

Dough: The dough can be made up to 3 days ahead and stored in the refrigerator, or frozen for up to 2 months. Thaw it overnight in the fridge.

Cookies: These are best eaten within a week of baking. Store them in an airtight container at room temperature.

1 cup (2 sticks / 226 grams) salted European-style (cultured) butter, such as Kerry Gold, room temperature

⅔ cup (70 grams) confectioners' sugar

1 large egg yolk

½ tablespoon finely grated lemon zest

1 teaspoon vanilla extract

⅛ teaspoon fine sea salt

2½ cups (325 grams) all-purpose flour

About 3 tablespoons thick jam (any kind)

1. In the bowl of an electric mixer fitted with the paddle attachment, cream the butter and confectioners' sugar together until smooth. Beat in the egg yolk, lemon zest, vanilla, and salt, scraping the sides of the bowl as necessary. Mix in the flour until just combined. Form the dough into a 1-inch-thick disk, wrap it in plastic wrap, and refrigerate it for at least 1 hour.

2. Between two sheets of parchment or waxed paper, roll the dough out ¼ inch thick. Leaving the dough between the pieces of parchment, transfer it to a baking sheet and chill it for 30 minutes, or until firm.

3. Heat the oven to 325°F and line two cookie sheets with parchment paper.

4. Remove the top parchment from the dough and, using a 2-inch round cutter, cut out cookies and transfer them to the prepared cookie sheets. (Reserve the scraps of dough and chill them to reroll later.) Press your thumb in the center of each cookie to make a shallow indentation, and fill it with about ¼ teaspoon of the jam (don't overfill the indentation or the jam might leak out). Reroll the chilled dough scraps and repeat.

5. Bake for 18 to 25 minutes, until the cookies are puffed and deeply golden, rotating the cookie sheets halfway through. Transfer the cookies to wire racks to cool.

Melon
with Sauternes

SERVES 4

---

2 small ripe Cavaillon or other melons, halved and seeded, at room temperature

Sauternes or other dessert wine, as needed, chilled

This isn't really a recipe, it's a PSA: pouring chilled sweet wine into the cavity of a succulent, juicy melon is about as perfect as dessert gets without having to do any work. I first had the combination in a little restaurant in a garden in Provence, and now it's what pops into my head whenever I hear the word *ambrosia* (which, as the mother of a Greek myths–obsessed child, is more often than you might think). When your melons are so ripe that you can smell them from across the kitchen, make this for dessert.

You can use any sweet wine here. A fortified wine such as Marsala or Port will also work nicely. Just make sure the wine is cold and the melon is at room temperature.

Fill the cavities of the melons with wine and serve one melon half to each guest, with soup spoons for eating. I like to serve these in deep plates or soup bowls to catch any overflowing wine.

Apricots and Red Fruit with Sugared Crème Fraîche

SERVES 4 TO 6

This is another not-really-a-recipe recipe that's all about flaunting a gorgeous array of ripe summer fruit. Here, a combination of berries, currants, and apricots gets piled onto a platter and topped with thick dollops of crème fraîche and a sprinkling of granulated sugar, which gives it all a pleasingly gritty crunch. Feel free to change up the fruit: anything juicy will work—peaches, blackberries, plums, pomegranate. The goal is for the sweet fruit juices to mingle with the tart richness of the cream in every mouthful.

Serve this as dessert with *sablés* (page 299) or other crisp cookies on the side, or all by itself for breakfast, substituting Greek yogurt for the crème fraîche if you really think you must.

6 ripe apricots, halved and pitted

½ cup (160 grams) small strawberries, halved (or quarter larger ones)

½ cup (60 grams) raspberries

½ cup (100 grams) red currants

About 1 cup (8 ounces/227 grams) crème fraîche

Sugar, as needed

Tiny sprigs fresh mint or lemon verbena, for garnish (optional)

1. Arrange the apricots on a serving platter and strew the red fruit all around them.

2. Dollop the fruit liberally with the crème fraîche, then sprinkle all over with the sugar. This is dessert, so be generous. Garnish with mint or lemon verbena sprigs if you like. Serve immediately.

Strawberry Champagne Soup with Fleur de Sel Meringues and Mint

SERVES 4 TO 6

As a child, I never understood the allure of cold fruit soups, which always struck me as glorified smoothies served up in a bowl. But as an adult, I've learned that spiking a bright and tangy fruit purée with champagne moves it away from any breakfast associations and into the realm of stunning, sophisticated desserts. This one is especially fancy, with its garnish of sliced strawberries that have been macerated in mint simple syrup and its fleur de sel–topped meringues dotting the surface. The mint syrup is the key to flavor here, adding a subtle but fragrant herbal note to the mix. Making your own fleur de sel–sprinkled meringues adds a particular sweet-salty nuance to the bowls of berry soup. But crushed store-bought meringues are easier and taste nearly as good if you sprinkle everything with a few grains of flaky sea salt right before serving.

FOR THE MERINGUES

2 large (60 grams) egg whites

Pinch of cream of tartar

Pinch of fine sea salt

½ cup (100 grams) sugar

Fleur de sel, as needed

FOR THE SOUP

½ cup (100 grams) sugar

⅓ cup (7 grams) fresh mint leaves, plus more for serving

2 pounds (910 grams) strawberries, hulled and sliced, divided

1 bottle (750 milliliters) inexpensive champagne or other sparkling wine

Toasted sliced almonds, for serving

1. Heat the oven to 275°F and line a cookie sheet with parchment paper.

2. **Make the meringues:** In the bowl of an electric mixer fitted with the whisk attachment, beat the egg whites, cream of tartar, and fine sea salt on medium-high speed until frothy, about 1 minute. Gradually add the sugar, 1 tablespoon at a time, and keep whipping until the meringue forms medium-stiff peaks.

3. Transfer the meringue to a piping bag (or use two tablespoons) and form 16 golf ball–size meringues on the prepared cookie sheet. Sprinkle the meringues with fleur de sel.

recipe continues

Thinking Ahead

Meringues: The meringues can be made up to 5 days ahead. Store them in an airtight container at room temperature.

Simple syrup: The mint simple syrup can be made up to 2 weeks in advance. Store it in a covered container in the fridge.

Strawberry purée: You can make the strawberry purée up to 3 days ahead and store it in a covered container in the fridge. It can also be frozen for up to 1 month.

4. Transfer the cookie sheet to the oven and immediately reduce the oven temperature to 225°F. Bake until the meringues are no longer tacky, 60 to 70 minutes. Then turn off the oven and let the meringues cool completely in the oven (this can take 2 to 4 hours, or you can leave them in overnight).

5. **Meanwhile, make the soup:** In a small pot, combine ½ cup of water with the sugar and mint leaves. Bring to a boil, stirring to dissolve the sugar, then reduce the heat and simmer for 5 minutes. Remove the mint simple syrup from the heat and let it cool completely; then strain it into a medium bowl.

6. In a blender, combine approximately two-thirds of the strawberries (save the prettiest ones for serving) with ¼ cup of the strained simple syrup. Blend until the mixture is completely smooth. Taste, and add more simple syrup if it's not quite sweet enough. Strain, and chill for at least 1 hour.

7. When you're ready to serve the strawberry soup, slice or quarter the reserved strawberries and stir them gently into the bowl containing the remaining simple syrup; set it aside to macerate while you prepare the servings of soup.

8. Divide the strawberry purée among serving bowls or coupes. Gently stir in champagne to taste. Float the meringues on top (you can crush them or leave them whole), and garnish with the macerated strawberries, fresh mint leaves, and toasted almonds.

Crème Fraîche Crème Caramels

SERVES 8

Adding crème fraîche to an otherwise classic crème caramel gives a distinct tang that helps mitigate the sweetness of the caramel syrup coating each wobbly custard. Be sure to cook the caramel until it's deep amber— you're looking for something that resembles the dark glossy coat of an Irish setter. It should taste sweet but balanced with an appealing bitter edge. Serve these flan-like puddings with crisp cookies for a contrasting crunch. I especially like the Black Sesame Palmiers (page 273) with these; their nutty bitterness pairs nicely with the flavor of the caramel.

2 cups (16 ounces/454 grams) crème fraîche, plus more for serving (optional)

1 cup (240 milliliters) heavy cream

1 cup (240 milliliters) whole milk

1¼ cups (225 grams) sugar, divided

1 vanilla bean, split lengthwise, seeds scraped out with the tip of a knife, pod and seeds reserved

2 whole eggs

5 large egg yolks

Pinch of fine sea salt

½ teaspoon honey

1. In a medium pot, whisk together the crème fraîche, cream, milk, and ½ cup of the sugar. Stir in the vanilla bean and the seeds. Bring to a simmer, then remove the pot from the heat and let the mixture steep for at least 30 minutes. Then return it to the heat and bring the liquid back to a simmer.

2. Meanwhile, in a large bowl, whisk together the eggs, yolks, salt, and ¼ cup of the sugar until smooth. Whisking constantly, gradually pour the hot crème fraîche mixture into the egg mixture, a little at a time, until it is completely combined. Immediately strain the custard into a container. Cover it with plastic wrap and chill it for at least 2 hours.

3. Place a rack in the center of the oven and heat the oven to 325°F. Have eight 6-ounce ramekins at the ready next to the stove.

4. In a small saucepan or skillet, combine the remaining ½ cup sugar, 2 tablespoons of water, and the honey and heat the mixture over high heat. Tilt the pan occasionally to evenly distribute the melting sugar; once it begins to bubble, reduce the heat to medium. Cook,

recipe continues

swirling the pan, until the mixture is a uniformly deep amber color, the color of an Irish setter, 5 to 10 minutes. You can best see the caramel color by spooning a little onto a white plate, so keep one handy.

5. When the caramel is the right color, working quickly, pour a little of it into a ramekin (just enough to cover the bottom). Tilt the ramekin immediately so that the caramel covers the bottom and some of the sides. Repeat with the remaining seven ramekins. Then pour in the custard, dividing it evenly among the ramekins.

6. Arrange the ramekins in a roasting pan and place the pan on the oven rack. Pour enough hot tap water into the roasting pan to reach two-thirds of the way up the sides of the ramekins. Cover the roasting pan tightly with foil and prick the foil all over with a paring knife to allow the steam to escape. Bake the custards for 30 minutes.

7. Pull back a corner of the foil to allow steam to escape (this keeps it from condensing on the underside of the foil and dripping back onto the custards). Re-cover the pan and continue to bake until the custards are set at the edges but jiggle just slightly in the center when shaken, 15 to 20 minutes longer. Transfer the ramekins to a wire rack and let them cool to room temperature. Then cover each one with plastic wrap and refrigerate them for at least 8 hours or overnight.

8. To unmold the crème caramels, run a small knife around the side of each ramekin, then invert the crème caramels onto dessert plates. Serve them with whipped crème fraîche if you like.

Gingerbread Mousse

SERVES 4 TO 6

I learned how to make this from my friend Eliane in Paris, who was like an aunt to me when I was studying in France. She invited me over to her chic fifth-floor walk-up on the Ile de la Cité for many meals that year, and introduced me to the French art of semi-homemade, which is of a whole other character than the American kind. I remember her once making a fabulous dessert from a piece of leftover spice cake (*pain d'épices*) and a pint of vanilla ice cream, mixed together into a glorious frozen parfait. This easy, fluffy mousse—essentially a mix of sweetened whipped crème fraîche and chopped-up spice cake—is my version of that dessert. If you're ambitious, you can make the *pain d'épices* yourself, but using store-bought soft gingerbread (or ginger cake) also works perfectly and is more in keeping with the original spirit of the confection. I also add chopped nougat and candied ginger for sweetness and crunch. If you can't get good nougat (or *torrone*, the Italian version), you can substitute ½ cup shaved milk chocolate or ½ cup chopped chocolate-covered almonds or hazelnuts. It's a completely different flavor, but it still adds the needed sweetness and texture.

FOR THE MOUSSE

1 cup (8 ounces / 227 grams) crème fraîche

1 cup (240 milliliters) heavy cream

2 tablespoons (15 grams) confectioners' sugar

1 teaspoon cognac

2 teaspoons vanilla extract

Tiny pinch of fine sea salt

FOR ASSEMBLING

5.25 ounces (150 grams; about ¼ of a homemade loaf) soft gingerbread or *pain d'épices* (purchased or homemade; see page 263), torn into pieces (about 2 cups)

2 tablespoons (30 grams) chopped crystallized ginger

¾ cup (80 grams) chopped soft nougat or *torrone*

Full-flavored honey, such as chestnut or lavender, for drizzling

1. **Make the mousse:** In the bowl of an electric mixer fitted with the whisk attachment, whip the crème fraîche, cream, confectioners' sugar, cognac, vanilla, and salt until medium peaks form.

2. **Assemble the dessert:** Crumble some of the gingerbread between your fingers (you want a combination of crumbs and bite-size pieces). Gently fold the cake and the ginger into the whipped mixture.

3. Serve the mousse in parfait or wineglasses or in small bowls, topped with the nougat and a drizzle of honey.

Thinking Ahead

Gingerbread mousse: This can be made up to 24 hours in advance; cover and refrigerate it.

Raspberry-Lavender Clafouti

SERVES 6 TO 8

Cherries are the classic fruit for a clafouti, and they're usually stirred into the batter unpitted, for ease of preparation. Here I use raspberries for the custardy baked pancake instead. They are softer than the cherries, but juicier, too, and meld nicely with the touch of lavender that I also add. It's a simple, casual sweet that can be pulled together in minutes and is lovely served either as a homey dessert or for an elegant brunch.

Thinking Ahead

Clafouti: This clafouti is best served within an hour of baking, while it's still soft and warm; but it is still quite good within 6 hours of baking (keep it at room temperature). Leftovers (stored in the fridge overnight) make a great breakfast when topped with yogurt and more berries.

Unsalted butter, for the baking dish

3 cups (350 grams) raspberries

½ cup plus 1 tablespoon (112 grams) granulated sugar, divided

1 teaspoon dried lavender buds

½ cup (120 milliliters) whole milk

½ cup (4 ounces / 114 grams) crème fraîche, plus more for serving (optional)

4 large eggs

Pinch of fine sea salt

⅓ cup (43 grams) all-purpose flour

Confectioners' sugar, for serving

1. Heat the oven to 375°F. Butter a 9-inch ceramic baking dish, a 2-quart gratin dish, or a 9-inch cake pan.

2. In a medium bowl, toss the raspberries with the 1 tablespoon sugar. Let them sit while you prepare the remaining ingredients.

3. In a food processor or blender, combine the remaining ½ cup sugar with the lavender; process until the lavender is mostly ground, about 2 minutes. Then pour in the milk, crème fraîche, eggs, and salt, and process to combine. Add the flour and pulse just to combine.

4. Arrange the sugared berries in the prepared baking dish, then scrape the egg mixture over them. Bake until the cake is golden and the center springs back when lightly touched, about 35 minutes.

5. Transfer the baking dish to a wire rack and let the cake cool for at least 15 minutes before serving. Then dust it with confectioners' sugar, slice it, and serve it with dollops of whipped crème fraîche if you like.

Lemon Verbena Ice Cream with Candied Lemon

MAKES ABOUT 2 PINTS

1 cup (240 milliliters) heavy cream
1 cup (240 milliliters) whole milk
1¼ cups (250 grams) sugar, divided
¾ cup (20 grams) fresh lemon verbena leaves
¼ teaspoon fine sea salt
3 large egg yolks
1 cup (8 ounces / 227 grams) crème fraîche
3 organic lemons

Once I began growing a lemon verbena plant on my deck a few years ago, I started infusing the citrusy leaves into pretty much any liquid that needed a vibrant boost—teas, syrups, custards, and fragrant ice creams like this one. The fresh leaves add a much zippier, stronger flavor than their dried counterpart and are worth seeking out—or growing yourself. If you can't get fresh lemon verbena, this recipe also works with fresh mint, and though mint lacks the citrus element of verbena, the candied lemon zest supplies the needed brightness. If you'd rather not make the candied lemon zest, you can leave it out. You'll get a milder, smoother ice cream without any of the chewy bits of citrus, but it's still delightful.

1. In a saucepan, combine the cream, milk, ¾ cup (150 grams) of the sugar, the lemon verbena leaves, and salt, and bring to a simmer. Remove the pan from the heat, cover, and let it steep for 1 hour.

2. Whisk the egg yolks in a medium bowl. Bring the steeped cream mixture back to a simmer over medium heat, and then slowly, whisking constantly, pour about half of it into the yolks to temper them. Pour the yolk mixture into the saucepan containing the remaining cream and cook, stirring constantly, over medium-low heat until the custard has thickened enough to coat the back of a spoon, about 5 minutes. Stir in the crème fraîche until smooth, and then strain the mixture through a fine-mesh sieve into a container, pressing on the verbena leaves. Cover and refrigerate for at least 4 hours, and preferably overnight.

3. Meanwhile, make the candied lemon zest: Use a vegetable peeler to peel thin strips from the lemons, trying to avoid peeling off the white pith underneath the yellow zest. (If some strips have a lot of pith, scrape the pith off with the side of a spoon.)

4. Transfer the zest strips to a small saucepan, add enough water to cover them by 1 inch, and bring it to a vigorous boil. Drain, and repeat this blanching one more time to remove some of the bitterness.

5. Return the zest to the empty pan. Add ½ cup of water and the remaining ½ cup (100 grams) sugar. Bring to a boil over medium heat, reduce the heat, and simmer until the strips are translucent, 15 to 20 minutes. Drain and let cool; then slice into very narrow strips.

6. Churn the custard in an ice cream maker according to the manufacturer's instructions, stirring in the candied lemon zest in the last minute of churning. Serve immediately, or transfer to an airtight container and freeze until hard.

Some people love chocolate, others love vanilla, but I'm crazy about chestnut, especially earthy, autumnal chestnut ice cream. This one, loaded with plenty of chestnut paste, has a particularly creamy, almost buttery texture that's smooth as silk. It's a sophisticated dessert that you can serve on its own or pair with scoops of the Darkest Chocolate Sorbet (page 318) or vanilla ice cream.

Chestnut and Armagnac Ice Cream

MAKES ABOUT 2 PINTS

2 cups (475 milliliters) whole milk

1 cup (240 milliliters) heavy cream

⅛ teaspoon fine sea salt

6 large egg yolks

¼ cup (50 grams) granulated sugar

1⅓ cups (352 grams) sweetened chestnut spread or paste

1 tablespoon Armagnac (or cognac or other aged brandy)

2 teaspoons vanilla extract

1. In a small pot over medium heat, bring the milk, cream, and salt to a simmer. In a heatproof bowl, whisk the egg yolks with the sugar. Whisking constantly, slowly pour about half of the hot cream mixture into the yolks to temper them. Then pour the yolk mixture into the pot containing the remaining cream. Return the pot to medium heat and cook, stirring constantly, until the custard has thickened enough to coat the back of a spoon, about 5 minutes.

2. Strain the custard through a fine-mesh sieve into a bowl. Whisk in 1 cup (264 grams) of the chestnut spread, the Armagnac, and the vanilla. Cover and chill for at least 4 hours or overnight.

3. Churn the custard in an ice cream machine according to the manufacturer's instructions. Scrape the ice cream into a container and dollop with the remaining ⅓ cup chestnut spread. Swirl the chestnut spread into the ice cream, then serve immediately or freeze.

Thinking Ahead

You can store the churned ice cream in the freezer for up to 1 week in advance.

Also shown: *Darkest Chocolate Sorbet*, page 318

Darkest Chocolate Sorbet

MAKES 1 SCANT QUART

This is about as close to fudge as chocolate sorbet gets, with a deep bittersweet flavor and a dense, almost chewy texture. The brown sugar adds a molasses note that accentuates the bitterness, and the combination of cocoa powder and chopped chocolate gives it body and depth. This one is for serious dark chocolate lovers only. Serve it plain or—as I adore it—with a fat dollop of unsweetened whipped cream on top.

See photograph on **page 317.**

Thinking Ahead

You can churn the sorbet and store it in the freezer up to 1 week in advance.

¾ cup (150 grams) granulated sugar

½ cup (100 grams) dark brown sugar

Pinch of fine sea salt

⅔ cup (65 grams) Dutch-process cocoa powder

8 ounces (227 grams) dark chocolate (at least 72% cacao), chopped

1 teaspoon vanilla extract

1. In a medium pot, combine the granulated sugar, brown sugar, salt, and 2½ cups (590 milliliters) of water and bring to a boil. Reduce the heat to a simmer and whisk in the cocoa powder. Cook, stirring occasionally, until the sugar has dissolved, about 5 minutes.

2. Meanwhile, place the chopped chocolate in a heatproof bowl. Pour the hot cocoa mixture on top. Let the mixture sit for 2 minutes to start melting the chocolate, then whisk until the chocolate is completely melted and the mixture is smooth.

3. Stir in the vanilla. If you want a perfectly silky sorbet, use an immersion blender (or transfer the mixture to a regular blender) to briefly blend the mixture and get rid of any chocolate lumps. You can skip this step if you don't mind a bit of chocolate chip–like texture in your sorbet. I like it both ways. Cover and chill for at least 4 hours and up to overnight.

4. Process the mixture in an ice cream machine according to the manufacturer's instructions. Serve immediately or freeze until hard.

Almond Milk Sorbet

MAKES 3 CUPS

These days, it's easy to buy all types of nut milk at any large supermarket. But making your own and churning it into sorbet is an entirely different experience. Fragrant and marzipan-y, yet not too sweet, almond milk sorbet is perfect for serving alongside cakes or crisp cookies or paired with scoops of chocolate sorbet for an understated dessert. For the best iced almond milk coffee you've ever had, drop scoops of the sorbet into glasses of cold brewed coffee. It also happens to be vegan, which isn't the case with all sorbets.

Thinking Ahead

You can churn the sorbet and store it in the freezer up to 1 week in advance.

1⅓ cups (185 grams) whole raw (unblanched) almonds
⅓ cup (65 grams) sugar
¼ cup (60 milliliters) light corn syrup
Few drops almond extract
Pinch of fine sea salt

1. Place the almonds in a medium bowl, add water to cover by at least 1 inch, cover the bowl, and let them soak overnight.

2. Drain the almonds and rinse them thoroughly. Place the nuts in a blender, add 2 cups (475 milliliters) of cold water, and process until smooth, 3 to 5 minutes. Strain the mixture through a fine-mesh strainer (or you can use a nut milk bag) into a bowl, pressing down on the solids; discard the solids.

3. In a small saucepan, combine half of the almond milk with the sugar and corn syrup. Bring the mixture to a simmer and stir until the sugar dissolves. Stir in the remaining almond milk, the almond extract, and salt. Transfer the mixture to a container and chill it for at least 3 hours, until very cold.

4. Churn the sorbet in an ice cream machine according to the manufacturer's instructions. Serve immediately or freeze until hard.

Marzipan Bonbons Two Ways: Rose and Lemon

MAKES 2 DOZEN BONBONS

Homemade marzipan is so easy to make and so much better tasting than the often stale candy you find in stores that there's really no reason to ever purchase the almondy stuff again. Plus you can flavor it in myriad ways, with liqueurs, extracts, elixirs, spices, and, in this case, rose water and/or citrus zest. If you can't decide which flavor you want to make, divide the marzipan mix and add ½ teaspoon lemon zest to one half and ½ teaspoon rose water to the other half. Or make a rose-lemon combination, adding both flavorings to the entire batch. If you don't feel like dipping these in chocolate, you can skip that step. But it really does add a pleasing bitterness next to the sweet, soft paste, as well as a slight crunch.

Thinking Ahead

You can make the bonbons up to 3 days in advance. Store them, covered, at room temperature.

1⅔ cups (200 grams) confectioners' sugar, plus more for kneading
1½ cups (145 grams) almond flour
1 large egg white
1 teaspoon rose water and/or finely grated lemon zest
Few drops almond extract
5 ounces (140 grams) bittersweet chocolate, chopped

1. In the bowl of an electric mixer fitted with the paddle attachment, beat together the confectioners' sugar, almond flour, egg white, rose water and/or lemon zest, and almond extract until it forms a smooth marzipan paste, about 2 minutes.

2. Turn the marzipan out onto a clean work surface. Dust the marzipan with additional confectioners' sugar if it seems very sticky, and knead it into a smooth log. Cut the log into 24 equal pieces. Roll each piece into a ball, working quickly before the mixture dries out. Leave the balls to dry, uncovered, at room temperature, at least 1 hour and up to overnight.

3. To dip the marzipan in chocolate, bring 1-inch of water to a boil in a medium pot. Put the chocolate in a heat-proof bowl, turn off the heat, and set it on top of the water. Let sit until half the chocolate melts, about 1 minute. Remove from the heat and stir until the remaining chocolate has melted and the chocolate is smooth. If needed, place the bowl over hot water again to make sure all the chocolate melts.

4. Dip each marzipan ball halfway into the chocolate, then shake off excess and place on parchment paper. Let the chocolate set at room temperature for at least 4 hours before serving.

Lavender Lemonade

SERVES 4 TO 6

Lemon and lavender is one of those perfect grows-together-goes-together combinations, with the acidity of the lemon taming any potentially cloying floral aspects of the lavender. Here they work in harmony, with the lavender adding a high note and a heady perfume to what would otherwise be a standard-issue summer beverage. Serve this as is to groups of all ages, or spike it with a little gin to make a grown-up cocktail that's a taste of summer in an icy glass.

4 large lemons

⅔ cup (130 grams) sugar, plus more to taste

6 sprigs fresh lavender, or 1½ tablespoons dried lavender buds

1. Use a vegetable peeler to peel large strips of zest from 1 lemon (avoid the white pith, which is bitter).

2. In a small pot, combine the sugar, lemon zest, and lavender with ⅓ cup of water. Bring it to a low boil, stirring, and simmer for 5 minutes. Remove the pot from the heat and let the mixture steep for at least 15 minutes and up to 30 minutes.

3. Meanwhile, juice all 4 of the lemons; you should have about 1 cup juice.

4. Strain the lemon-lavender syrup through a wire-mesh strainer into a large pitcher, then stir in the lemon juice. Stir in about 3 cups of water or to taste (the lemonade should be slightly stronger than you like; ice will dilute it). Taste and stir in more sugar if needed. Serve over ice in tall glasses.

Thinking Ahead

Lemon-lavender syrup: You can make the syrup up to 2 weeks ahead. Store it in a covered container in the fridge.

Lemonade: This is best served within 24 hours of making.

Red Currant–Lemon Verbena Cordial

MAKES ABOUT 1½ CUPS

This ruby-colored tonic flaunts the best of red currants, with all of their tangy-sweet flavor but without any seeds. It does take an afternoon to make, but you can double the recipe if you're rich in red currants.

Be gentle when you're making this. The less you press down or otherwise agitate the currants while they drain, the clearer and more jewel-like the cordial will be. But if you can't bear to waste those last drops of currant-flavored liquid, squeeze them into a separate bowl and use this cloudy elixir to spike lemonade or seltzer.

To turn the cordial into an elegant aperitif, pour a splash or two into a pretty glass and top it with chilled sparkling wine, white wine, or rosé. I like to garnish the glasses with more red currants, still attached to their stems, and some lemon verbena sprigs.

Thinking Ahead

Cordial: The cordial will keep for a month or even longer. If you see mold growing, you'll know it's time to throw it out.

12 ounces (340 grams) red currants
½ cup (100 grams) sugar
2 large sprigs fresh lemon verbena

1. Wash one or two glass jars or bottles (you will need to accommodate about 1½ cups of liquid) very well with hot soapy water or run them through the dishwasher. You want the jars to be as clean as possible before making the cordial.

2. Pull the currants off their thick stems, but don't worry about any little stems that remain attached. You should have about 2 cups of mostly de-stemmed currants.

3. Put the currants in a pot, add ¾ cup of water, partially cover the pot, and bring the water to a simmer over medium heat for 3 minutes. Then remove the pot from the heat and let the currants infuse for 1 hour. They will look sort of gray when they are done.

4. Line a colander with cheesecloth or, if you have a muslin jelly bag or a nut milk bag, you can use those. Place the colander over a large bowl or a large measuring cup. Pour the currant mixture through the cheesecloth and let it drain without squeezing the fruit (if you squeeze, the liquid will turn cloudy). Let it drain for about 1 hour, pressing very gently. You should have about 1 cup of juice.

5. Add enough water to the juice to make 1½ cups. Pour it into a pot, add the sugar and lemon verbena, and bring it to a simmer, stirring occasionally, for a few minutes. Remove it from the heat and let it infuse until it tastes lemon verbena-y enough, 20 minutes to 1 hour. Discard the lemon verbena sprigs.

6. Let the cordial cool completely. Pour it into jars or bottles and refrigerate it for at least 4 hours before using.

Acknowledgments

So many people joined me on this journey to France, and I'm so grateful for their help. Let the thanking commence!

Janis Donnaud, my agent and fellow Francophile. *Merci beaucoup, comme toujours.*

The always stellar team at Clarkson Potter: Doris Cooper, Marysarah Quinn, Derek Gullino, Mark McCauslin, Kate Tyler, Erica Gelbard, Stephanie Davis, and Lydia O'Brien.

The graceful and superlative photographer Laura Edwards, her helpmeet, Bob Cooper, and their adorable little assistant, Hannah (and who wouldn't adore having a baby on set?).

The divinely inspired food stylist Joss Herd, with help from Harry Eastwood, who are not only amazingly agile in the kitchen, but also hilariously funny. Lily Starbuck aided and abetted them along the way. We did have a good time, didn't we?

Ever-stylish and supremely organized prop stylist Tabitha Hawkins, who literally gave me the shirt off her back to wear for a photo.

I couldn't have created these recipes without my superbly talented recipe testers: Jade Zimmerman, who did the bulk of the work here, with help from Adelaide Mueller, Sarah Huck, and again, Lily Starbuck.

My dear friend Zoe Reiter, who brought her good humor and verve to our photo shoots, delighting us with her presence.

My brilliant editors at the *New York Times*: Sam Sifton, Emily Weinstein, and Patrick Farrell, who challenge me to think more deeply and clearly in all of my writing. Thanks for your enthusiasm and support during the writing of this book.

And finally, my husband, Daniel, who loves France as much as I do, and our daughter, Dahlia, who doesn't, but grimaces and bears it. *Je vous aimes de tout mon coeur!*

Ratatouille Sheet-Pan Chicken, **page 176**

Index